T0196050

SHADOWY REMAINS OF UTAH TOWNS

A GUIDE TO HUNDREDS OF UTAH GHOST TOWNS

Penny Spackman Clendenin

Archway Publishing books may be ordered through booksellers or by contacting:

Archway Publishing
1663 Liberty Drive
Bloomington, IN 47403
www.archwaypublishing.com
844-669-3957

Front Cover Photograph: Nielsen Grist Mill, outside of Bicknell Utah,
Photo by Penny Clendenin

ISBN: 978-1-6657-1320-7 (sc)
ISBN: 978-1-6657-1321-4 (e)

Library of Congress Control Number: 2021920307

Print information available on the last page.

Archway Publishing rev. date: 05/19/2022

Table of Contents

Chapter 1   Beaver County 1-9

Chapter 2   Box Elder County 10-33

Chapter 3   Cache County 34-35

Chapter 4   Carbon County 36-48

Chapter 5   Daggett County 49-51

Chapter 6   Davis County 52-53

Chapter 7   Duchesne County 54-58

Chapter 8   Emery County 59-65

Chapter 9   Garfield County 66-70

Chapter 10   Grand County 71-80

Chapter 11   Iron County 81-89

Chapter 12   Juab County 90-100

Chapter 13   Kane County 101-104

Chapter 14   Millard County 105-117

Chapter 15   Morgan County 118-122

Chapter 16   Piute County 123-126

Chapter 17   Rich County 127-128

Chapter 18   Salt Lake County 129-141

Chapter 19   San Juan County 142-149

Chapter 20   Sanpete County 150-154

Chapter 21   Sevier County 155-156

Chapter 22   Summit County 157-165

Chapter 23   Tooele County 166-184

Chapter 24   Uintah Count 185-191

Chapter 25   Utah County 192-204

Chapter 26   Wasatch County 205-206

Chapter 27   Washington County 207-217

Chapter 28   Wayne County 218-221

Chapter 29   Weber County 222-226

Preface

I have always been fascinated by ghost towns and the history and stories they tell. This fascination led me to write the *Shadowy Remains of Utah's Towns*, which is a comprehensive guide to many of the ghost towns in Utah. Some of the places are semi-ghost towns, some under water, others were at one time considered a ghost town, but are now thriving again, such as Park City, and some are just a distant memory.

Many years of research went into writing *Shadowy Remains of Utah's Towns*, to give you the most accurate information possible. Research included; books, internet, museums, experts, people familiar with the area, and a personal trip to as many locations as possible.

There are so many fascinating details and interesting stories to be learned and enjoyed from reading about and visiting Utah's ghost towns. Visiting Utah's ghost towns is a great way to learn Utah's history and a fun and inexpensive way to spend time with family.

I hope you enjoy reading, *Shadowy Remains of Utah's Towns* and I hope it inspires you to get out and experience Utah's ghost towns.

—Penny Spackman Clendenin

Acknowledgements

I would like to thank my dad, John Spackman for taking our family ghost town hunting when I was a young child. This led to my fascination and desire to "hunt" ghost towns. The pictures from the 1960s and 1970s, included in this book were taken by my dad, John Spackman.

I would like to express my gratitude to my husband, Rod Clendenin. We have spent many fun-filled, exciting hours "hunting," walking, studying old maps, riding our 4-wheelers, and even camping in some of the ghost towns in this book. Thank you for going on this adventure with me.

Many of the recent pictures in the book were taken by Penny Clendenin.

I want to give special thanks to all of the people who were willing to take time out of their busy lives to answer my questions, help me find information, and help me locate hard-to-find ghost towns. I would also like to thank Tim Chapman for proof reading and editing, Doug Crawford for technical computer help, and to Holly Woodruff Fuller for proof reading for me.

I am very sad that my son Kyle and husband Rod passed away in 2019 before I was able to get my book published, they both encouraged me to get it published.

If anyone has any comments they can E-mail me at penny@rodsbestauto.com

CHAPTER 1
Beaver County

Adamsville was located on the north side of the Beaver River, nine miles west of Beaver City. It was first settled in the spring of 1862 by David B. Adams and three other families. The settlement was named Adamsville in 1867 after its founder. A stone church was built the following year. It was soon joined by a schoolhouse with a row of benches around its walls and the teacher's desk in the center; next came a store. In 1914 the town's population was 121. A land development company purchased most of the area to build Minersville Reservoir. The water soon backed up and flooded Adamsville, forcing people to leave. The church was taken apart in sections and moved to Beaver, while other buildings were moved to nearby ranches and farms. When Minersville Reservoir filled to capacity, Adamsville ceased to exist. In 2012 there were a few ruins remaining.

Photos taken by Penny

Arago was a town located ten miles southwest of Milford near Shauntie in the Star Mountains. Shauntie seems to have been a center for early mining towns on the west side of Picacho Peak near the head of Shaunite and Moscow washes.

Arrowhead was a community of an organized group of miners. Cabins and clapboard shacks were built in the cedars and pinions at the foot of the mountain below the Arrowhead Mine. Although it remained a bachelor camp, it was a pleasant place, high above the desert heat and shaded by tall pinions. The main camp, where the post office and general store were located, was near the Cougar Spar Mine, in the next canyon north. There the mining companies built several large boarding houses, barns, a blacksmith shop and offices, as well as numerous cabins and smaller structures.

Beaver Bottoms was located seven miles north of Milford, a small settlement along the river.

Photo take by Penny

Blueacre was a small mining camp five miles northwest of Hickory at the south end of the Beaver Lake Mountains. It gave promise of becoming a copper mining center and a number of substantial homes and buildings were built. The settlement received its name from the blue lupine flowers that grew in large numbers in the spring time. The mine's resources were depleted and Blueacre was abandoned in 1906.

Bradshaw City was founded on the story of John Bradshaw and his dream. One night Bradshaw had a dream that he saw a cave high on the mountain and a pack rat's nest filled with gold nuggets. His dream was so real that he told friends about it, but they laughed. Bradshaw set out on foot to find his dream mine. As he hiked north from Minersville, he tied string on cedar trees so he wouldn't get lost. He had never been in the mountains before but followed landmarks he recognized from his dream. He found the cave high on the mountain. He climbed up to it and inside he found a pack rat's nest with handfulls of yellow nuggets. The inside of the cave was a great limestone stone cave with stalactites, and the ceiling was heavily encrusted with sparkling crystals of silver and gold.

Cabins were soon built in the canyon below the cave. A boarding house, saloon and general store were across the canyon. The small camp was a wild one. It only lasted a few years because it didn't take long to strip the cave. As of 2018, just inside the cave mine where sunlight filters down through the opening, there was an old forge and the fire-blackened walls from an underground blacksmith shop. Across the canyon at the edge of the hillside is a single tombstone marked, "John Hayes, 1866." The town was located seven miles north of Minersville.

Cruz was a railroad camp.

Elephant City was located one mile southwest of Star City. The road turns north and climbs a steep hill to an old cabin standing near the ruins of the Vicksburg mine. Elephant City was a popular place for miners to gather, as the camp baseball field was located there. On Sunday miners from other camps and mines would meet at Elephant City to play ball. Liquor and beer flowed freely because there was no water at Elephant City. During the 1870s and 1880s it was a thriving camp. Some mines near the city were Golden, Era, Estelle and Maude. The town's post office was located at the Crown Point mine.

Florida was an early mining boomtown in the San Francisco Mountains northwest of Milford.

Fort Cameron was first known as "The Port of Beaver," established in 1872. It was named Fort Cameron on July 1, 1874 when it was designated a regular army garrison as a result of the tragic Mountain Meadows Massacre. Home to the 8th Infantry, it was two and a half miles square, located on the north side of the Beaver River two miles east of Beaver City. It was a well-built place of hand-cut stone and mortar that included four barracks, a commissary, a hospital and a row of officers' quarters. In 1883 the fort was disbanded. The buildings were sold and reopened as Murdock Academy, a branch of Brigham Young University. Several new buildings were added. The school closed in 1922 and most of the buildings were dismantled for the stone. Mormon churches at Milford and Minersville were built from the stone. Today what remains of Fort Cameron is listed on the U.S. National Register of Historic Places, and rests at the edge of a golf course in Beaver, Utah.

Fortuna was a mining camp in Fortuna Canyon, northwest of the north end of Beaver Valley.

Frisco was located 17 miles west of Milford, in the San Francisco Mining District. The District was organized on August 12, 1871. Frisco was developed as the district post office and commercial center, as well as the terminus of the Utah Southern Railroad extension from Milford.

In 1880 the population was 800. Frisco was one of the wildest mining camps in the west and boasted the richest silver mine in the country, with 21 saloons, hotels, gambling halls, its own newspaper, a red light district that would have rivaled many towns in the west, and two to five murders or shoot-outs per day. In Frisco water was scarce and alcohol was cheaper than water.

The town began in 1875 with the discovery of the fabulous Horn Silver Mine and at its peak 6,000 people called Frisco home. Murders were daily faire at Frisco. Two men killed each other over a 50-cent bet, and as many as a dozen men were killed each night. It got so out of hand that the founding fathers hired a marshal, who made his policy clear the first day. He would have no jail, make no arrests and there would be no bail or appeals. Outlaws were given two choices, get out or get shot. Some didn't think he meant business, but they changed their minds when he killed six men his first night on duty.

Mines located in the San Francisco Mining District were the Horn Silver, Blackbird, Cactus, Carbonate, Comet, Imperial, King David, Rattler and Yellow Jacket. By 1885 over $60,000,000 was taken from the mines. The ores contained lead, copper, silver, gold, and zinc, with some arsenic and antimony. By 1933 a major part of the district, including Frisco, was controlled and owned by the Tintic Lead Company.

The great Depression essentially put an end to the area, but some sporadic development work continued into the 1940s and 50s. While the camp is now gone, the Frisco charcoal kilns remain and are listed in the National Register of Historic Places in 1982.

Frisco

Grampian was located at the south end of the San Francisco Mountains just north of present-day U-21. It was a mining town near the town of Frisco.

Greenville was located about four miles southwest of Beaver on U-21. In 1860 a group of families, including Samuel Edwards, came from Parowan and Cedar City to settle. The community was named for the region's lush growth of pasture and meadow grass.

Both Photos taken by Penny 2013

Harrington was located four miles west of Milford at the north end of the Star Range. It was a mining town that grew up around the Harrington silver mine.

Hay Springs was located 15 miles southwest of Minersville. Hay Springs was a settlement for freighters and travelers in route to and from the eastern Nevada mines; it was also part of an early horse ranch.

Hickory or Old Hickory was a mining camp started in 1882, five miles North West of Milford. Mines in Hickory were Hickory, O.K., Rob Roy, and Montreal. The Hickory Mine produced 40% copper and eight ounces of silver to the ton. A stamp mill was installed in 1883, which was sold and moved to Nevada a year later.

Indian Creek was an Indian village on Beaver Creek in the late 1800s.

Laho was a railroad camp on the Union Pacific Railroad between Thermo and Upton.

Lincoln was a mining camp that was Utah's most historically significant, a long-forgotten camp that grew up around the workings of the Lincoln Mine, five miles north of Minersville. It is unknown how old the diggings are. When Mormon Bishop James Rollins and his party discovered the ancient workings in 1858 they described them as "an old Spanish mine." They were very old, but still intact. They explored the workings, finding rusted remnants of tools left behind. They also found a vein of what they thought to be pure lead, which they needed for bullets against Johnston's army. The Rollins party wondered why the bullets they cast were so hard. When the ore was assayed they found it to be nearly pure silver.

The town had a population of 500, with over 100 homes and many businesses. Other mines in the area included the Pioneer, Rattler, Golden Gate, Dunnerburg, Yip-Yap, Home Ticket, Richmond, Coral Reef, and December Mine. There were several smelters built near the mine.

Lower Beaver was located seven miles downriver from Beaver. In early 1859 a settlement was formed, and the settlers lived in dugouts or cellars. An early name of the settlement was "Old Cellars."

Manderfield 2013 Photo by Penny

Manderfield was a small settlement five miles north of Beaver on I-15. Manderfield was originally settled in 1865 by the Ephraim Twitchell family. In 1910 the community was named for J. Manderfield, a railroad man. A small church remained there in 2013.

Moscow was a mining town southwest of Milford at the head of Moscow Wash in the Star Mountain range, settled in 1870. The mine was called the Burning Moscow Mine.

Mercury Springs was a terribly isolated camp. A long dusty road leads to the old camp today. Miners at Mercury Springs were first interested in silver, but gold finds attracted more people and after that mercury discoveries brought still more miners to the rugged Needles Range. Even later tungsten was mined in great quantities, but over the years fluorspar has probably bought more whiskey, bread and beans than anything else.

Directions: From Cedar City, travel north three miles to where a narrow, paved road turns northwest and follow it 31 miles to Lund. Crossing the track, 14 miles beyond on a dirt road, a side canyon on the right hides the old Red Bud Mine, an interesting place to stop and explore. Six miles further (20 miles from Lund) a narrow track to the left leads 11 miles to the Arrowhead Mine, where some cabins can be found. Old buildings are built into the mountainside. To get to the main camp, return to the road from Lund and continue north for six miles to where a second side road turns to the left. Some remains are hidden in the cedars and others along the forest. Iron pyrite and violet fluorspar can be found here and at the Arrowhead Mine Camps. Numerous beryl crystals free for the taking can be found on the Holt Bluebell property at the 9500 foot peak above the Cougar Spar mine.

Murdock was a railroad camp.

Newhouse was located 30 miles northwest of Milford, at the end of a dirt road that leaves U-21, six miles west of Frisco. A few prospectors lived here in the crude cabins and dugouts as early as 1870. But the camp never amounted to much until 1905 when Samuel Newhouse purchased the Cactus Mine.

Newhouse established a model city building comfortable stucco homes for his miners. He rented them for $10 a month including all utilities. Newhouse built the Cactus Trading Company, Cactus Club, Cactus Dancehall and Cactus Café. He also allowed only one saloon that was built a mile from town. There was a clubhouse at the center of his city, containing a well-stocked library, pool tables and a small bar, but it was a very proper place, no drunks were allowed. The town had no red-light district, saloons, or gambling; schools and parks were built instead. When the railroad laid track into town, they stopped at the saloon, wanting its influence and the people it brought no closer than that. Newhouse offered a $50 prize to the parents of the first child born at Newhouse, and at Christmas time he provided free gifts for all the children in town.

The mine produced $3,500,000 in silver, gold and copper. In five years the mine began to decline and the region became a center for sheep men and cattlemen, who built large sheep-shearing pens. In 1914 the Cactus Mill was torn down, and in 1921 several of the town's buildings burned. In 1922 the silent movie "The Covered Wagon" was filmed at the town.

Newhouse

North Creek was a small community northeast of Beaver on North Creek from which it receives its name.

Opal was an end of line railroad camp.

Pine Creek was located at the north end of the Tushar Mountains, on US-91. It was settled in the late 1860s. A stage station was built here. There were also cabins, a small store, and a U.S. mail drop.

Pine Grove Creek was located on the western slopes of the Wah Wah Mountains. Pine Grove Creek was a small town settled by the Dodd brothers.

Shauntie was the center of the Star Mining District, about 12 miles southwest of Milford in the Star Mountains. It was the earliest mining settlement established in the county. Shauntie had over 40 houses of various types and several businesses including a hotel, several saloons, its own post office and stores.

A two-stack smelter was constructed in 1873 and was replaced with a larger smelter in 1874. As many as 100 workers were employed there, processing 3000 tons of ore containing $325,000 of silver and $10,000 of gold in just three or four years. The smelter burned in 1875, but was quickly rebuilt, processing even more ore. In 1876 the town of Shauntie was destroyed by fire, but was soon rebuilt and attracted the attention of mining men from all over the west. The veins in the Star Districts proved to be shallow, and closed down by 1877.

Shauntie and the other camps were left abandoned for thirty three years. In 1910 there was a small resurgence when some of the mines were re-opened to mine the low grade ore. Shauntie again was the center of activity. The post office was changed to Moscow in honor of the Burning Moscow mine, then to Talisman, but the locals still called it Shauntie. By 1920 the low-grade ore was mined out, and the few people that stayed to carry on small-time mining moved to Milford. Nothing remained of Shauntie in 2012.

Shenandoah was located 12 miles southwest of Milford, the southernmost camp in the Star Mountains. Shenandoah was a mining camp known as North Camp in the 1870s. Some of the mines were Wild Bill, Mowitza, Red Warrior, Hooster Boy, Cedar Tailsman and Silver Bug. The only water in Shenandoah was what could be dipped out of the mine shafts or from melting snow. There are no streams or springs in the Star Range. Nothing remained of Shenandoah in 2012.

Smyths/Read/Reed was a railroad siding 12 miles north of Milford where John Smyth developed a ranch. The ranch then evolved into a small settlement. The community was also known as Read (Reed) for a short period of time. Smyths is slowly being buried by drifting sand dunes, but the remains of an old windmill can be seen.

South Camp was one of the leading camps of the Star District, with houses, stores and saloons. Back in its day the stage coach ran west through South Camp to the Nevada diggings. Many wanted men passed through the rough town. Directions: South Camp was located eight miles southwest of Milford in the Star Mountains. A dirt trail turns to the right and a steep climb for about a mile leads to the ruins of South Camp. Nothing remained of South Camp in 2012.

Star City was the namesake of the Star Mining District and was located six miles southwest of Milford. During the 1870s Star City grew from a tent town into a mining camp. More than 1,600 claims were located in the Star District. Some of the mines were Little May, Rebel, Copper King and Osceola. Water was scarce in the boomtown; in the winter miners melted snow, during the summer water was peddled door to door at a cost of ten cents a bucket.

Miners claimed it was cheaper to drink beer. Businesses and saloons prospered in Star City, but few women chose to live there due to the lack of water.

Sulphurdale/Morrissey was established in 1870, but mining did not begin in large scale until 1883. The mining company built 30 homes, a school, a two story hotel, stores and company offices. Despite the heavy mining activity, high quality sulfur was difficult to find. In 1883 a thermal plant was built to process the extracted sulfur. Sulfur production slowed in the 1940s and 1950s and in 1966 the mine and mill shut down. By the end of the 1970s, the town was abandoned. Sulphurdale was just south of Cove Fort. The schoolhouse and a couple of homes remain in the town proper. In the 1990s there was a watchman and a locked gate, but beyond the gate several remnants of the old town remained.

Sulphurdale 2013 Photo by Penny

Thermo was a siding on the Union Pacific Railroad southeast of the Shauntie Hills. The name comes from the hot spring thermal activity of this area. Nothing remained of Thermo in 2012.

Troy was a small settlement, located five miles south of Milford on the Beaver River. A smelter was needed, so in 1875 the owner of the Mammoth mine at Shenandoah built a smelter at Troy. In 1888 the mill was destroyed by fire.

Upton was a railroad camp. Nothing remained of Upton in 2012.

Wah-Wah was mining camp 60 miles west of Milford.

CHAPTER 2
Box Elder County

Appledale was an expansive development of homes and orchards which failed when the irrigation water leached alkali and salt to the surface, killing the apple trees and crops.

Belfour was eight miles west of Corinne. It consisted of several gambling hall tents, 100 feet long and 50 feet wide. There were a number of similar saloon tents, as well as dozens of smaller ones where Irish laborers stayed when they weren't working or drunk.

Beppo was the fourth railroad town east of Lucin.

Blue Creek/Deadfall/Hell's Half Acre was the Union Pacific's camp east of Kolmar. It was officially called Blue Creek for a spring of beautiful blue water found there, but nearly everyone called it Deadfall. It was not uncommon for two or three men to be shot or knifed every night. One report said there were 24 men killed there in 25 days. Whiskey was sold everywhere at Deadfall. Men earned their money working like horses and spending it like asses! The town died and nothing was left except dozens of nameless graves whose locations are now unknown. A school was built in Blue Creek, and it later became a farming community with scattered houses and a post office. It was located 15 miles southeast of Snowville where ATK is located.

First Home in Blue Creek

dead Fall

Boone was a railroad town, between Terrace and Lucin.

Booth Valley was a small community between Promontory and Promontory Summit. Booth Valley had its own school house.

Boston Terrace/Newfoundland's was located in one of the most isolated mountain ranges in the west, completely surrounded by the Great Salt Desert. The old mining camp is largely unknown. Long after most of the Utah Territory had been mapped, Box Elder County's desert ranges were unexplored and unknown. Mormon stockmen called the little known ranges the New Found Land, but avoided the barren, waterless slopes. During the late 1860s silver was discovered in the mountains of the New Found Land, and a group of Swedish miners started a little mining camp on one of the desert ranges they called the Newfoundland's. The Swedish had an agent in Ogden who they sent the ore to and he sent them supplies and banked their profits. After a year, they went into Ogden to discover the agent had skipped town. They never returned to the mine.

In 1880, the Box Elder Mining District started searching the Newfoundland's and located several promising silver outcrops. They reopened the mine of the Swedish and renamed the town Boston Terrace. For nearly a decade miners stayed at the isolated camp, until the richest and most easily mined ore was gone.

There were buildings clustered at the northwest tip of the range near the Nephi Mine. In 1905, almost overnight Boston Terrace was deserted. In the 1950s there were still locked cabins from the 1800s. The water is tainted with arsenic. There are no roads to speak of, the only access being along the Southern Pacific tracks from Lakeside on the south or Lucin to the north.

Directions: From I-80 west from SLC, turn north about five miles past Delle to the small railroad workers' town of Lakeside; from there follow the railroad tracks past the Desert Pumps to the northern tip of the mountains. Cross the tracks where an unmarked dirt road leads in a southerly direction toward the Newfoundland Mountains. This road loops around the mountain range, but the military has closed it at the south end. A cable car ore shuttle system can be found in Dells Canyon. To reach Boston Terrace, travel north from Lakeside or south from Lucin to the Union Pacific rail line. Travel west, turning to the south where the road crosses the track. Stay on the main road, traveling southwest nearly 12 miles. The town's turnoff is located at N41.20.370 W113.40.294; proceed east from there up the mountain. This road requires four-wheel drive. As the road climbs, tailings of the mines can be seen. The rock house is located at N 41.11.083 W 113.22.781. The mines are to the south about 100 yards. This area has no water and is extremely desolate so be properly prepared.

Bovine was the second Central Pacific camp in Utah. It was located 12 miles east of Lucin and 20 miles from the Nevada line. It was named for the large herds of wild cattle which roamed the area. When the rails reached Bovine, the railroad provided an outlet to market the cattle, and soon large corrals and shipping pens were built. The rough town of Bovine served as a section station. In 1869, facilities included a section house, train car body, Chinese bunk and cook house, and a water tank. Thousands of Chinese laborers worked on the railroad at the towns along the railroad. The Chinese had their opium dens and countless dugouts and rough cabins. The town came to an end but the station remained active for several years as a shipping point for cattle and a supply town for ranchers.

Buel City was a tiny town built up around a smelter in 1871 at the eastern foothills of the Pilot Peak Mountains. Between 1870 and 1917, over $3.2 million of metals gold, silver, copper, lead, and zinc was mined.

Camp Cedar Swamp was established near Promontory in 1863. It was a temporary camp of California Cavalry on the northeast shore of Great Salt Lake.

Camp Church Buttes was a camp established in 1865 near the Great Salt Lake.

Cedar Creek was located near the dry stream bed of Cedar Creek, as it comes from the Raft River Mountains, eastward into Curlew Valley. Farmers and ranchers moved into the area in the 1860s and 1870s and by the first decade of the twentieth century a small community had developed. By the 1910s there were 20 families in the community. The community has a school, church house, a home post office, and a place called the "Halfway House," which was a small log inn and store. Some of the homes were attractively furnished; others made do with comic papers for wallpapering in the upstairs rooms. In 1916, the new school teacher was so homesick she couldn't sleep. She spent the first night roaming around her attic bedroom reading the wallpaper.

Around 1920 to 1925 farming became extremely difficult. Travelers were now bypassing Cedar Creek and finally the residents all moved away. Directions: after the Snowville exit take State Highway 30 west about 15 miles. At the split in the road, travel right on Highway 42. At Strevell take gravel road about three miles toward Naf, Idaho but before reaching Naf take a gravel road south about three miles.

Cedar Springs was a ranching community.

Clear Creek/Nafton was located in the Park Valley area, three miles southwest of Strevell, on the north central side of the Raft River Mountains. Clear Creek was a small ranching community that received its name from the creek. An earlier name was Nafton for a Mr. Naft, who established a cattle and horse ranch there around 1900-11. Maps from 1953 list the area as Nafton while later maps show it as Clear Creek.

Colin was the 15th railroad town east of Lucin.

Connor was a railroad siding and workers' camp, 14 miles west of Corinne.

Copperfield/Copper Hill was a small mining camp at the north end of the Desert Range, 30 miles across the Salt Flats northeast of Wendover. It came about in 1870 when copper galena ore was discovered in the newly organized Lucin and Silver Islet Mining Districts. Among the early mines were the Tecoma, Empire, Rising Sun, Mary Ann and Bald Eagle claims. Ore from the Goldstone mine assayed up to 50%. At the Black Warrior Mine, horn silver value was $4,000 a ton. A smelter was built near the Salt Lake but the wagons often became bogged down in the mud. Mining in Copperfield came to an end because it was not profitable.

Corinne/Burg on the Bear was a thriving railroad terminus during the building of the transcontinental railroad. It was settled in 1868 by Mark A. Gilmore and friends, with the intent of becoming a "gentile" community, trying to distinguish itself from Mormon communities. By March 1869, 500 frame buildings and tents housed about 1500, and an additional 5000 railroad laborers were quartered in construction camps. A whole block was set aside for a University as the town was meant to be large and important.

In about 1869 one of the first water systems in the territory was installed and the first non-Mormon church building in Utah was erected by the Methodists. Other businesses included a small sawmill, cigar factory, brick yard, an Epsom salts factory, a flour mill, several meat packing plants, two theaters, and department stores. A large expensive hotel covering half a block and a large opera house were in use for many years. There were several banks and huge warehouses for various freighting companies. There were 28 saloons and two dance halls, assorted gambling dens, and several hotels for the "ladies of the night." Still, in 1871, new businesses began, which included cement and tile works and a newspaper. By 1872 there were several wholesale and retail liquor dealers, tobacco stores, billiard halls, breweries, livery stables, auctioneers and Chinese laundries.

In 1903 the Southern Pacific Railroad built a trestle across the Great Salt Lake from Ogden to Lucin eliminating the route through Corinne. By 1920 the population was down to about 500. In 1871 a smelter was built in town to handle the ores coming up from Eureka and Ophir. Much of the ore was transported on steamboats; most notable was "City of Corinne", a three-deck, 100-foot-long craft. It was eventually run aground due to the fluctuating lake. It was then used only for excursions stopping up and down the lake at various resort beaches such as Garfield and Black Rock and some in Davis County. The old ship was eventually run ashore at Black Rock and used as a hotel-resort for many years. (See Davis, Salt Lake & Tooele County.)

When railway routes were changed, Corinne's population declined, which gives Corinne the classification of a ghost town, even though the residents are very much alive. Corinne had a fascinating divorce process. A couple of lawyers by the names of Johnson and Underdunk started a machine divorce mill. For a $2.50 gold piece and a crank of a handle a divorce certificate came rolling out, signed by the Corinne City Judge. The involved people filled in the blanks and the divorce was legal. In fact, to make things easier, you could just send in the $2.50 with names, etc., and the lawyers would do the cranking. Remote control divorces, the world's record for speed, ease and low cost! The only problem was, like many other projects started in Corinne they were either immoral or ill-founded. This scheme was illegal and the courts were up to their ears in later times trying to untangle some 2000 of those Corinne cases.

Cropley was a railroad town, north of Evans.

Dathol was a railroad town, six miles northwest of Corinne.

Dove Creek was located in the Park Valley area. It was a labor camp for Chinese workers on the railroad. It is said to be haunted by the sound and voices of the Chinese workers who lived and died there.

Elinor was a railroad town north east of Kelton.

Etna was five miles southwest of Grouse Creek, east of the Nevada border. There is no longer an established community today. First settled in 1875, its early name was West Fork. A permanent name was required before mail could be delivered, so Charlie Morris, the mail carrier, chose Etna. In 2013 there Were some remnants of the town. Photo by Penny

Evans was a small community and siding on the old Oregon Short Line Railroad, two miles west of Bear River City. The Utah-Idaho Sugar Company named the siding to honor Mase Evans, manager of the company.

Fort Bear River was a fort built during 1867 in Bear River City. It was a Mormon settlers' ten-acre fort, enclosing several log cabins.

Fort Calls was located seven miles north of Brigham City on U-89 at the base of the Wellsville Mountains. It was settled in 1854 and named after Anson V. Call, who built the fort. The Fort was 125 feet square with walls eight feet high and three feet thick. By 1858, 35 families lived in or near the fort. In 1862 a school house was built. With the Native American troubles over and the railroad at some distance the people left to start their own farms. A large rock monument was built with stone from the fort seven miles north of Brigham City.

Fort Davis was built in about 1851 in Brigham City. It was a Mormon settlers' fort built to protect against Native Americans. It was later called "Old Fort" after Call's Fort was built.

Fort Malad was a settlers' fort, built across the river from Portage at the former town of Washakie in 1855-1858.

Golden was located six miles west of Park Valley, just outside and south of the national forest in Century Hollow Canyon. It was a silver camp that began at the turn of the century. Claims were the Planetary, Deer Trail, Elamigo and Susannah Mines, and Vipont. The first ore from the mine was rich in gold, so the camp was named Golden, but as shafts were sunk deeper, the ore changed from gold to silver, with values of up to 1,000 ounces to the ton.

A five stamp mill at the Century Mine produced $500 a day. Everything looked so promising that the original Century Mill was replaced with a larger 16-stamp plant in 1906, and the next year one of the first Chilian Rod Mills was installed at the Susannah Mine. The Century Mine had three levels. The first work was done at the discovery near the top of the hill. Ore was first hauled from the second, or middle level, and from the third, or top level, down the steep hillside by teams of horses or mules and wagons. There was a big room which had been dug out inside the mine where the mules were stabled. The population was around 500, with several log cabins, a store, post office, assay office, saloons, cook kitchen, and tool sheds. In 1907 the mines closed, miners left daily, and the town died. Golden had a rebirth in 1910 when several of the mines were reopened.

Golden June 2015 Photo by Penny

Gravel Pit was located east of Ombey and originally served as a construction camp. In 1869 there was a 16 foot by 30 foot section house and 10 foot by 20 foot kitchen at Gravel Pit. Other facilities included a Chinese house, water tank, and a train car body.

Groome was the seventh railroad town east of Lucin.

Grouse Creek/Cookville was located in Grouse Creek Valley on the west banks of Grouse Creek. The area was settled in 1876 and received its name from the creek. The original name was Cookville for the Cook family that first settled. Benjamin F. Cook dug the first well in the vicinity. The first settlers built dugouts and later log houses with dirt roofs. The closest place to get mail, groceries and supplies was Terrace, a railroad town, 25 miles across the mountain or 40 miles around the mountain.

In 1879 the Grouse Creek LDS Ward was organized and meetings were held in homes until a log social hall was built in 1891. In 1912 a new chapel made of native sandstone was completed. It was a beautiful building with stained glass windows and a basement for recreation, (demolished in 1983). In 1882 a school was started and held in a log tithing granary. Later a log building was built, and then a four-room school was built of native sandstone. It was remodeled in 1980. Kindergarten through grade 10 was available, but upper grades had to board away from home. There were no doctors in the rural area and only a few midwives. There is now an ambulance service and trained EMTs.

School in Grouse Creek Home in Grouse Creek

<u>Grouse Creek Fort</u> was located in Grouse Creek, built in 1878. It was a Mormon settlers' settlement of closely-spaced log cabins for defense.

<u>Hampton's Ford</u> was a stage station, ferry and bridge. The bridge was built in 1866. It was the main stage coach line between Ogden and Montana. Later it became Collinston, Utah.

Hardup was a very small settlement at the mouth of Crystal Hollow and the east end of the Raft River Mountains. Six miles north northeast was Curlew Junction. It's reported that stills were operating there during prohibition.

Hogup was the ninth railroad town east of Lucin.

Iowa String was located along 6800 west between Utah Highway 83 and the Box Elder County Fairgrounds in Tremonton. Several families moved to the area from Iowa & Illinois. They built a hall which served as school and church in 1899.

Jackson was the third railroad town east of Lucin. It lay on the western end of the Lucin Cutoff, just west of the Great Salt Lake. Jackson was never much more than a railroad siding, named by the railroad for a prospector who operated a mine in the area. On February 20, 1904, during a collision between two Southern Pacific trains, a carload of dynamite exploded, destroying everything within a half a mile radius, including the majority of lives within the town of 45.

Junction was located just north of Lynn and had its own school.

Kelton/Indian Creek was located in the Park Valley area. The site was first settled under the name of Indian Creek. When the post office was established in 1869, it was named Kelton after an early stockman. It quickly grew into a prosperous town with several fine hotels, stores, homes, a whole row of saloons and gambling halls, and a telephone exchange. The town was inhabited from 1869 to 1942. Once an important section station on the First Transcontinental Railroad, Kelton was dependent on the railroad throughout its history. The town suffered a serious setback in the 1880s when its busy stagecoach route to Boise, Idaho was discontinued. Another setback occurred in the 1900s when the building of the Lucin Cutoff bypassed the town from the main rail line. On the morning of March 12, 1934, Kelton was hit by the most powerful earthquake ever recorded in Utah. At a magnitude of 6.6, only two people were killed. Great fissures and holes opened in the earth with muddy water gushing from them. Houses and other buildings were severely shaken, and the Kelton schoolhouse was leaning at such a angle that it had to be abandoned.

As late as 1937 Kelton was still an important local shipping point, and a population of 47 remained. The end of Kelton came when the Southern Pacific Railroad completely dismantled the old railway line in 1942, and contributed the hardware to the war effort. The last residents of Kelton left, taking some of the houses with them. Nothing remained of the town in 2015.

In the 1870s and early 1880s, the Wells Fargo stage line running between Kelton and several gold mines in Idaho and Montana was robbed more often than any other stage line in the Old West. Treasure hunters still search for the unrecovered dollars rumored to be cached in the nearby City.

Kelton Depot Kelton Hotel

Knowltonsburg was located on the south side of the Newfoundland mountains in an area known as the Saddle. The camp was named after Chris Knowlton, an early prospector. Prospectors arrived in 1871 and in 1872 the Newfoundland Mining district was organized.

Kolmar was the largest and liveliest of the new towns. It was the last camp before Promontory. Just west of Kolmar and north of the old roadbed, about two-thirds of the way up to Promontory Range, is the Chinese Arch, a natural rock formation named in honor of the 10,000 Chinese laborers. People lived in two old railroad cars that were built together end-to-end. It had a water trough filled by a spring from the mountains to the east. It was used for only a short time. Also, nearby was the "Big Trestle" where two large wooden elevators, scales, a storage building, and a platform were built.

Kosmo/Cosmo was known to have had one of the wildest fights in railroading history, between the Irish and the Chinese. In the end there was still some question as to who had won the fight.

Many years after its railroading days, Kosmo became the site of a large potash plant. At that time the preoccupied town boasted more than 40 houses and several stores. Now it is only a swampy marshland. Two sidings, about one-half mile apart, were constructed there. Kosmo West was built in 1912 in conjunction with potash activities and the original Kosmo East, constructed in 1901, and served area ranchers. Potash, used in the manufacture of gunpowder, had been chiefly supplied by Germany. With the advent of World War I, potash became difficult to acquire. The Salt Lake Potash Company began building ponds, canals, a rail spur, and processing station at West Kosmo, a half-mile from Kosmo. Three bunkhouses, a cookhouse, garage, stock corral, general store, blacksmith shop, and coal house were constructed and a train car body served as the depot. In 1924, there were 200 people in Kosmo.

Lake was located five miles southeast of Kosmo, entering the record books on April 28, 1869. On that day the Central Pacific track layers established a record which has never been broken. They put down ten miles of track in only 12 hours. The starting point was just south of Lake's Station and ended four miles beyond Rozel Station. It was accomplished with great precision as well as speed. 16 railroad cars of iron rail were unloaded in only eight minutes. The actual placing of the rails on the cross ties was done by "eight strong Irishmen" as fast as the heavy rails could be carried to them by the Chinese. Those eight men lifted 3,250 rails that day, or more that 125 tons each. Lake contained a section maintenance facility, a siding, and was built in February 1877. Lake was inhabited by Chinese, population 17 in 1870, 25 in 1876, 100 in 1879. The census for 1879 may have included the Chinese, often ignored in early census reports.

Lakeside was located on the western shore of the Great Salt Lake. In 1901 the settlement developed and was inhabited by people who worked for the Southern Pacific Railroad that crossed the lake. Today the area is restricted to federal government military use.

Lakeview was located directly north of Saline. The Lead Mountain is the site of Lakeview and the lead-silver mines of the early twentieth century.

LaMay was a railroad stop on a rise of land in the Great Salt Lake Desert north of Wendover. Although called an island, it was surrounded by salt beds, mud, and alkaline flats.

Lampo was a rest stop for those traveling. It was the place to water horses, and a place for travelers to drink and rest. The water was cold and sweet.

LaMay Lampo

Last Chance was a railroad town on the slopes of Promontory.

Lemar was the fifth railroad town east of Lucin.

Little Valley was a community which bloomed and faded with the construction of the Southern Pacific Causeway in the late 1950s. The construction camp town of Little Valley was built two miles from the boat harbor and shipyard, with the old Lakeview mines quarry site to the south, west of Promontory Point. The town boasted schools, shops, homes, dormitories, warehouses, and a supermarket for 1,000 people. There were five flat-top barges and a fleet of tugboats to haul the barges. The abandoned tunnels of the mines honeycombed the mountain not far from Little Valley. They were blasted in the largest man-made non-atomic explosion up to that time. The causeway was completed in July 1959.

School at Little Valley Barges at Little Valley

Tug Boat in Little Valley, all 3 Photos taken 1961 by John Spackman. This is my family I am the one on top kneeling down in White and red.

Loy was the eighth railroad town east of Lucin.

Lucin/Pilot Peak was the first Central Pacific camp in Utah. It was located about seven miles from the Nevada line. When the end of the track moved further east, Lucin became a supply town for ranchers and farmers in the Goose Creek area. During the 1870s prospectors discovered gold, silver & copper in the mountains. Rich mines brought a lot of miners to the area and for several years the town enjoyed a boom. Lucin was founded in the late 19th century, about ten miles north of its current location, to provide a water stop for railroads to replenish their steam locomotives. The town was moved in 1903 to serve as a stop for the Lucin Cutoff. Historically, the town's population consisted mainly of employees of the Central and Southern Pacific Railroads. In 1936 the town was abandoned, and then resettled by a group of retired railroad workers and their children.

Lucin Cutoff is a railroad line that included a railroad trestle which crossed the Great Salt Lake, built by the Southern Pacific Company between February 1902, and March 1904 across Promontory Point, it bypassed the original Central Pacific Railroad route through Promontory Summit where the Golden Spike was driven in 1869. By going we

Phone booth Photo
by Penny

st across the lake from Ogden, Utah to Lucin, Utah, it eliminated 43 miles and avoided curvatures and grades. In 1944 it was the site of a train wreck in which 48 people were killed. The trestle was eventually replaced in the late 1950s with a parallel causeway. Directions: Take I-80 west from SLC through Wendover to Oasis, Nevada. At Oasis take Nevada Highway 233 through Montello, Nevada and back into Utah where the road becomes Utah Highway 30. About ten miles past the state line is a sign for Lucin. There are two gravel roads on the right. Take the first one for five miles to Lucin. Cross the railroad tracks and continue on the same road for about two miles. Turn left and proceed about two miles, then turn right for about a mile to the Sun Tunnels.

The nearby **Sun Tunnels** is a large work of art created by Nancy Holt in 1976. Very interesting place to explore.

Sun Tunnels Photo by Penny

Lynn was a small agricultural settlement at the north end of the Grouse Creek Mountains on the South Fork of Junction Creek. In the 1920s the settlement had mail service, an LDS church and a school. There are no services left in Lynn and only two families live there year round and four to six families in the summer. A few buildings could be found in Lynn in 2013.

Photos by Penny

Matlin was a railroad station about 12 miles east of Terrace, where a share of the Chinese railroad workers built section facilities and a small Chinese community. Population records document 15 people living in Matlin in 1870 and 25 in 1876. Completion of the Lucin Cutoff in 1904 prompted the abandonment of Matlin. As of 2012, all that remained was Sake jugs, opium bottles and lost coins from the Chinese playing Fan-Tan.

Medec was a railroad town between Lucin and Bovine.

Metatarsus was a railroad town.

Midlake was the 14th railroad town from Lucin, at the middle of the Lucin cut off. The town of Midlake was built on a platform 80 feet long by 40 feet wide, suspended 15 feet above the lake. Midlake had a store, a telegraph office, and a row of houses. The population even reached 30 at one point, all men except for three telegraphers. They didn't do much but eat, sleep and work; no booze was allowed. Mail, groceries and other needed supplies were brought in by rail.

Monument/Parker's Camp was an end-of-track camp, with tents, shacks and empty box cars. The camp was home to nearly eight thousand "Celestials" who labored there. Years after the last Chinese laborer was gone and forgotten, a salt works was built at Monument. The salt plant closed after several drought years shrunk the lake, causing the plant to be miles from shore. Browning Arms Company held a rabbit hunt at Monument killing 8,000 rabbits in one day making it the rabbit hunting capitol of the world.

Muddy had at least three stills operating during prohibition. It was located on Muddy Creek north of the Rosebud Ranch, in the Park Valley area, south of Yost. Muddy had its own school.

Nella was a railroad siding built in 1902 for service to local ranchers. The siding was removed by the railroad in 1906, and re-laid again in 1916. In 1917 a train car body and freight platform were present.

Nerva was a siding on the U.P. Railroad, three miles south of Willard. In 1915 farmers asked the railroad to build the siding for the local sugar beet industry. At first the railroad refused, thinking they had a lot of nerve in asking for it. Eventually the siding was built, but the railroad named it Nerva to express their feeling about the project.

North Promontory was a small community on Promontory with its own school house.

Old Terrace was a site on the Central Pacific. In 2004 nothing remained but a sign and a wood and metal squared-off space that could be a cemetery. Old Terrace is located about a mile northeast from Terrace.

Olney was the tenth railroad town east of Lucin.

Ombey was a fuel station, a place where engines stopped to load up wood to fire their boilers. It was named for the Ombey Mountains. The Ombey siding was completed in 1881. Railroad profiles show a section house, tool house, and Chinese bunk and cookhouses. For a few months Ombey served as home to thousands of Chinese laborers, many of whom lived in dens and burrows dug into the hillsides. The caved-in dugouts can still be found.

Painted Post was a railroad siding on the slopes of Promontory.

Park Valley was located on U-30 south of the Raft River Mountains. It was first settled in 1869 by William Cotton Thomas, who migrated from Brigham City and developed a cattle ranch near Dove Creek. The heavy growth of trees along the creek and the view of the valley inspired the name, Park Valley. Settlers, mostly ranchers, numbered several dozen. Mormons started moving into the area, so a meeting house was built. A store was added, a typical log protective fort and log schoolhouse were erected. More people moved in and more stores and a hotel were built. In the late 1890s a gold vein was located six miles west of Park Valley, bringing many boomers that moved into Park Valley which increased the populating by the dozens. A five-stamp mill was built near the mine. At Park Valley's peak the population was about 500. By 1914 the boom was dead and abandoned homes, shacks, and homesteads filled the town and dotted the plains. There were only a few families living in the Park Valley area in 2013. Photo by Penny

Pegion was the first railroad town east of Lucin.

Penrose four miles south of Thatcher and southwest of Tremonton, settled in 1890. The agricultural community was named for Charles W. Penrose, a noted editor, poet, composer and Mormon Church official. The settlers farmed beets, wheat, corn and hay. The Malad Valley branch of the Oregon Short Line had a spur from Tremonton to Penrose.

Peplin was located four miles beyond Ombey by rail. While the slow work on the long horseshoe-shaped cut through the mountains was being dug, Peplin bustled with activity. Peplin consisted of a siding, a small bumper spur, a train car body and a loading platform. Hastily built joss houses and opium dens served the Chinese while shacks and cabins replaced the little white tents usually used for shelter. The residents often built into rocky cliffs and hillsides.

Promontory/North pass/ Ives Pass was an early construction camp near the point where the Central Pacific Railroad from the east and the Union Pacific Railroad from the west met on May 10, 1869.

Before May 10, Promontory was a single muddy street; lined on one side with canvas and rough-cut lumber shacks, frame false front lunch counters, candy shops, saloons, gambling dens, stores, hotels, a school house and numerous tents. The other side of the street was the railroad with its typical buildings; depot, water tower, office shacks, and dormitory cars, with some tents and a few shacks beyond. It was a typical Rail Road camp until it was decided that it would become the meeting place for the two railroads. The majority of the residents in town actually lived in converted boxcars on the sidings of the two railroads.

Promontory served as the terminus for each railroad, handling many tons of freight and transferring some 30,500 passengers by the end of 1869. During the last few months it was a terminus town, the place was a real "hell town," full of outlaws, gamblers and prostitutes. Confident men got on the trains at Corrine and Kelton, warmed up to the passengers, and then led them into crooked casinos when the trains reached Promontory.

Briefly, besides a siding, early railroad facilities at Promontory included a turntable installed in late 1869, a foreman's house, section hands' housing, a coal shed, water tower, tool house, and depot. Being a local center for shipping of wheat and livestock, until about 1942, several businesses and homes were constructed including the Houghton Store and the school house. During the decades of use, three school houses were built, two being destroyed by fire. The roundhouse was in ruins by 1937 and the Houghton Store (with a post office, restaurant and boarding house) ceased operations about 1942 when the rails were removed. Buildings still standing in 1966 were moved or destroyed with the construction of the Golden Spike National Historic Site. The status of the town varied from complete abandonment, to cattle town, to an honored site under the National Park Service (The Golden Spike National Historical Site.)

Promontory Point was located at the southern tip of the Promontory Mountains.

Quarry was a railroad town.

Rambo was the 13th railroad town east of Lucin.

Red Dome was a station five miles east of Terrace, located at the point where the rails turned northward after they had followed a due east course along the edge of a dry, barren hillside. It was a short lived place, where for only a few weeks' great piles of rails and cross ties stood alongside the long rows of little white tents used by the Chinese. The railhead had hardly moved to the next line camp before the tents were taken down and the transient's camp left behind, leaving little to mark its site except discarded sake jugs, opium bottles and coins lost while playing Fan-Tan. In May 2004 nothing remained except a sign.

Romola was a railroad town southwest of Kelton.

Rosebud was located in the Park Valley area in the Grouse Creek Mountains, in the Rosebud mining district to the south of Yost.

Rosette/Victory was a small ranching community five miles west of Park Valley. Rosette had a school and post office with Jonathan Campbell as the first postmaster. He named the town in 1871 for the wild roses in the area.

Rosette

Rozel/Camp Victory was an important stop for trains bound for Promontory Summit, which was eight miles to the east. "Helper" engines, stationed in Rozel assisted freight-laden trains up the Promontory Mountains. Railroad structures included a section house, train car body, water tank, bunkhouse, and cookhouse. Local informants indicated the presence of a hotel in the early 20th century. There was a population of 25 people in 1870.

Indians had frequented the site of Rozel for centuries before the coming of the railroad, to obtain the natural asphaltum which seeps to the surface there, which they used as a medicine. The asphaltum is similar to natural rubber, seeping from the ground at a temperature of 130 degrees; it quickly cools, congealing in pipe lines and storage tanks. A large plant was built in the town but it didn't last.

Russian Settlement was located just south of Park Valley, where a monument marks the site, one of Utah's strangest towns. In 1914, a band of Russian peasants came to start a new life. Legend claims they traded valuable property in San Francisco for the desolate acres in Park Valley which were owned by an old Chinaman who won the land in a Fan-Tan game. Before long they had put up houses, churches and schools in the strange architectural style of Czarist Russia.

The Russian settlement was laid out in a similar fashion to villages in the Russian Empire. A main street running east to west centered the town. Houses, barns, outbuildings, wells, and root cellars were constructed. The lumber came from a Pacific Land and Water sawmill located in the nearby Raft River Mountains. Livestock was purchased from local ranchers, and crops were planted. For six long years the Russian peasants battled the hostile desert. After repeated crop failures and a death to match every birth they gave up and moved.

Today the little cemetery hidden in the sage and a caved-in well are all that remains. Between 1910 and 1914, the Salt Lake City-based Pacific Land and Water Company acquired about 180,000 acres of property in Box Elder County to resell. The company misrepresented this arid land in advertising, describing it as "amongst the richest in the state of Utah" with the local climate as "energizing," and it was claimed that the heavy growth of sagebrush indicated that the land was fertile for farming. Land was sold for $17.50 per acre, financed at seven percent interest, with 20 percent down and the remainder paid annually over five years.

By August 1914, the number of school-age children had reached 40, prompting Box Elder County to establish a one-room school and provide a teacher. A portable school house was built on the west end of the main street, and the teacher, was paid by Pacific Land and Water, the school closed by 1915, the abandonment of the town, beginning in 1915. In August 1916, the stove from the school house was sent to the Lucin School, and in September the entire school was disassembled and shipped to Promontory. By the end of 1917, Russian Settlement was a ghost town.

Directions: From Park Valley turn east at the State Highway maintenance buildings, and travel southeast on a gravel road for about seven miles. Nothing remains of the town.

Saline was located west of Promontory Point on the old FAA landing strip, the site of the Lake Crystal Salt Plant. It also has a siding for loading salt onto the railroad. Saline had its own school house. The buildings were demolished and buried in the 1990s.

Scandia was situated somewhere between the Great Salt Lake and the Nevada border.

Seco was located seven miles east of Kelton. Seco was an end-of-the-track camp with tents and shacks. Seco was established in June 1873 as a section station to accommodate the moving of facilities from Ten-Mile which is about four miles east. The work crews and inhabitants of Seco were Chinese. Nothing remains to mark the site. There is an iron door over a cave in Box Elder County rumored to be near Seco where outlaws stashed their loot.

Speery was a grain transportation center where Thiokol is now located.

Standrod/One Mile was located at the southern tip of the Raft River Valley and is tucked back in a large canyon on the north slope of the east-west Raft River Mountains. The town was settled in 1870 and built on the Utah-Idaho border 12 miles west of Strevell, Idaho.

Standrod was first known as "One Mile" in the early 1870s. There was a store, post office, and brick school house added in 1903. The first white men in the area were cowboys employed by various cattle barons. The railroad planned to go through an area close to Standrod, so settlers moved in, building a schoolhouse on the state line in the middle of town that served not only as a school, but a place for all community affairs including meetings, a church, and a place for dances, a store and blacksmith shop were also built directly on the Utah-Idaho border. However, the railroad never arrived.

The first white settlers in the area found the winters hard and supplies difficult to come by. The morale of these people rose and fell, but they didn't turn back. They were strong faithful people who still enjoyed dancing and singing and each other's company. People began arriving to settle Standrod at a rapid rate in 1900. Homesteading filled the flats with cabins between Standrod and Raft River. Droughts and poor soil prevented them from making a living and soon drove them away.

Prior to 1900, people got their mail seven miles away. There was a prosperous saw mill up One Mile Road. In the 1970s two old saw mills were still standing east of Standrod. Also standing were three large brick homes built prior to 1900. Agriculture is still the main source of income for the people. Hay is the main crop, but some grain is also grown. Cattle and sheep graze on the fertile mountain sides. The town is accessed by gravel roads.

Stanrod 2016 Photo by Penny

Stokes was a railroad town four miles north west of Corinne.

Strong Knob was the 11th railroad town east of Lucin.

Subon was a railroad town.

Surban was a railroad town.

Teck was the second railroad town east of Lucin.

Ten-Mile was a section station established in 1869. The name is derived from the distance west from the original Lake section buildings. The closest siding was two miles east at Monument. Railroad profiles locate a section house, train car body, and water tank at Ten-Mile. Railroad documents indicate that the section facilities at Ten-Mile were moved to the Seco town site in 1873. There were at least three stills operating at the site during prohibition.

Terrace was established in 1869 as a Central Pacific Railroad operations base. Rose Bud Springs fed the tanks at Terrace; it was an important point for fueling and watering locomotives. A 16-stall round house, machine shop, coal sheds, water tanks, and an eight-track switchyard were located at Terrace. The town included Wells Fargo and Company Express, a telegraph, railroad agent, a school, bath houses and reading rooms or library, 13 saloons, a dance hall, and a soda fountain. A China Town was located on East Ridge at the east end of Terrace. Chinese lived in dugouts or shanties and also had a Buddhist Church. A post office operated from 1872 to 1904. Water was carried to Terrace by a twelve-mile long aqueduct from a spring in the Grouse Creek Mountains and stored in three tanks. Terrace's population was more than 200, not counting the six to eight thousand Chinese laborers. Many of the Chinese remained or returned to operate stores and build a China Town second only to San Francisco. Opium was sold openly for $7 a bar. Terrace still had a population of 900 thirty Years later, by that time nearly all were Chinese. Terrace remained the Central Pacific's largest town and maintenance station in Utah. The town was abandoned in 1942 when the railroad closed its facilities and moved the division to Montello, Nevada. Directions: Driving 28 miles southwest of Park Valley on Highway 30, the highway intersects the old Railroad Grade road. Travel northeast about two miles along the Railroad Grade road. In May 2004 nothing remained but a sign, some bricks and lots of glass. At the Lone Hill Cemetery 60 people are buried.

Tresend was a railroad town, located five miles from Midlake.

Umbria was a railroad station and a short-lived town established in 1869.

Union was a small temporary settlement during the early 1900s. It was located about two miles southwest of Tremonton. A schoolhouse was built in the town.

United Order was a railroad town located five miles from Corinne.

Vipont was a gold and silver mining settlement established in 1899 in the extreme western part of Box Elder County. Mining continued into the winter of 1918 with three carloads of gold and silver ore shipped from Vipont to smelters in the Salt Lake Valley. A boarding house and an office building were erected, and necessary supplies were brought in to keep 16 employees working throughout the winter. In the spring of 1919 additional workers built a concentrating mill that was 150-ton capacity. The employees of Vipont did well financially. In the spring of 1923 it was reported that Vipont had more than 300 men working with the smallest wage being $4.50 per day. Vipont grew from a crew of 300 men to 600 men and a total population expansion from 500 to 1,500 within a year. At first a 100 horse power engine generated electricity until the power line was built from Oakley to Vipont in 1921. The installation of hydroelectric power and lights, telephones, air drills, aerial tramway, and flotation at the mill ushered in a new era for the district. A 14,200 foot long tramway was built from the Vipont Mine down the steep mountain front to the new concentrating mill. In 1900 a post office was established and discontinued in 1905. The mine was reopened in 1920 when the owner uncovered an ore body with values of 12,000 ounces of silver to the ton, and it was then mined until the 1930s. The Vipont mine and ghost town are located in the far northwest corner of Utah at the head of Birch Creek. Directions: Travel north of Grouse Creek, Utah toward Oakley, Idaho on the Grouse Creek road. About two miles beyond the Idaho border is the Birch Creek turnoff. The Birch Creek road then angles back to the southeast and reenters Utah as it continues up the Birch Creek drainage to its headwaters in the Vipont area. The town site is not far from the City of Rocks and Granite Pass on the old California Trail.

Walden was a railroad town used from 1898 to 1906.

Washakie was located off I-15 near the Utah/Idaho border 50 miles north of Brigham City. Years ago the town was the cultural center for the Utah's Shoshone. In 1873 many of the northwestern Shoshone Tribe converted to Mormonism. In the 1880s the church settled the people into Washakie, a ranching community. In time the number of people in the cemetery outnumbered the living. The town died after WWII. Just west of town was the graveyard. The church, with pews and broken windows, and also a house were all that remained of the town in 2013.

LDS Church 2013 Photo by Penny Home 2013 Photo by Penny

Watercress was located about 28 miles southwest of Park Valley on U 30 then left about five miles to the railroad grade. Watercress was a water station and had a high water tower which was kept filled with spring water, piped from springs to the north where watercress grew in abundance. It was an important stop because it was the only place steam engines could get water supplies before continuing into the desert ahead. Track was laid rapidly near Watercress. Railroad documents from 1926 record other facilities at the town, including corrals, a barn, a stock pond and water tank, and a loading platform. Watercress was abandoned around 1940.

Woodrow was a small town located west of Yost.

Wyben was a railroad town.

Yost/George Town/George Creek/ Junction was one of the most remote Box Elder County towns, located on the north central slopes of the Raft River Mountains, 115 miles northwest of Brigham City. The settlement developed in the 1880s with a post office added.

In 1880 a sawmill was built near Park Valley and west to Vipont, which supplied lumber for several years to railroads and to the gold and silver mines. Yost was made up of mostly members of the LDS faith, with 15 LDS families in 1882. A year later, the settlement grew to about 35 families. In 1886 the first joint school house/civic hall/church house was built of logs. In 1900 a large rock church house was built, and a brick school house was added in 1908. By 1910 the population had increased to 251 people. Yost incorporated on August 19, 1935 during the Great Depression. At the time, Yost's boundaries were the largest in size in the state of Utah. Due to poor land quality for farming and ranching, the population declined and the town of Yost dis-incorporated on January 6, 1984. Photo by Penny

Zias was a single-track railroad town that served the area ranchers.

Miscellaneous

Railroad towns along the Lucin Cutoff starting from Lucin going east were Pigeon, Teck, Jackson, Beppo, Lemay, Newfoundland, Groome, Loy, Hogup, Olney, Strong Knob, Lake Side, Rambo, Mid Lake, Colin, Saline, Promontory Point, & Bagley, which was in Weber County. Boarding houses were built on a platform raised on piles well out of the way of storm-waves from the Great Salt Lake. There the men lived until their work was finished. The railroad company furnished supplies and cooks, and the men were paid $4.00 a week plus their board. The men worked ten hours seven days a week. There was not much to do but work and sleep, no place to spend money, and no liquor was allowed. All stores and all packages coming out to the work men were carefully searched, and any liquor found was promptly confiscated. Workers were allowed to bring wives and children with them. They were housed in box cars called "Out-fit" cars placed on temporary sidings. The company maintained a hospital, staffed by a surgeon near the work site.

CHAPTER 3
Cache County

Buster City was located in Public Grove Canyon. In May of 1892, predictions were that Buster City would soon have a population of 500 as soon as word got out about the discovery of silver and lead. By the end of May over 75 men were at work in the mines, while houses and stores were being built. Stage routes from both Logan and Ogden were quickly added.

Camp Relief was an army post located east of Lewiston and south of Franklin, Idaho, established in 1864.

Fort Logan was a Mormon Volunteer Militia Fort located in Logan. It was constructed in 1895.

Fort Richmond was a Mormon settlers' fort which was built in 1859 when Brigham Young visited Richmond and noted that the people were too scattered. He advised them to build a fort, where they could better protect themselves against the Indians.

LaPlata was a booming silver-mining town on the border between Weber and Cache Counties. The first ore in the area was discovered in July 1891, by a mountain shepherd, who showed his foreman what he found. The foreman recognized it as silver-bearing and took it to be assayed in Ogden. The sample was 45% lead, with a silver concentration of 400 ounces per ton. The two quietly registered a mining claim, but the secret got out. Several more high-grade ore pockets were found, and a silver rush began.

This was the first major Utah mining claim ever found north of Salt Lake City. By August 1891 more than 1000 miners had arrived, and the number soon reached 1500. Lines of cabins and stores stretched along either side of the creek, forming a town called La Plata (Spanish for "silver"). There were about 70 buildings in all, including two stores, saloons, a bank, and a post office.

Because La Plata was populated largely by locals who had temporarily become miners, it differed from most western mining camps. It never had a cemetery, as there were never any killings in town. When a few prostitutes tried to set up business, they were driven out. The Thatcher Brothers Bank in Logan bought the original claim, called the Sundown Mine. Ore was shipped north to Logan, and then transported by rail to Salt Lake City.

Both Cache and Weber counties were petitioned to build roads to the site; the Cache road was completed first and was somewhat less difficult to travel, although there was no easy route to La Plata. La Plata's high elevation made for harsh winters, and few people stayed after the 1891 season. In January of 1892, only 150 inhabitants remained. By then the richest ore had started to run out; the highest concentrations of silver were found on or close to the surface. The return of warmer weather brought a second, smaller rush; the population was back up to 600 by July 1892. By the summer of 1892, companies rather than individuals controlled most of the mining, and Utah farmers who had rushed in to get rich found they couldn't compete with the experienced miners who had come from all over the Western United States.

The 1893 financial panic closed many silver mines nationwide. A few mines remained open at La Plata, continuing to produce lead, until its price also dropped. The town did not last through 1894, although some sporadic mining activity continued as late as 1906. Some old cabins remained in the 1990s.

Mineral Point was a small off-shoot of LaPlata, located high on a ridge directly above Porcupine Reservoir. There were several houses and mine buildings of which nothing remains.

Porcupine City was at the foot of James Mountain. By spring of 1892 the Porcupine Mine and Milling Company had a force of 25 men working in their mines. Houses and businesses were built here, but nothing remains.

Smithfield Fort was constructed in Smithfield during 1860-1862. It was a Mormon settlers' fort built after the settlement was already created. In July 1860 the settlers were attacked by Indians and two white men were killed. The settlers moved closer together and eventually 68 houses were constructed within the fort walls. The town was originally named Summit.

Willow Valley was settled in 1863, by Mormon pioneers from the Salt Lake Valley. In 1879, lead was discovered and the Willow Mine was opened. In 1885, the settlement was abandoned because of dry conditions and a lack of water.

CHAPTER 4
Carbon County

Blackhawk was a tiny mining village east of Hiawatha with its own post office. Nothing remained in 2014.

Castle Gate began in 1886 when the Pleasant Valley Coal Company started mining operations. The name of the town was inspired by the large rock formation at the mouth of Price Canyon.

    The first houses for employees were old box cars provided by the railroad. Later homes and buildings were constructed. There was a business called the Wasatch Store where employees were required to shop or lose their jobs. n 1916 Castle Gate had its own 22-piece brass band. There was a hospital that was operated by the mining company; the miners were charged a nominal fee deducted from their pay to use the services. There was a school for the lower grades; the upper grades were bussed to Price.

    There were two Castle Gate mines, Castle Gate #1 (1888) and Castle Gate #2 (1912) that were found to have the finest coal in the region. On March 8, 1924, the Utah Fuel Company's Castle Gate Mine #2 exploded, killing 172 miners. It was the third-deadliest disaster in the history of coal mining in the United States at that time.

    Castle Gate was dismantled in 1974 and the residents were relocated to a new subdivision at the mouth of Spring Canyon, west of Helper. On April 21, 1897, Butch Cassidy and Elzy Lay held up an employee of the Pleasant Valley Coal Company in a daylight robbery at the busy railroad station in Castle Gate, making off with $7,000 in gold. In 2014 there was a big coal plant where Castle Gate use to be, and a historical marker on the Highway.

Clear Creek is located about five miles south of Scofield on Mud Creek, at the south end of Pleasant Valley. Clear Creek was founded in the 1870s as a logging camp that supplied lumber to the nearby mining town of Winter Quarters. About twenty years after Clear Creek was founded, coal was discovered beneath the town, and a mine was developed.

In 1898, the Denver and Rio Grande Western Railroad built a spur line from Scofield to the mine at Clear Creek. Two years later, the Utah Fuel Company built 25 homes, a hotel, a store, a hospital, a school, a workshop, and a water plant in the town. From 1910 to 1920, 2,000 tons of coal was being mined per day. Clear Creek had about 600 residents. In 1930, the need for coal began to decrease. By 1955, the mine cut production and the town's population had decreased to 150.

In the 1950s a ski resort was developed at Clear Creek, but it didn't last long because of sparse snowfall. The resort closed just a few years after it opened. As of 1986, four families lived in Clear Creek year-round. Recently some of the old houses have been bought and rejuvenated as summer homes. During deer season the population doubles.

Home at Clear Creek

Coal City/Great Western was nicknamed Dempseyville after Jack Dempsey, a boxer who lived there while training for fights. In 1885 Coal City was first settled as a farming community, but the elevation and dry desert foot hills were unsuitable. Then ranching was tried but there was too little feed for the cattle. When coal was discovered in the area, a coal camp was established.

In August 1921, the permanent town site was platted and renamed Coal City, after the coal in the area. The town was incorporated in 1921. Most of the houses were tents. A log school house served Coal City in 1925, and was replaced by a brick schoolhouse in 1927. Later that year, a couple of stores and a bakery were constructed, making up the business district. A few dozen homes were constructed around the stores. The town began to decline in 1935 and by 1940 it was uninhabited.

Directions: Travel about two miles south of Helper, then nine miles west on Consumer

Road. At that point, a few yards up a dirt road to the right is Coal City. In Oct. 2016 there were a few ruins across the fence and a historical marker up the hill to the south.

Coal City 2016 Photos by Penny

Consumers/Gibson was a coal town that boomed in the 1920s. It was a tent town originally named Gibson. The name was changed to Consumers after the Consumers Coal Company. Many company houses were built along both sides of Gordon Creek, and many miners built their own houses or shacks farther up canyon. By 1937, Consumers had a hospital, an amusement hall, a store, service station, post office located in the mining offices and a four-story apartment building. The only homes with indoor plumbing were the mine officials' homes. The town was abandoned in 1960s, but the mine was still being worked in 2016 It is located up Consumer Road which is north of Helper and a few miles west of Coal City. In 2014 there were a few foundations and some mining equipment remaining.

Fort Nine Mile was an old Indian fort. It was located in Nine Mile Canyon, on the Carbon and Duchesne County borders.

Franham was named for an early surveyor in the region. Franham was settled in 1887. It was located seven miles southeast of Wellington.

Hale was a coal town on the Rio Grande Railroad, located about two miles downstream from Scofield Reservoir on the Price River. The reservoir now covers the upper part of the town.

Heiner/Panther was a tiny coal camp founded in 1911 that was originally called Panther. Located near the mouth of Panther Canyon, the camp was also known as Carbon. They finally named it after Moroni Heiner, Vice-president of the U.S. Fuel Company.

The town consisted of about 100 people of several different nationalities. Heiner grew to about 600 people by 1923. The houses were owned by the mining company and the residents did everything they could to make them homey. By 1917 there was a post office, a Co-Op store, and a one-room school house, then in 1923 they built an eight-room school house that served the people until the 1950s. There was a tramway leading to the mines. The town faded in 1950 when coal prices dropped.

Located north of Helper, nothing remained in 2014.

Hiawatha was one of many coal mining towns that dotted the hills and valleys in the Price/Helper area. Hiawatha was incorporated in 1911 and in the 1940s had a population of 1,500. There were many nationalities and many small towns that made up Hiawatha: Greek Town, Jap Town, West Hiawatha, East Hiawatha, Flat Town, Tram Town, String Town, Railroad Town, Silk Stocking Row, and what became known as Uptown where the stores were. There was an amusement hall, a library, a school, two churches, and a dairy. Hiawatha's business district was a shopper's dream in the late 1910s, with many stores. The Hiawatha Mercantile was the cutting edge of homemaking technology, advertising the latest in washing machines and irons.

Production dropped, people moved away, and Hiawatha was unincorporated on November 20, 1992. The town was located on SH-122, nine miles west of SH-10 at a point eight miles south of Price. In 2006 the road leading to the old town was gated, prohibiting a closer view, but several buildings were visible.

Kiz was first settled in the 1890s by two ranchers who soon abandoned their land, due to drought. In 1906 the first of the more permanent settlers arrived, but most of the homesteaders came in the period from 1910 to 1916. A sheepherder filed the first legal claim to the land in 1916, and by then there were two dozen families who were aware of the valley's desert climate, set about the difficult task of dry farming. Trying to save all the available water, they dug numerous wells, although there was no stream nearby, and they built a large reservoir for irrigation.

In 1921 the American Legion promoted the valley as a home for World War I veterans to establish themselves, making claims of available irrigation water that never actually arrived. It is not known how many people this advertisement brought, but by 1924 there were enough children to establish a school which was held in unused granaries until a proper school was built. The population reached its peak in 1925, and a post office was established in 1926. There was also a small general store.

Kiz did experience successful harvests some years, but water was always in short supply. In 1930 there was another severe drought, driving most of the residents away. The school burned down in 1932, so the students started attending school in Sunnyside. By 1940 Kiz was a ghost town.

Directions: Kiz is located 15 miles east of Price, about seven miles east of Wellington on U.S. Highway 6-50, then five miles northeast into Clark Valley. The town's cemetery and a few empty foundations remain.

Latuda/Liberty was located six miles up Spring Canyon. A coal developer, Frank Latuda started the Liberty Fuel Company on the canyon wall in 1914. Latuda began as a tent town, and then the name changed to Liberty in 1918, as 20 homes were constructed around the mine. In 1920 a two-story mine office was built, and the top floor was a hotel for visiting stockholders, as well as a doctor's office. A school house was built in 1923 and shops lined the streets. In 1927, an avalanche roared down the mountain, wiping out an entire row of company houses and killing two people. By the 1940s there was a population of 400. This was a company-owned town, and at the request of the post office the town's name was changed back to Latuda. The town grew modestly until 1964 when the mine closed down most of its operations, causing the town to be completely abandoned by 1967. Some remnants of the town were visible in 2006.

Latuda 2015 Photo by Penny

Little Standard was a small town with tents and shacks, located across the canyon from Mutual, about one mile up the left hand of South Fork Canyon. One large tent housed a 14-bed bunk house, and miners lived in the town for more than 12 years. When the company mine closed in 1938, the residents left and the tent city dwellers took over the pretty homes at Mutual.

Martin was a part of Helper until 1918 when angry citizens petitioned to make it a separate community. A long narrow line of houses joined it to the larger town down-canyon. One night there was a fight that spread into the streets and involved a whole neighborhood, but the authorities of Helper couldn't get through the snow and mud to the upper canyon. Citizens were tired of depending on Helper and voted to start their own town, but Martin police and other services were worse than ever. Martin had an old stone hotel and tavern, built of hand-quarried rock by one-armed Ross Gigliotti. The building was still standing as of 2014, although it was crumbling with trees growing up through it.

Mutual was named in 1912 for the Mutual Coal Company. Mutual was located eight miles northwest of Helper, being the most extreme western town in Spring Canyon and the last to develop. Mutual was known for its fine built and well-kept homes, having had many three and four-story buildings. The town developed in 1920 and had several mines where

the residents worked, including the Day, Vulcan and Western mines. In 1938 the mines were closed but the store continued operating until 1958 to service the other mines in the area. In the 1970s there was a family that still lived in Mutual. They had no electric or gas lines, but there was enough loose coal to last a lifetime.

Photo by Benny

National was a town about three miles from Coal City. Coal was discovered in the area in 1908, but large-scale mining didn't begin until the National Coal Company purchased the mines in the 1920s. All of the buildings in National were constructed of the same brick material and the businesses and saloons all looked alike. In 1921, the National Coal Company, together with the Gordon Creek Coal Company, built a railroad line from Helper to the mining operations. In July 1938, the National Coal Company discontinued mining operations in the area. The mine was sold under foreclosure by the end of the year and all of the mining equipment that had value was sold. Mining continued under a new owner for a short time, but the town was soon abandoned. In 2014 a few foundations and deteriorating buildings could be seen in National.

New Peerless was located three miles north of Castle Gate, about a mile up canyon from Royal. Coal was discovered in the area as early as 1900, but was not feasible to mine until 30 years later. It started during the great depression when life was hard, and the population never exceeded 300. A salvage firm removed many of the buildings. Along the present canyon highway an old stone wall remained, and in a side gulch the mine's old powder magazine could still be seen.

Nolen was located six miles from Castle Gate, settled in 1883 by coal miners. It was one of the earliest coal camps in the state, but didn't last long because the coal had to be hauled too far through bad conditions. A freeway now winds through the canyon bottom alongside the Price River where Nolen was once located.

Peerless was located three miles west of Helper on Spring Canyon Road. Peerless was settled in 1912, a town that grew up around the Peerless Mine. In 1917, the Sweets sold the property to the Peerless Coal Company. Coal shipments began over the Denver and Rio Grande Western Railroad in 1918. As the mining continued, the population in the 1920s and 1930s grew to about 300, with about half working in the mines. The community included 30 homes, a store, a school, the mine office, a post office, a school house and a pool hall. Coal production peaked in World War I, when 2,000 tons of coal was mined daily. In 1938, coal mining activity began to decline and people began to leave. By World War II, the mine was operating very little and only a few people remained. The mine closed in 1954, and the town was abandoned. A few foundations and filled-in mine shafts remain.

Rains began in 1915 as a typical town with businesses on both sides of the street, including a school, a boardinghouse and a store. There was a double row of 60 company houses that lined both sides of the street. About 500 people lived in the town, which had all the modern conveniences except indoor plumbing. Life was difficult but also joyous; there were dances, free movies and talent shows. The mine was shut down about 1958. Some foundations and walls remained at its location seven miles from Helper and one-mile up Spring Canyon from Latuda.

Photo by Penny

Royal/Rolapp/Cameron/Bear Canyon was a 1900s coal mining town. Originally called Bear Canyon, the town was renamed Cameron, Rolapp, and finally Royal, changing names each time a new owner took over. In 1917 there was a population of about 200 with a general store and post office. By 1940 the population was 350, the store had enlarged and there was a school, a church and saloons. Royal had a reputation of being a wild place. It was located about 11 miles northwest of Helper and one-mile northwest of Castle Gate. As of 2018 all that remained of Royal were some stone walls and a few mines. Photo by Penny

Scofield was established in 1879, as an outgrowth of Winter Quarters. There were many homes that surrounded the city center of stores, churches, business offices, a city hall, post office and jail. By 1890, there were 700 residents. The men worked in the mines the Kinney, Union Pacific, Blue Seal, Utah, and Winter Quarters mines as well as several small one or two man operations, which was one of Utah's richest coalfields. There were several saw mills in the canyon. In 1920 the city at 2000 residents, twelve stores. Thirteen saloons, four large hotels and served as the business center for the Valley of 6000 to 7000 people. A miners' strike of major proportions hit in 1922, and the town has been in a steady decline ever since. In 2010 the population was 24. In 2016 there were many building to see.

School Scofield historic jail

Spring Canyon/Storrs was a town located one mile up canyon from Peerless. In 1895, a wagon road was constructed in order to make coal transportation easier. In 1912, Jesse Knight purchased 1,600 acres of land west of Helper, organized the Spring Canyon Coal Company, and constructed 60 homes. Knight also constructed a railroad in 1913 to the Denver and Rio Grande Western Railroad line in Helper. Knight named the new town Storrs, after the mine superintendent, George Storrs. Knight was a Mormon and ban saloons and gambling houses from being constructed in the town. In 1914, a school and a church were constructed for the townspeople, who were mostly members of the LDS Church. By 1924, Storrs had 1,000 residents, a hotel, and a heated swimming pool, well-built sandstone houses with hot and cold water, offices, and stores. Storrs had its own bakery and dairy.

By the end of 1914, a thousand tons of coal per day was being shipped. George Storrs was eventually charged with mail fraud, and the town's name was officially changed to Spring Canyon. In 1940, the Spring Canyon mine was ranked as the fourth largest coal producer in Utah. By 1946, the Spring Canyon mine had transported and mined eleven million tons of coal. However, the need for coal began to diminish, and by 1954 only a small group of miners remained in Spring Canyon. The mine closed in 1969 and Spring Canyon was abandoned. In 1975 every building in Spring Canyon was demolished. The railroad trestle is the only remnant of the former coal mining town.

Standardville was established after coal was discovered in Spring Canyon in 1912. The town's layout was planned with well-maintained lawns, bushes, and poplar trees. This became the "standard" for coal mining towns in Spring Canyon, and the town was named Standardville. As Standardville's population increased, a company store, several apartments, a butcher shop, a barber shop, a hospital, a recreation hall, tennis courts and an elementary school were constructed. In the 1930s the population was about 550. Although it was considered the standard for mining towns, Standardville still had problems with crime. On June 14, 1922, several miners went on strike and attacked a train carrying several new miners. The striking miners then fled and were pursued by mine guards. The shooting that occurred killed a mine guard and wounded two others. On February 6, 1930 an explosion caused by gas occurred in the Standard Mine. Of the 29 miners that were working in the mine, 20 were immediately killed by the explosion. A cave-in killed three rescue workers while they searched for the miners, but nine survivors were able to escape. The explosion had a large impact on the community, but, the the town continued to grow. When World War II ended, the demand for coal decreased, and the mine was unable to meet its payroll. In an attempt to save the mine, miners worked only for food. This attempt was unsuccessful, and after the mine went bankrupt, it shut down in 1950 and people began to relocate elsewhere. A few families remained until the 1970s, after which Standardville was abandoned. The town was located five miles northwest of Helper.

Standardville 2015 Photos by Penny

<u>Stewart</u> was a company town built by the Stewart Coal Company in 1914. This firm possessed no mines of its own but bought coal from other Carbon County mines, such as Royal Mines.

<u>Sunnyside</u> is located on U-23 at the base of the Book Cliffs. The town was first settled in 1897. Tents were the first dwellings, later replaced by company housing. It had an earlier name of Verdi after a nearby railroad camp. There was a Liquor House by the railroad yards. There were many houses, they had a School, company housing, Italian Camp, meat market, amusement hall, boarding houses, company store, pay office and a depot.

Company Housing Italian Camp at Sunnyside

Sweets was an impressive place in the 1920s, its buildings extending almost to the edge of National. There were wild times at Sweets. For several years the miners and their families lived in a tent town. The Cochrane family lived in one half of the lamp shack. As the miners prepared for work, they would enter the lamp shack and pass through the Cochranes' living area. At its peak the population was 200 residents. A high trestle was built across the narrow canyon above the town to bring coal from the Sweets Mine. Directions: Sweets was located two miles up canyon from National on the main fork of Gordon Creek, 14 miles from US 6-50. From National follow Gordon Creek up the main canyon instead of turning right to Consumer. Nothing remains of the town.

Watts 2014 Photo by Penny

Wattis was a coal mining town up Serviceberry Canyon, located eleven miles southwest of Price. Mr. Wattis and Mr. Browning of Ogden established the community in 1917 in order to operate the nearby mines. Shipments of coal began when the railroad was completed to the camp. In 1918 a permanent town was built by the company, with row houses, bunk houses, an amusement hall, a Japanese camp and several businesses. By1965 the town was abandoned but the mine continued into the 1990s.

Winter Quarters was the first commercial coal town in Utah originally called Peaceful Valley, where a few pioneers lived and grazed their cattle. The community changed in 1875 with the discovery of coal. By 1877, hundreds of miners moved in and a town suddenly emerged. The winter of 1877 came early and was very severe, keeping the miners snowbound until the following February. The town was renamed Winter Quarters.

Most of the first miners were Mormon converts from the coal districts of Wales, England and Scotland. One of them, David Williams, leased the Winter Quarters Mine from the Pleasant Valley Coal Company from 1880 to 1885, operating in the dual capacity of mine manager and bishop of the local LDS Ward.

As the town grew, the need for a railroad increased. In 1879, Milan Packard, a merchant from Springville, financed the construction of a railroad from Springville to Winter Quarters and Scofield. The railroad was named the Utah and Pleasant Valley Railraod until it was purchased by the Denver and Rio Grande Western Railroad in 1883.

By 1900, there were 2000 families living in Winter Quarters. The town's main street was over a mile long with many businesses, most of which were made of stone. The mine was considered the safest in the state. On May 1, 1900, while the town was celebrating Dewey Day, an explosion occurred in mine #4, caused by coal dust. One hundred men were killed by the explosion and intense heat. Carbon monoxide spread to mine #1, killing 99 more men. Rescue crews consisting of men from Clear Creek, Castle Gate, and Sunnyside, along with locals from the valley, worked for almost a week recovering bodies. The final death count reported by the Pleasant Valley Coal Company was 200, though other reports reported 246 deaths. That one moment of time left 105 widows and 270 fatherless children behind. Almost 150 miners were buried in the cemetery in nearby Scofield and two special funeral trains carried the rest of the victims to burial grounds in Utah and other states. The state inspector's report concluded that the cause of the explosion was an accidental ignition of black powder, which ignited the coal dust in the air. The Pleasant Valley Coal Company supplied each deceased miner with a coffin, burial clothes, and $500 to each family who was affected by the mine explosion.

CHAPTER 5
Daggett County

Bridgeport was a small ranching community in the eastern part of the County, near the Colorado border. The store, saloon and post office were located on the north side of the Green River near the mouth of Jesse Ewing Canyon, at the western end of Browns Park in Colorado. Bridgeport was developed and operated by Charley Crouse, an early Browns Park pioneer. The post office operated from 1902 to 1940. No remnants of the community could be found in 2014.

Browns Park or Brown Hole was a large area of land that was partly in Utah and partly in Colorado. The BLM has preserved a place on the Utah side of Browns Park called the **John Jarvie Historical Ranch**. John Jarvie settled the area in 1880 and opened a general store, trading post and became the town postmaster. A year later he started a ferry operation across the Green River, and also mined and had livestock in the area. There is a cemetery located at the ranch.

The area was used by mountain men, Indians, fur trappers, travelers and local residents. Ann Bassett (Etta Place of Butch Cassidy & Sundance Kid fame) was a resident of Browns Park. From Highway 191 about a mile north of the Vernal turn-off, a sign marks Browns Park and Diamond Mountains. In July 2014 the ranch could still be viewed, as well as a stone house that was built by outlaw Jack Bennett, a museum, a two-room dugout where John and his wife first lived, the blacksmith shop and corral, and a water wheel. Also visit the general store where John Jarvie was murdered; the store has the original safe that was robbed. Browns Park is listed on the National Register of Historic Places.

Dug Out Home Photo by Penny

Fort Davy Crockett was one of the first forts built in Utah. The site of Fort Davy Crockett (1837) is located in Brown's Hole. It consisted of three rows of log cabins in a U-shape and was protected by adobe walls. The valley was a trappers retreat, outlaw hangout, and favorite location for wintering stock. In 1944 it was burnt to the ground by Indians.

Greendale was a large ranching/homesteading area in the Uinta Mountains in the south-central part of the county. A United States post office operated at Greendale from 1915 to 1916. Enough families lived in Greendale to support a one-room school in the 1920s and 1930s. Major changes came to the Greendale area in the 1950s and 1960s due to the construction of Flaming Gorge Dam. The region received its first paved roads, which increased land values and helped encourage most of the ranch families to sell out.

"Uncle" Jack Robinson's cabin at
Greendale, Utah. He was a "Mountain man",
His cabin is the oldest in Utah.

Linwood was a small, unincorporated village in the north-central part of the county near the Wyoming state line. The town was located along Henrys Fork of the Green River about five miles east of the county seat of Manila. Linwood was first settled in the 1890s. The nearby bottomland was used for irrigated agriculture. Sheep ranches operated in the more arid lands to the north. The town was in decline by the 1920s, due to farm consolidation and road improvements, which made larger communities more easily accessible to local residents. In the late 1950s the Linwood area was purchased by the Federal Government as part of its land acquisition for the Flaming Gorge Reservoir project. The remaining buildings in Linwood were razed or moved, and the town site is now under Flaming Gorge. A United States post office operated at Linwood from 1903 to 1958.

Sweat Ranch was a family homestead to the south of Dutch John. They raised and sold cattle, as well as producing prosperous crops on their plantation. A signposted near a popular camp site and ranger station in the Flaming Gorge National Park is all that remained as of 2018.

Photo taken in 2019 by Penny

<u>Sweett Ranch</u> is listed on the National Register of Historic Places, and maintained as an interpretive site by the United States Forest Service. The 397-acre Swett Ranch began around 1907. It was operated with only horse-drawn equipment for 60 years until it was purchased by the US Forest Service in 1970. The ranch consisted of three pioneer homesteads. A visit in 2014 was enjoyable. Still remaining were two cabins, the main house, spring house, outhouse, root cellar, pig pen and chicken coop, horse barn, work shop, wood shed, two blacksmith shops, a granary, milking barn and farm equipment.

Saw Mill at Swett Ranch was operated by a Model T Ford engine 2014
Photo taken by Penny

CHAPTER 6
Davis County

Bountiful Fort was built to protect against Indians. Construction began in 1854 and continued for two years, but it was never completed.

Farmington Stockade was located in Farmington, established in 1854. A palisade was erected around this Mormon settlement.

Kaysville Fort was located in Kaysville from 1854 to 1858. It was built by Mormon settlers but was not completed and never used.

Simkins was an end-of-the-line railroad town.

Vigilini was an end-of-the-line railroad town.

Resorts

Lake Park was a resort on the east shore of the Great Salt Lake that began July 15, 1886, located between Lake Side and Lake Shore. Railroad magnate Simon Bamberger built the resort as a proven way to increase passenger traffic on his trains. It was promoted as one of the "most attractive watering places in the West." Some 53,000 people visited Lake Park in its first season. Based on 1886 lake levels; it was probably located about two miles west of today's Lagoon. It boasted an open-air dancing pavilion, a small Victorian-style hotel and a string of cabanas along the beach. A sailboat racing and rowing club also had headquarters at Lake Park. By 1895, the resort was suffering from low water levels, the shore became blue-colored mud. Guests had to walk a third of a mile or more to reach the water. Bamberger decided to move the resort inland to a swampy area. Five of the resort's original buildings were moved. The park reopened as "Lagoon" on July 12, 1896.

Lake Shore was a small resort located a few miles southwest of Lake Park. It opened in 1879 and had some dressing rooms. Not much is known about the resort. Lake Shore was reached by the Central Railroad system.

Lake Side was a resort on the Great Salt Lake located southwest of Kaysville. It opened in 1870 and was probably the first-ever attraction along the lake's shore. The resort offered 25 cent rides to the City of Corinne (later changed to the General Garfield), a steamboat, and going to Lake Point on the south shore. There were numerous church and family outings held at the resort. The low lake level in the early 1890s caused the closure of the resort.

The Garfield

Syracuse Resort staged bicycle races on a nearby dirt track. Artesian wells and water tanks served the resort. It had a dance pavilion suspended on pilings. Trains were known to sometimes strand people at the resort. For example, on July 8, 1889, a group from Ogden had to spend the night after the evening's only train left early. Syracuse Resort closed in 1892 from a two-fold problem; a dispute over ownership of the land and the receding water of the lake, leaving it mired in mud.

CHAPTER 7
Duchesne County

Altonah is in the upper bench land adjacent to the south central Uinta Mountains. There were three miles south of Altamont. The site was originally settled in 1906, but was named Alexander after Robert and Milton Alexander who were early settlers. After the town site was finalized in January 1912, its name was changed to Altonah which refers to its altitude. There was also an early temporary name Queen City.

Courtesy of the Uintah County Library - Regional History Center

Antelope was a long, strung-out community along Antelope Creek, about two miles south of Bridgeland. It was first settled during the 1905 land rush.

Basin was located about three miles north of Roosevelt. In about 1905 several people attempted to settle this site but failed. Today it is an agricultural region.

Bluebench was a small settlement outside Duchesne.

Blumesa was a small settlement that began in 1914, located seven miles northeast of Duchesne.

Bridgeland is a scattered agricultural community nine miles east of Duchesne on U-86. The community center was located where the highway crosses the river on an important bridge built in the early 1900's. Mileage was measured from this point during the early days of the town. The bridge drew neighboring communities Antelope and Arcadia closer together. The Bridgeland Camp ran from 1934-1939.

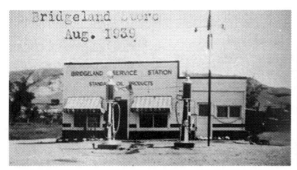

Cedarview was a small agricultural community surrounded by rolling cedar-covered hills. The town was first developed in 1912 on U-121, five miles south of Neola. The area currently supports ranching, gas and oil production.

Cresent was located four miles north of Roosevelt and east of the State Highway. In about 1905 several people attempted to settle here but failed.

Emigrant Springs was an early stage station located about two miles south of Cedar Creek.

Falls was a small community that disappeared according to *A History of Duchesne County.*

Harper is located in Nine Mile Canyon in the southern part of the county. This stagecoach town came into existence in 1886. The nearest inhabited town is Wellington. Alfred Lund came from Nephi in the spring of 1885 with his cattle and was the first homesteader in Argyle Canyon. Lund's first home was a log cabin which stands in ruins on the south side of the creek. Tom Taylor also homesteaded this ground before the Army built the road through to Fort Duchesne in 1886. In the 1890s, the government was freighting to Fort Duchesne over a road which passed through Nine Mile Canyon. During the years 1888 to 1895 there were 600 soldiers at Fort Duchesne who hauled their supplies over this route. Ed Lee purchased Taylor's homestead and it became known as "Lee Station", a stagecoach stop. The army installed steel telegraph poles in the canyon around 1886 that were American Civil War surplus. This telegraph line became the telephone line into the Basin in 1907 and remained until 1917. The poles have since served a local line until the 1990s.

According to government maps, in the 1890s the name of the settlement is "Nine Mile," but some traditional accounts called it "Minnie-Maud," named for two girls who lived there. When the post office was established the town was named Harper. Sometime before 1895, residents of Nine Mile Canyon struggled to keep a school district going. The first school house, built of logs by residents, sat in the mouth of Argyle Canyon. Until 1916 there were two schools, one in Carbon County and one in the Duchesne District. From 1916 to 1924, one school was maintained, which was closed in 1931 and moved to Wellington in the 1930s where it later burned. As of 2006 only a few structures remained, including the old stagecoach stop and some other log dwellings. The two-story Harper Hotel was destroyed by fire in the late 1980s or early 1990s, only the stone foundation remains. Most of the town site is on private property, so permission is required to explore the area. In 2006 many ruins could be seen from the road.

Harper 2006 both photos were taken in 2016 by Penny

Hartford was located between Myton and Roosevelt. It began during the 1905 land rush in the northern part of the county.

Hyland was located between Myton and Roosevelt. It began during the 1905 land rush in the northern part of the County.

Ioka is a small community that was first established in 1907, located on U-87, five miles northwest of Myton. It was named for a Ute headman and means "bravado."

McAffee disappeared according to *A History of Duchesne County*.

Meadowdell disappeared according to *A History of Duchesne County*.

Midview was located about two miles north of State Highway 121. It began from the 1905 land rush in the northern part of the County.

Montwell was a temporary community located near Monarch. It was first called Wells for the many artesian wells in the area.

Mount Emmons was located near Altonah and Boneta. In 1914 E. A. Daniels laid out the town site and named it Banner. The name was later changed to Mount Emmons.

Palmer disappeared according to *A History of Duchesne County*.

Smith Wells was a collection of small stone or wooden buildings. Owen Smith hand-dug the well and added a store and a home. It was a main stopping place for travelers.

Starvation was located five miles west of Duchesne. In 1905 the Uintah Indian Reservation was opened by the federal government to homesteaders. The land in the river bottoms of the Strawberry River was very desirable. The first pioneers into the area started clearing the river bottoms and the community began to develop in 1911. In 1915 a post office was established in Starvation and was called Strawberry. The first school was built around 1911 named the Strawberry School. On July 26, 1922 the school burned down from the sparks left by campers, but the school was rebuilt and running by 1923. In 1924 the school was closed and the students were bussed to Duchesne. The land was bought by the Bureau of Reclamation in 1970 to make way for Starvation Reservoir. The settlement is now underwater except for a cemetery that lies on a plateau southwest of the community.

Stockmore was located 11 miles upstream from Tabiona. Almost overnight it became a small town of tents and hastily built wooden buildings. Included were a general store, four saloons, a butcher shop, a barber shop, a livery and an assay office, all necessary businesses for a new mining town. For a time there was a hotel where dances were held. After several lots were sold, the town site proved to be unsuitable, as most prospective buyers either bypassed the region or settled lower downstream in the Hanna area. This community was planned for development during the land rush of 1905. A Mr. Stockman and Mr. Moore "founded" the town and advertised lots for sale by displaying gold nuggets that came from "Stockmore." Stockman and Moore fled when federal marshals entered the scene. A forest ranger station stands at the site.

Upper Strawberry/Riverside had limited farm land, but the community grew. Those that did not own land worked as farm hands, ranch help and miners. In 1921 residents changed the name to Riverside. In the fall of 1920, two bridges were built, this allowed for auto travel all the way through the community. Eventually the mines closed and the big farms sold out. In the 1930s the CCC came in and replaced the original bridges with heavier cable support bridges. As the roads improved and the commute to the community of Duchesne became easier, the Riverside School closed down. The community eventually lost its identity as Riverside and became a bedroom community of Duchesne. In 1952 high waters along the river flooded the canyon and washed out the CCC bridges and a few houses. The community spent the summer completely isolated until the county built new bridges in the fall. 1952 brought the first power lines into the canyon. Before that some of the farmers used wind turbines and batteries for lighting. Phone service was brought in by Uintah Basin in 1978.

Photo by Penny

Utahn was settled in 1905 on the Duchesne River, nine miles north of Duchesne and three miles west in the river bottoms on State Highway 35. Originally it was a compact group of log cabins and a church house. After a few years the people built more substantial homes. The town saw its peak in the late 1920s with about 200 people. People became discouraged at the low production of the land and began to move out.

Woodbire disappeared according to *A History of Duchesne County*.

CHAPTER 8
Emery County

Austinville was a farm of more than 2000 acres and was developed by the Austin brothers. Austinville boasted its own school for a brief period around 1916.

Cedar was a settlement on the Denver & Rio Grande Railroad.

Cliff was a settlement on the Denver & Rio Grande Railroad located north of Woodside.

Connellsville was located three miles up Coal Canyon, near the head of Huntington Canyon in the northwestern corner of Emery County. It was a coal mining and coke manufacturing center. Connellsville was the first settlement in Emery County, inhabited from 1874 to 1878. The population was small, with only a few dozen miners and coke-oven workers. By 1878 the project was deemed a failure, and the town was abandoned. The town now lies beneath the waters of Electric Lake. Utah Power funded an archaeological survey of the area and reconstructed one of the coke ovens on a new site above the water line.

Desert was a settlement on the Denver & Rio Grande Railroad.

Desert Lake was located six miles east of Cleveland on the north end of the lake. In 1885 several families moved from the town of Cleveland, Utah to an area they called Desert Lake, and built a 500-foot embankment dam to impound a 300-acre irrigation reservoir. In 1896, the dam broke, causing significant damage. The LDS Church provided $1000 to rebuild the dam, and also to extend a ditch to Cleveland. In 1900 the population was 127. In 1906 the Desert Lake area was surveyed and an LDS church, a general store, several homes, and a school were built. The general store also served as the town's post office. A problem throughout the valley occurred as farmers irrigated land, which dropped the water table and caused alkali in the soil to rise. The alkaline soil eroded adobe structures and caused many crops to fail. The residents moved about six miles away and founded the town of Victor. Desert Lake was inhabited from 1885 to about 1910.

Emery/Muddy Creek was located on Highway 10 about 15 miles north of I-70. This is a semi-ghost town with about 250 people that still live there. There is also a gas station and a grocery store there. The town was first called Muddy Creek after the nearby creek. It was later named Emery in honor of George W. Emery of Tennessee, who was appointed governor of Utah Territory in 1875. In 1879, people had settled in Muddy Creek Canyon, establishing a town that was known as "Muddy" for short. The first settlers were able to get mail once a month, in the summer, and not at all in the winter. The mail was brought by horseback from San Pete County, through Salina Canyon by anyone who might be going through. In 1882, mail service to Muddy Creek was improved to once a week, making a 60-mile trek from Price, Utah. The post office also served as a doctor's office, with Wiley Payne Allred, a former bodyguard of Joseph Smith's, using his in-laws post office as a place to set broken limbs, extract teeth and apply herbal remedies.

Grassy was a settlement on the Denver & Rio Grande Railroad.

Lawrence was a small Mormon farming community, on Roper Wash, five miles southeast of Huntington. It was first settled in 1879 and named for the St. Lawrence River. A Post office and Church was built. The church was built in 1888 or 1889 and was demolished in the 1950's.

Several homes were built in the town. Stores were operated for brief periods. Lawrence had a population of 107 in 1890 and 160 in 1900. It was a hiding spot for Butch Cassidy after the Castle Gate holdup.

Mohrland was a coal mining town in Cedar Creek Canyon that began on a small scale sometime before 1896. In 1907 an investment group bought the mine and surrounding land. They incorporated as the Castle Valley Fuel Company and surveyed a town site called

Mohrland. Coal started shipping by April 1910, and despite Castle Valley Fuel's financial problems, the town continued growing. A business district was soon established which included a hospital, company boarding house, Wasatch Store, a post office and several saloons. In 1915 ownership of the mine was transferred to the United States Fuel Company. By 1920 Mohrland had over 200 houses, a large amusement hall and a school, the population was about 1000. Mohrland was a company town and the mine owners essentially ran the town, and they worked to make it a pleasant place to live. The streets were lined with shade trees, and a small stream ran along the canyon bottom. Employees' benefits included medical services, as well as regularly scheduled dances, films, and other social events. Mohrland's company baseball team was popular and successful. In the spring of 1915, as champions of the Carbon County league, they played an exhibition game at Price against the Chicago White Sox, drawing an audience of over 10,000, but losing by a score of 17 to one. The most successful years were the early 1920s, but by 1925 coal prices and profits were down. On March 1, 1925, U.S. Fuel closed down the mine without warning, leaving Mohrland's residents without jobs and without credit at the company store, many people had no money or food. The company reopened Mohrland just as suddenly in September 1926, and the town struggled back to its feet. In 1930 the population was 620. Coal production continued to become less profitable during the Great Depression. In 1938 U.S. Fuel announced a decision to close Mohrland. The buildings were sold to a salvage company for $50 each. Very little of the town was left behind. Directions: Travel south from Price on U-122 and follow it to Hiawatha. From Hiawatha a dirt road leads west for five miles to a fork. The right fork leads up canyon one mile to the old town site. In 2006 several remnants of the town could be seen.

Mohrland 2006 All 3 Photos taken by Penny

<u>Moore</u> was a community at the edge of the San Rafael Swell, elevation 6,247 feet. The population was five at the 2000 census. It was originally named Rochester for a town in New York. At about the same time, Emery was digging the Muddy Canal and financial investors from the eastern states became aware of the lush productive farmland on the flats east of the Muddy River headwaters. The investors saw the potential and formed The Independent Canal Company to claim water from the Muddy Creek and coax this arid land into producing grain like in the Midwest. Shares were offered to residents of Emery County. They began digging and blasting to build a new canal that would irrigate farmland and provide water. The town had a store, brick school, and post office. In 1940 the community was renamed Moore after postmaster L.C. Moore who became the land development project leader for the area in 1907. Most residents have moved into neighboring towns but have kept their farmland which continues to produce great crops. These pioneer settlements of the late 19th century were also the crossroads for other historic civilizations, such as the Fremont culture. Several rock art panels surround Moore, such as the Rochester Rock Art Panel.

RochesterRock Art 2014 phot taken **by** Penny Rochester School 1914

Moore 2014 Photo taken by Penny

Nolan was a railroad town.

Quitchupah was a small settlement near Muddy Creek. First settled in 1882, the small community erected a frame school house that also served as a center for social activities. A cloud burst in the early 1900s caused severe flooding, causing the people to move away.

Sphinx was a settlement on the Denver Rio Grande Railroad.

Temple Mountain was a small village that was built up in 1910 where a vein of uranium was located at the base of Temple Mountain in 1904. During WWI most domestically used uranium came from Utah and Western Colorado. Some of the ore was sent to Paris, France for Marie Curie's radium experiments. After the war and the depression all mines closed in the country. Experiments during and after WWII triggered the 1950 boom, the mines were again opened. Most of the new workers brought their own house trailers, while a few lived in the 50-year-old stone cabins, and some prefabricated homes were erected. Temple Mountain Junction was the business center with a store, service station, café, pool hall and some dwellings added in the late 1950s. The children were bussed to Green River to school. In 1962 the uranium boom was over, miners hitched up their mobile homes and disappeared. The Junction lasted till 1968. Directions: Temple Mountain Junction is on State Highway 24 about 37 miles south of Green River. The mine site is seven miles west on a largely paved road through San Rafael Reef.

Marie Curie stayed here when she came to Temple Mountain

Victor was established in 1910. A dam burst, flooding the soil near Desert Lake with alkaline water that preventing farming. Residents of Desert Lake had to relocate to a more fertile area in order to continue farming. They chose a spot six miles east of Elmo, and the town was named Victor. Homes and a schoolhouse were built in town. Farming was more difficult at Victor because the area was much drier than Desert Lake. Sand dunes located near the town were often blown onto farmland and the buildings. In 1920, the continuous lack of rain caused the residents of Victor to leave. The schoolhouse and some foundations remain at the town site.

School at Victor

Wilsonville was located about three miles southeast of Castle Dale. The Wilson families were first to settle in this area. A mail route was established between Ouray, Colorado and Salina, Utah over the Old Spanish Trail. The route covered 250 miles and took six weeks by horseback. Sylvester Wilson contracted to handle mail over this route with a post office established at Wilsonville. He established a rest station with extra horses at Thompson Springs, north of Moab and hired others to carry the mail. Wilsonville Post Office, with Sylvester as postmaster, was established in 1879 and was discontinued in 1882. The mail bag for Wilsonville was left in the crotch of a tree at the Wilson homestead until Sylvester built a split-log post office. The building still stands even though it has been moved over a rise to Rock Creek Canyon on the south. It has been used as a granary and for storage. The railroad reached Price, Utah and the horse-carried route was abolished, which marked the end of Wilsonville.

<u>Woodside/Lower Crossing</u> was settled in 1881 and became a thriving farming community and livestock loading station. The first resident was a local prospector by the name of Henry H. Hutchinson. Other settlers arrived the following year and soon established a small community with stores, a cafe and blacksmith shop. After damming the near-by Price River for irrigation, a variety of food was grown including vegetables, turkeys, cattle, sheep, sugar beets and honey. They called the town "Lower Crossing" for the D & R railroad which crossed the river at this point. The name was changed to Woodside for the numerous cottonwood groves in the area. At one point the community included a railroad hotel and depot. A school built in 1892 served as a town gathering place. In 1897, following a train robbery at Castle Gate, Butch Cassidy hid in a network of tunnels under a house outside of town. Railroad facilities improved and nearby Helper became a more convenient town. In the late 1920s livestock shipping facilities and the depot were removed from Woodside. The occasional flooding of the river caused the farmers to search for better lands. After the cafe and store burned down in 1970, Woodside became a ghost town. Woodside is located between Price and Green River on US-6. At one time, a geyser in the center of Woodside erupted about every 20 minutes. The railroad company was drilling a well when water shot up. Vandals threw some big rocks into the geyser hole and plugged it, causing the geyser to stop erupting. There was also a dry ice house near Woodside. The people that ran the business had a carbon dioxide well for dry ice making. The cemetery lies to the northwest. In 2014 remnants of the town could still be seen

CHAPTER 9
Garfield County

Asay Town/Aaron was first settled in 1872 by Joseph Asay, his wife Sarah Ann, and family. Joseph was the first postmaster in Asay and he also ran a small store. The area was a farming community in the late 1800s but the high altitude and short growing season resulted in poor crop yields. Directions: The town lies about six miles south of Hatch where Asay Creek crosses US-89. The site is on private property, about a mile off US-89, west of Bryce Canyon. Several buildings remained in 2013. There was a fairly intact cabin and several farm out-buildings. The entire site was very overgrown. Beware of an open, uncovered well off the south end of the cabin.

Asay town 12/2013 photo taken by Penny

Bromide Basin was a large 1890s gold camp with tents, houses and boarding houses at the base of Mount Ellen in the Henry Mountains. A sign posted in 2013 read: "Not allowed in the area, active mining."

Castle was a small settlement on the Sevier River, between Cedar Breaks and Panguitch Lake. The area was pioneered in 1872 by Meltiar Hatch and his two wives. The family operated a cattle ranch. The town was named for the spectacular castle-like topography of the surrounding cliffs.

Clifton/Cliff was a small farming hamlet. Several villages were settled in this area during the mid-1870s, but an erratic water supply and flooding forced the settlers to abandon the villages. Clifton was named by Willis E. Robinson for the surrounding cliffs. Clifton is located south of Cannonville on Utah Route 12 near Georgetown.

Clifton 2012 Photo taken by Penny

Eagle City was located at the fork of the canyon two miles below Bromide Basin at the head of Crescent Creek in the Henry Mountains. The area is very remote, with beautiful scenery. Eagle was a large 1890s gold camp, with a store, doctor's office, a hotel, boarding house and a saloon. The Bromide Mill burned in 1911. WWI caused the demise of Eagle City. Only Frank Lawler remained another 60 years at the camp. Lawler believed the Lost Josephine Mine to be in the Henrys. There was some mining activity as late as 1988. Directions: Travel south from Hanksville about 22 miles, taking a dirt road on the right. After about three miles there will be a sign for Little Egypt. The road will form a "Y", keep to the right. After

about three miles cross a small stream and take the right fork that will lead into the Henry Mountains. After climbing several miles, there will be a "T" in the road. Turn around and go back about a quarter mile, watching for old landings dug into the hillside to the north. Along the road some old house lumber can be spotted. The city was located where there are large trees and a small stream along the road. One building on the side of the mountain remained in 2013.

Georgetown was established in 1877 as a small ranching and farming community. By 1894 it had a population of nearly 200; it also had a school, store and post office. By the 1940s Yellow Creek dried up and the people moved to Cannonville. The saints who named the settlement for their church leader had high hopes of establishing an oasis in the desert, but they are pretty rare in Garfield County. Georgetown was built on the Kane county line. Directions: Travel two miles south from Cannonville on a paved road to the Kane County line, then take a hard right (west) on a dirt road. Travel one mile to the town site, the grave yard rests on the north side.

Georgetown 11-2013 photo taken by Penny

Greens was located north of Escalante in Main Canyon. The Green family lived in this small community.

Henderson was located four miles North of Widtsoe. The small colony began in 1915 named for William Henderson who donated land for the town center. There was a post office and a church-school building. By 1924 the town had disappeared. Nothing remained of the site in 2013.

Hillsdale was located on US-89 about six miles from Hatch. The community was settled in 1871 under the leadership of George Deliverance Wilson. Wilson and Johnson established a saw mill in that same year to supply lumber for the 20 families that moved into the area around 1871. By 1886 the people began to move away because of the cold climate and water uncertainties. A handful of people stayed on for another 50 years running cattle. In 2013 one of the old cabins was made into a tackle shop, and a few other cabins in the area were in ruins.

Hillsdale 2013 Photo taken by Penny

Losee/Loseeville/New Clifton was a small Mormon farming village with a church and school house. It was located two miles east of Tropic, on the Yellow Creek. A post office was granted in 1886. Yellow Creek dried up and people moved to Cannonville around 1900. Only the cemetery located in the middle of a field remained in 2013.

Osiris was located approximately 13 miles north of Widtsoe. The settlement was established in 1910 by an earlier Panguitch sheep man who donated land for the town site. Later W.E. Holt from

nearby Widtsoe built a rock-walled creamery, flour mill, a telephone exchange and many homes on the site. He then renamed the town Osiris (for the King or god of the dead) in Black Canyon. The altitude and insufficient water resources prevented the growth of reliable vegetable crops, and within ten years the settlement was abandoned. The buildings remaining in Osiris are privately owned and should only be viewed from Highway 22 which runs past the old creamery.

Old Creamery Osiris, 12-2014
Photo taken by Penny

Panguitch Fort was a Mormon settlers' fort from 1865-1868.

Spry was located eight miles north of Panguitch. The settlement was established in 1872 and had several early name changes as clusters of families were absorbed into the settlement. Early town names were Fort Sanford, Lowder Spring, Tebbs Springs, Tebbsdale, Orton, Bear Creek and Cleveland. When Jesse LeFevre became postmaster in 1908, he renamed the established community to Spry in honor of Utah Governor William Spry.

Ticaboo was a mining town located South of the Henry Mountains. The small settlement was a company town with a mill for processing uranium from nearby mines. By the time the town and mill were completed, the price of "yellowcake" (processed uranium ore) had dropped and the mill was shut down. As of 2018 rusting machinery, abandoned shafts, and scattered debris are all that survive as relics of the uranium booms of the 1950s.

Warm Creek was was a village located along the east side of a stream by the name on the Kaiparowitz Plateau. A coal vein was discovered and a group of pioneers was sent to develop it. The coal was mined and transported to the Colorado River where it was floated downstream by barge to civilization. The village was made of sandstone blocks with stone corral fences and was established shortly after Bryce Canyon was discovered in the 1860s.

Widtsoe/Adairville is located on the east fork of the Sevier River, approximately 16 miles northeast of Bryce Canyon. One of the first settlers in the area was Isaac Riddle, who built a temporary ranch in the valley; in 1876. It became a stop for the Hole-In-The-Rock pioneers in 1879. Jeddah Adair, along with one of his plural wives, Julia Ann, and eight children eventually bought the land and moved onto the property in 1902. They practiced a new farming technique called dry farming. Other settlers moved into the area when they saw Adair's success.

In 1910, Julia Adair donated 40 of her acres for the beginnings of a town. It was established as "Winder." The standard of living was low; water had to be brought into town in barrels. By 1914, the town grew when it added another 160 acres. The town had two hotels, an LDS church, confectionery, four stores, a post office, and a three-room schoolhouse, with a population of 310. In 1915 running water was piped into town. In April, 1917, Winder changed its name to Widtsoe, in honor of LDS Church Apostle and dry farming expert John A. Widtsoe. In 1920 the population was approximately 1100. The town reached its heyday in the early 1920s.

In 1923 W. F. Holt bought the Widtsoe Hotel, built over ten homes, constructed dams and irrigation canals, provided funds for telephone lines, and brought in high-altitude lettuce seed (which was considered to be the best iceberg lettuce in the world.) Holt spent nearly $300,000 in the area. Severe drought, erosion of the land, drastic climate fluctuations, and large numbers of rodents took their toll. People began to leave and by 1934 only 40 families remained. That spring the residents' plight was critical and they requested federal aid. The Federal Resettlement Administration stepped in and bought out the townspeople and homesteaders in 1936. The Widtsoe Cemetery was still in use with the most recent additions being infant twins buried in 1999. In 2013 there were some old buildings remaining along with new cabins and old mob

Widtsoe 2013 Photos by Penny

CHAPTER 10
Grand County

Agate was located 38 miles east of Green River on US 6/50 south of Cisco. It was a settlement along the Denver & Rio Grande railroad. Little is known about Agate except that Johnnie Pace was a school board member representing the Danish Flats and Agate Schools.

Archeron was a railroad town near the Utah-Colorado boarder. It had an artesian well, but the water was poor and could not be used. The town ended in 1890 when a new railroad track south of town was laid.

Castleton was a mining supply center located at the far end of Castle Valley. This little town was the center of activity for a large area that included Miner's Basin and the ranches of Fisher Valley. In 1879 there were some cabins along Castle Creek built by prospectors and stockmen. At one time, Castleton boasted a boardinghouse, two hotels, a store, a post office, two saloons, restaurants, livery stable, blacksmith and cobble shops, deputy sheriff, physician, mine offices, a school, a Sunday school and homes. The first school was held in a saloon. There was a post office from 1900 to 1920. The town died after the 1907 national financial panic killed the mines. Castleton is located seven miles south east of Castle Valley. In 2014 there were a few foundations and an old dilapidated log building remaining.

Cisco was an ore and coal shipping, outfitting, and supply center that was settled around 1887. At one time the town served as a saloon and water-refilling station for the Denver and Rio Grande Western Railroad. At one time there were two stores and a hotel in Cisco. The children had to walk three miles to the pump house to school. For 60 years Cisco depended on the pump house and railroad for water. When the railroad changed from steam to diesel they refused to continue pumping water. Cisco survived long enough into the 20th century to be assigned a Zip Code. Unfortunately for history and railroad buffs, the ghost town's easy access and proximity to the freeway have lured vandals; the relics are heavily damaged. Cisco is about six miles southwest of I-70 at Exit 220. Cisco spreads nearly a mile, with a cluster of buildings at the central point. Several old buildings remained in Cisco in 2014, and one appeared to be lived in.

Cisco Nov. 2014 Photo taken by Penny

Cisco Nov. 2014 Photo taken by Penny

Cottonwood was a settlement along the Denver & Rio Grande Railroad. In the 1930s this tiny map dot was a busy town with several hundred people, and was located on what was US-6/50. Cottonwood was located a few miles northeast of Cisco.

Crescent/Cresent Junction was an end-of-the-line railroad camp that housed Italian construction crews. There was also some mining in the location in the early 1900s to mid-1940s. Crescent was located 20 miles east of Green River.

Crystal Carbon was located about 18 miles northwest of Cisco. The Crystal Carbon lamp black factory was the only manufacturing plant of its kind in the state and one of a very few in the entire Rocky Mountain region. The factory buildings and a nearby group of houses made up a neat little town at the foot of the Book Mountains. The plant consisted of two rows of long, narrow houses built of tin, each about 12 feet wide and 150 feet long. There were 36 of these buildings, 18 in a row. The factory began operations in 1927. Thousands of jets burned steadily. The product commonly known as carbon black is nothing more than gas soot. Much precaution was taken to prevent its escaping into the air, but when some did all the white-faced cattle had black faces. Nothing remained in 2014.

Dalton Wells Camp was in existence from 1933 to 1943. The Dalton Wells CCC Camp worked in conjunction with the U.S. Division of Grazing. The camp was also used during World War II as a relocation and isolation camp for a small number of Japanese-Americans.

Dalton Wells Camp

Daly was located about four miles east of Green River, Utah. It was believed to be either a railroad or an agricultural community.

Danish Flats was a small farming community of Scandianvian immigrants. It was located near Cottonwood Wash in the area of the old narrow gauge tracks north of Cisco, in the Cisco Desert. It is believed the community exisited from about 1908 to the early 1920s. There was a schoolhouse in Danish Flats that also served as a social center. Nothing remained in 2014.

Dewey was located about 15 miles from Cisco on SR-128 or 32.5 miles up the river from Moab on SR-128. Richard Westwood moved his family to Dewey in 1904 to run the ferry. The first school was held in a family's cabin from 1904 to 1906. Mrs. Westwood had to sign up for classes to meet the quota for a school. In 1906 Grand County built a school made of native lumber. The walls were covered with unbleached muslin to keep the dust, wind and bugs out. Miners built cabins under the trees near the river and panned for gold. Farms and ranches were plentiful in Dewey. The bridge was completed in 1916, causing Mr. Westwood to lose his job as ferry operator. The cable bridge was 502 feet long and ten feet wide. There was a post office from 1898 to 1902 and the little school stood for many years. In the 1980s a new bridge was built and the old one was used for walkers and bikers. The old bridge burned in 2008. Only the upper part of the old bridge remaineds.

Photos taken 2014 by Penny

Dolores Triangle was a small settlement where several homes were located in a triangle area and many people made homes on the river bottoms. The community had a post office from 1913 to 1919.

 **Elgin** was a small agricultural community where 30 families lived in 1905. At one time Elgin had a post office, railroad depot, school and a store by 1909 there were two schools a fruit growers' association, a bonded abstractor, a good telephone system, exceptional fruit land and a population of 225. The post office operated from 1898 to 1918. There was a ferry to Green River. In 1917, the price of coal rose, and two years of harsh winters destroyed the orchards. By the 1920s the town was abandoned. Elgin was located across the bridgeFrom green River.

Elk Mountain Mission was a settlement located in Green River. In April 1855, 41 men under the leadership of Alfred N. Billings were called to establish an LDS mission in the Elk Mountains. They left Salt Lake City May 7, 1855, arrived at Grand River June 11 and selected the site for a settlement. By July 15, they had built a fort 64 feet-square with sturdy stone walls. At first the missionaries were successful, baptizing over a dozen Ute Indians, but tensions arose and an attack rendered three of the pioneers dead, James W. Munt, Edward Edwards and William Behumin, who were buried within the fort. A historical monument stands at the Moab Chamber of Commerce.

Fort Moab was a fort that was abandoned after repeated Indian attacks. It was utilized from 1851 to 1855, and the area wasn't resettled for another 20 years.

Halfway Stage Station served travelers between Moab and the railroad at Thompson. The railroad was 35 miles from Moab. At the halfway house horses were changed, meals were served and travelers could stay overnight. The trip from Moab to the train took eight hours, travelers would stop to eat, and freighters stayed the night.

Harley Dome was a small community on I-70, exit 227 near the Colorado border. The town was named after Harley Basker who drilled a gas well on a dome in the Cisco desert. This was the beginning of what developed into the Harley Dome Oil scandal. In 1969 Dynamic Industries Incorporated bought the oil rights to hundreds of acres in the area and sold shares. In 2014 there were big oil companies in the area.

Hittle's Bottom was a post office stop for mail carriers. In the early 1900s, the Tom Kitsen family lived here. Tom carried the mail with his team of horses from the Cisco post office to the Castleton post offce. He used this place as a halfway stop to change his teams. In 2014 some remnants of the cabin and a gravesite remain, along with a plaque. It is located in a picnic area on SR-128, 22 miles from Moab.

Remains of the cabin at Hittle's bottom 11-2014 Photo by Penny

Little Grand was a railroad station/settlement along the Denver & Rio Grande Railroad. The settlement was located east of Green River at the Floy exit. Nothing remained in 2014.

Marrs was a farming community located on the Cisco Desert near Westwater. A post office was located in Marrs from 1910 to 1913.

Mesa was a mining town located in the La Sal Mountains on Wilson Mesa. The town was settled in 1891 and enough miners came to the area that in 1900 a school was built. A post office served the community from 1907 to 1913. A historical marker in this area marks the spot where on June 15, 1881 a band of hostile Indians killed eight settlers.

Miner's Basin/Basin was a small gold-mining town at an elevation of 10,000 feet, located up the side of a steep tree-covered mountain where there is a road that leads to a valley of lush meadows. About 20 cabins were built in 1898, there was also a stamp mill and 125 ton cyanide mill east of the camp. Miners Basin developed and eventually reached a population of 75-80 people. There were two saloons (A blind man, Sam McGrew ran one of the saloons), two restaurants, a blacksmith shop, boarding house, hotel, post office, shoemaker, general store, livery stable, sheriff's office, and a Sunday school. In 1907 a new 125 ton cyanide mill was built in the canyon east of town. The mines barely reached 50-150 feet. The 1907 financial panic killed the mines and the town died. Everyone moved away except Gordon Fowler, who stayed for the next 50 years, always promoting Miner's Basin. He kept the old cabins in repair, with fresh chopped wood in each cabin and beds made. He stayed until his death in 1966, then Bill and Edith Connors moved into his old cabin, located 18 miles east of Moab. Directions: Starting at Castle Valley Junction, travel ten miles to Castleton, where the road forks. Follow the La Sal Loop road to the right, traveling south and west for about five miles. Miners Basin is about four miles up a treacherous road, which was impassable in the winter of 2014.

Picture Gallery was an agricultural settlement along the Grand River bottomlands north of the Dolores River. It was named for the scenic beauty in the area. The settlement began in the 1880s and later a post office and other facilities were established on Coats Creek, near the Utah-Colorado boarder. There was a school located in the settlement for about three years.

Pindhook was located in the La Sal Mountains near Miner's Basin. It was mining camp of one log house and about 25 tents. At one time it had a tent school and a saloon.

Pinto was a settlement along the Denver & Rio Grande Railroad.

Polar was a mining camp located in the La Sal Mountains.

Richardson was a settlement developed in 1879 on Professor Creek, two miles from the Colorado River. In 1879 Professor Richardson settled at the mouth of Professor Creek. He built a small cabin and later converted it into a store. Richardson was the postmaster and a teacher in a small school in Professor Valley. There was a post office in Richardson from 1886 to1905, located 17 miles northwest of Moab on SR-128. Uranium was discovered near this point in 1898 and was stripped from this site for eight to ten years. By the side of the Colorado, there is a solitary grave enclosed by a rough pole fence. To the east in Richardson's back yard, are the beautiful red spires of the Fisher Towers.

Sagers was a railroad town located a few miles northwest of Cisco.

Sego/Neslin/Ballard was an early 1900s to 1950s era coal mining camp and once had 500 people. The camp was located in Sego Canyon, about six miles north of Thompson Springs. There were company houses, a two-story hotel, and many other businesses and houses. There was an Italian, Japanese, American, Greek and a Negro section in Sego. Three better homes were built in a separate section, one each for the superintendent, the doctor, and the storekeeper, who was also the postmaster. The store keeper was considered very important. He was responsible for scrip (money) bought by the miners, which could only be used in the Sego store. Prices were double those in Thompson, but few people had a way to travel. The miners were threatened with the loss of their jobs if they bought outside of Sego. Just above the store were a clubhouse and a boarding house for unmarried office workers. Near the entrance to the mine tunnels there was a Greek boardinghouse, a few dwellings, three gambling houses, and a coffee house which was the pool hall for men only, but every Saturday night there was a dance. In 1928 Sego was the busiest coal camp in Utah. In 1947 the Sego Coal Mine closed. In 1955 the houses were taken to Moab and sold. Sego Canyon has numerous petroglyphs. The town was first known as Neslin until April 1918.

Directions: from Thompson Springs. Take the gravel road exiting north, about five miles past badly marred pictographs. At the end of a narrow dirt road, which twists and winds its way up the canyon, there are a few remains. Scattered through the greenery are dugout cabins, an explosives bunker, and many foundations. There is a cemetery on the windy ridge just below the town. Sego has been abandoned for many years, but smoke still comes from the mine shafts from the fires that have burned for years. In Sego the miners could build cabins wherever they wanted. All along the canyon and its side gulches are places where cabins or shacks were built. Under high ledges, dugout homes can be spotted. In 1955 the houses were taken to Moab and sold. Sego Canyon has numerous petroglyphs.

House in Sego 2014 Photo by Penny Sego Company Store 2014 photo by Penny

Solitude was located about nine miles east of Green River. It was either a railroad community or an agricultural community, according to *A History of Grand County*.

South Mesa was an agricultural community. A tramway was rigged up to lower crops over the edge of South Mesa. Logs were cut and lowered to build eight towers in a straight line down the face of the cliff. Each tower contained eight-inch pulleys rigged to the two arms of the towers. A two-foot binder wheel was placed at the bottom of the tram. The cable was equipped with 12 hooks that carried a total of 1200 pounds at a time. A road was finally built, and then improved in 1971.

Thompson Springs/Thompsons was located about a mile north of I-70 at exit 185, about 27 miles east of Green River. It was the most active rail hub in eastern Utah. The town of Thompson Springs was an agricultural community around 1890. It had a hotel, pool hall, railroad station, store and a single-story brick motel, the Silver Grill Café, and other buildings which included the old Sego School which began in 1907. E. W. Thompson lived near the springs and operated a sawmill near the Book Cliffs. Stockmen from both San Juan and Grand counties ran their cattle and sheep in the area. In spring the sheep were sheared and then the sheepshearer's ball was held. The town was also a prominent shipping point for cattle. The original name for this settlement was Thompson Springs, and then it changed to Thompsons then back to Thompson Springs. In 2014 many empty buildings and houses could be seen, with a few still inhabited.

Thompson Spring 2014 photos by Penny

<u>Thompson Spring Canyon</u> has a lot to see it is a great place explore. It is up the road from the town of Thompson Springs.

Thompson Springs Canyon Utah by Penny Clendenin

Utaline was a settlement along the Denver & Rio Grande Railroad.

Valley City was a small hamlet located on U.S. Highway 163 about five miles south of Crescent Junction and U.S. Highway 6-50. A few miles south of Crescent Junction are the remains of a rock and dirt cellar, which is all that remains of a once-thriving farming community. The company raised enough money for a cement dam but the secretary-treasurer of the company spent the money on horse racing so a dirt dam was put in. In 1908, 20 people were setting out sixty acres of orchard when the dam was washed away in a storm, and the people moved away. Several years later they rebuilt the dam and raised fruits and vegetables. There was a school in Valley City for a few years. By 1930, flash floods finally forced the last settlers to move.

Victor was located in Mill Creek Basin. Mining interests in 1900 planned to apply for a post office but it never materialized. No other information could be found about Victor.

Webb Hollow was in a little valley at the foot of Bald Mesa. "Hi" Allen settled here and prospected, spending most of his time panning for gold but he found very little. J.H. Webb bought out Allen's improvements and filed on the homestead. He staked some mining claims, and he and his son-in-law panned out thousands of dollars in gold.

Westwater was located southwest of the Utah-Colorado border. The ranching community began in the late 1800s and became a railroad town in the 1890s. A large number of the people were Chinese, Japanese, and Mexicans working on the railroad track. There was a school, two stores, and an eating house. A post office was constructed in 1887. Mining also took place near Westwater. After mining and railroad construction in the region declined, the town was abandoned and the area was used for grazing. Directions: Travel on I70, taking exit 227. Turn on Harley Dome road and follow it for about eight miles. In 2014 a few scattered ranches in the area could be found.

Whitehouse was a settlement along the Denver & Rio Grande Railroad. At one time there was a depot and other buildings, along with a camp that housed Chinese workers.

Wilson Mesa was a small settlement in the rocky red and yellow cliffs east of Moab on the Sand Flat Road; posted Moab's dump is posted as the "most Scenic dump in the world." A road winds its way up Little Spring Hill, through Malloy Park, and then onto North Mesa of the LaSal mountains. At one time, there were log cabins and pole corrals. School was conducted in the early 1900s for three years, and then people moved to Moab during the school months. There was a post office from 1907 to 1912 and reopened from 1915 to 1923. Nothing remained in 2014.

CHAPTER 11
Iron County

Aberdeen was a small settlement not far from Cedar City. The town was poor and was soon abandoned.

Avon was a railroad siding between Lund and Iron Springs on the spur into Cedar City.

Beryl was one of the three largest railroad towns of Iron County. A hotel and warehouse served homesteaders and freighters and a section house accommodated the railroad crews. Enough homesteaders and railroaders lived in or near Beryl to build a school in the 1920s. The school grew to 30 students of diverse races and nationalities, including Japanese, Italian, and Native Americans. Beryl was nine miles northwest of New Castle. It was named after the semi-precious stone found in the vicinity. As late as 2012, many traces of the old town could be seen.

Both Photos by Penny 2011

Beryl Junction was located 13 miles south of Beryl. This area was part of the New Castle Reclamation Company property from 1909 to 1915. The company built a hotel so that prospective homesteaders could be picked up at the Beryl railroad station, brought to see the agricultural development and housed at the hotel. Mormon apostle David O. McKay, an officer in the company, invested in land at the Junction. Although the reclamation project was unsuccessful, modern irrigation and deep-well pumping have turned the area into a rich agricultural valley.

Buckhorn Springs was a watering place along the old California wagon road. In 1887 John Eyre became the first settler, and then between 1907 and 1922 some 20 families made their homes here to try dry-land farming. One family was Lewis Farnsworth's family; Lewis' son was Philo, inventor of the television. The Buckhorn Branch of the Paragonah LDS Ward was organized in 1910. The first school was established in 1907 and the last in about 1922. Years of drought drove most of the farmers out in the 1960s. The settlement was located three miles north of the I-15 rest stop between Beaver and Parowan.

Cedar Fort was a protective fort built between 1853 and 1854. Nine of 16 city blocks were enclosed, and the fort walls were made of adobe which was three feet thick at the base, nine feet high and one foot wide at the top.

Chloride was a mining camp where silver chloride was discovered in 1890 in Chloride Canyon on the western slope of the Antelope Range. The camp was located 23 miles west of Cedar City, and mining continued sporadically from 1890 to 1910.

Desert Springs was a stagecoach inn and freighter's camp which was built at Desert Spring at the junction of roads from Beaver, Iron Springs, Mountain Meadows, and the Nevada mining camps. Ben Tasker, cattle rustler and outlaw used Desert Spring as his headquarters. The Desert Spring Cemetery is three miles north of Modena on the west side of the road to Hamlin Valley. Ruins of the stagecoach stop are opposite the cemetery on the east side of the road. Tasker sheltered rustlers and outlaws at his hideout, which was complete with a trap door leading to a stable under the house where horses were kept, ready for a quick getaway.

Duck Creek Camp was a camp that worked in conjunction with the U.S. Forest service. Duck Creek was near Cedar Breaks.

Ford was a railroad siding and sheep-shearing station five miles southwest of Lund.

Fort Louisa was the name of a fort that was later changed to Fort Parowan. George A. Smith officially named the new location "Fort Louisa," in honor of Louisa Beaman, the first documented woman to marry into Polygamy.

Fort Paragonah was constructed in 1855. The fort's first story was 100 feet square and the second story was finished in 1857. The fort occupied the center of town until the early 1860s.

Fort Sanford was built downriver form Panguitch in the spring of 1866 when the Blackhawk war broke out. About 50 men were sent from Beaver and Iron County. Within a short time they erected a picket stockade. They built eight-foot-high walls from juniper posts which they planted in a vertical stockade style, enclosing five acres with good grass so livestock could be protected. They also dug a deep ditch around the perimeter to prevent attackers from scaling the walls. Men at the fort endured many skirmishes with the Native Americans and many hardships guarding the captives, carrying messages, watching stock, and helping settlers move houses into the fort. All was accomplished, but in June the order came to abandon the settlement.

Gold Springs was an early gold mining camp in 1897 near the Utah-Nevada border, ten miles northwest of Modena. There were homes, stores and a hotel in Gold Springs. The ore at the mines was so rich that armed guards were used when it was shipped to Salt Lake. Gold Springs was abandoned as the resources were depleted. The population in 1910 was 45. Telephone service was established in 1917-18. The mine was reopened in 1930 and the homes were renovated or new ones built. The town was half in Utah and half in Nevada. Gold Springs and the Jennie Mine were destroyed by the Utah division of Natural Resources in 2004 and the area was bulldozed.

Grimshawville was a small agricultural community. William H. Grimshaw wandered through Cedar Valley in 1902 looking for the tallest sagebrush. He found it north and west of Enoch where he homesteaded. He and his wife brought honeybees and planted corn and alfalfa. Soon they went into the seed business with what was described as phenomenal success. Many families moved to the area, but later a water shortage caused the fields to die out. Grimshawville became part of Enoch Town in 1956.

Hamilton's Fort/Walker Fort/Fort Sidon began as a wooden structure. In 1854 the settlers built an adobe fort enclosing a quarter acre called Fort Sidon. By 1860 the settlement was known as Hamilton's Fort, located four miles south of Cedar City. The settlement was founded in 1852 and known as Shirts Creek after the creek the fort was founded on. The fort and creek were both named for Peter Shirts, a noted Mormon Pioneer and scout. After the Native American wars of 1853, Shirts sold the fort and land to his neighbor, John Hamilton. At that time it was known as Fort Walker, supposedly in honor of the noted Indian Chief Walker. During the Native American wars with Chief Walker the settlers moved into nearby Cedar City. When the settlers returned in 1857 they renamed the settlement Sidon after a City in Asia. In 1869 the settlers moved one-half mile north of the old fort and renamed the site Hamilton in honor of John Hamilton. Located five miles south of Cedar City, the fort was three-feet thick and enclosed all the settlers' cabins.

Hamlin Valley was settled in the early 1920s. Homesteading dry farmers from the Midwest built a schoolhouse/community center in the south end of the Hamlin Valley about 17 miles north of Modena. It was open from about 1920 to 1926. There were 28 students attending the school in 1922. The valley was more suited for livestock range than farming.

Heist/Escalante was railroad siding town five miles northeast of Modena.

Iron City/Iron Town/Old Iron Town/Iron Mission was settled in 1868 when Mormon pioneers moved in after the Cedar City mining operation had failed nearly ten years earlier. By 1870, the town had close to a hundred residents. The settlement grew up around the iron works. Ebenezer Hanks, president of the company, owned the town site. The town grew until by 1875 there were close to 200 residents. Iron City seemed prosperous, but the iron company was unable to overcome financial obstacles created by the money panic of 1874, and the lack of suitable transportation to northern Utah. In 1877, the iron operation closed. Charcoal kilns, the foundry, and blast furnace lie in ruins among many other foundations. The site was added to the National Register of Historic Places in 1971. At its peak, the settlement included a brick schoolhouse, blacksmith, post office, boarding house, butcher shop, pattern shop, machine shop, general store, and a foundry. Originally the iron works included two charcoal kilns, 2,500-pound capacity furnaces, a pattern shop, and an arista, which was a grinding device. Most families moved away after the Iron Works closed down in 1876. By 1880 there were only fifteen residents, and it became Utah's first ghost town. The town is located about 20 miles from Cedar City on U-56. In 2012 many remnants could be observed.

Furnace at Iron Town   Horse-driven arista for grinding ore   Kiln

Photos by Penny

Iron Springs was settled as the Cedar Cooperative Sheep Company built a long narrow building for shearing known as the "old rock house." Shearing at Iron Springs was a big event which attracted many of the county's men and boys, who camped in tents or wagon boxes. When the railroad spur was built into Cedar City in 1923, the rails came first to Iron Springs, where a depot was built. Iron Springs was at its height when the Pioche and Desert Mound mines were producing between the years of 1924 and 1936. There was a post office in the branch store of the Cedar Mercantile Company, and the Iron Springs School operated from 1924 to 1930. The mine employed about 40 men at the time, and Iron Springs had its own baseball team which competed against other towns and camps.

Johnson Fort was a Mormon settlers' 165-foot square adobe-walled fort, with a two-story bastion in the southeast corner, constructed in 1851 in Enoch. The town was originally named Johnson Springs until renamed in 1890.

Kerr was a railroad siding north of Lund and ten miles south of Nada.

Latimer was an end-of-the-line railroad town, located between Kerr and Nada. District records show that school was taught there in 1917 and 1923.

Page Ranch house 2013 Photo by Penny

Little Pinto/Pages Ranch was located six miles northeast of Pinto, three miles across the Iron County line. It was an off-shoot of Iron town. Little Pinto is also known as Pages Ranch. Only about a dozen people resided there. Pages Ranch was located where the road from New Harmony intersects with the road to Pinto. Robert Richie began ranching this area in 1850s, then his grandsons Daniel and Robert Page were raised on the ranch and in 1890 took it over. In 1900 Daniel Page constructed a large brick ranch house which is still standing, and listed on the National Register of Historic Places. In 1900 there were 32 people living in this corner of the county. Sophia Page and her children operated the ranch for 30 years, using the house as an informal hotel for travelers and the boarding house for men working in nearby iron mines. The Page Ranch House was once an important stop along a freighting and travel route through Iron County, Utah.

Lund was a town established in about 1898 as a station stop on the Los Angeles and Salt Lake Railroad, later Union Pacific Railroad. It was also a community center for early twentieth century homesteaders. The area's population was never large; however, most early settlers were unsuccessful due to the region's harsh and arid climate. Lund's population remained extremely small until 1911, when the valley was opened to homestead settlement. The Lund town site was plotted in 1913. A population decline began in the 1920s, due to

the failure of most of the homestead-era farms. Lund's most dramatic event was in February 1922, when a freak flood struck the desert valley and partially inundated the town. Lund gained importance as a railroad junction in 1923, when the Union Pacific constructed a branch line from Lund to Cedar City. A post office operated in Lund from 1901 to 1967. The last passenger trains stopped in Lund in 1969, and the depot building was razed the following year, marking the end of the town's railway

Photo by Penny 2013

prominence.

Marchant was settled during the 1930s, when a few Japanese farmers moved to the area eight miles north of the Beryl crossroads and two miles east of U-98. They enjoyed productive farms for a few years and built the Marchant School, which was used from 1934 until 1940.

Midvalley was a farming center in the middle of Cedar Valley west of Enoch. School was held there between 1914 and 1920.

Modena began when the railroad was established through the area in the late 1800s. B.J. Lund and his business partners started freighting and other ventures. They were freighting to St. George, Utah, Pioche, and Delamar Nevada. By 1903, a U.S. Weather Bureau office had also been established in Modena. One source states that an Italian laborer named the railroad camp after Modena, Italy. Another source relates that a Chinese cook during the serving of dinner would call out periodically, "Mo'dinna, mo'dinna." Lund soon bought out his partners and in 1903 incorporated under the name of B. J. Lund & Company. The name "Lund" is still found on several buildings in town including the General Merchandise & Hotel building. The change from steam to diesel by the railroad brought about the demise of Modena, which today is almost a ghost town. The town served locals and others working the silver, iron ore, and beryl rock mines around the area. A stone school building is one of the more imposing structures in town. Just north of town is the Modena cemetery. Facing the railroad are two classic structures. One is a chocolate brown, bare windowed, single-story false-front building, while the other is a well weathered two-story, with peeling paint advertising it as the "BJ Lund & Co. General Merchandise and Hotel.

Other buildings of note include the white clapboard Last Chance Saloon, Forces General Store, single pump gas station/post office, and a few other structures. Modena is on U-56, about nine miles east of the Nevada border and fifty miles west of Cedar City.

Both Photos by Penny 2013

Nada began as a railroad siding on the Iron-Beaver County line. In 1912 a hostel or temporary hotel provided accommodations for those seeking "free" 160-acre ranches on newly surveyed land in Iron County opened to homesteading. Land locators met the trains and guided hopeful landowners to see the potential of the area. The Culmsee family chose a claim near the Nada sidetrack, where they moved in 1913, visualizing not only a homestead but a community. Culmsee obtained a post office for Nada. The population was split between two counties so they didn't always qualify for a school, but Mrs. Culmsee and later her son Carlton, taught local children anyway. It took years of hard labor and the drilling of a well to make a partial success of family's farm. But after Culmsee's death in 1936, the wind and the desert reclaimed the community of Nada. The town sat atop an ancient Indian ruin. With the constant wind, arrowheads, grinding stones and pottery are often exposed. For 20 years settlers tried to farm that part of the desert, but crops either burned up or were blown away.

New Castle received its name from the surrounding cliffs which looked like a castle. The homesteaders came from Pinto in 1893, but it was 1903 before the first home was built. The town was established and officially named New Castle in 1909. A telephone line was established in 1909 and schooling began in 1913. The site is located 27 miles west of Cedar City at the mouth of Pinto Canyon.

Pikes Diggings was named after an old prospector called Pike. During the early 1890s gold was discovered on Buck Mountain, near the western end of Iron County. Soon the camp had rough log cabins and dugouts. The camp became the center of the Stateline Mining District.

Pleasant Valley was founded in 1851 on the Utah/Nevada border. A mail route to California was established during the Pony Express days. The area housed a sleeping station when the Pony Express was discontinued. The station was abandoned for a few years; then, in 1870, two men stumbled across the area while running cattle to California. They settled in to ranching at the site and named the area Pleasant Valley.

State Line was a mining town at the South end of Hamblin Valley. Gold and silver was discovered in Stateline Canyon in 1894 and soon a town sprung up. Then in 1896 the Ophir mine was discovered and a large population boom took place. By 1903 there were approximately 300 people living there and there was a general store. But as with most mining towns the ore started to play out around 1910 and by 1918 only 18 people remained. Minor mining activity has continued in the area ever since. Directions: Turn north on a good dirt road in Modena on Highway 56. Then drive into Hamlin Valley and turn west toward the Nevada border on a four-wheel-drive road marked as Stateline road.

Stevensville was settled in about 1910, when the Stevens brothers and their families began farming there. The settlement was located in northern Cedar Valley four miles northwest of Enoch. Alfalfa flourished on the farms during years of good precipitation.

Sulphur Springs was a stagecoach and freighter stop built at Sulphur Springs on the road from Beaver to Pioche in the 1870s. By 1880 this strip was busy with freight wagons and stagecoaches hauling between Nevada mining camps and the railroad at Milford.

Summit was a small hamlet settled in 1853 on the divide midway between Parowan and Cedar City. Summit was first laid out as a herding ground. In the spring of 1858 people moved in and began farming. In 1877 the Summit LDS Ward was organized. A log schoolhouse was replaced with a one-room concrete building, and then by a two-room brick school in 1920. The school went through the seventh grade.

Tomas was a railroad siding west of Modena.

Uvada was the last railroad siding in Utah, and terminus of the railroad from 1899 until 1905 when the tracks were extended across Nevada to California. The town lies in both Nevada and Utah, southwest of Modena.

Yale was originally named Prout. The name was changed to Utana in 1920, then to Yale in 1923. The settlement was a railroad siding, located five miles southwest of Beryl. Between

1915 and 1927, some 75 families made their homes in Yale, and school was held from 1921 to 1924.

Zane/Sahara was a siding on the Union Pacific Railroad, five miles northeast of Beryl. The settlement was named for Zane Grey, the noted western author. Southern Utah was the setting for many of Grey's novels as he traveled extensively throughout the isolated regions. Nothing but a sign remained of the settlement in 2012.

Zenda was an end-of-the-line railroad town.

CHAPTER 12
Juab County

Black Rock Station/Butte Station/Desert Station/Rock House Station was an old Pony Express Station located 14 miles southwest of Dugway Station along the northern edge of the county east of Callao. Travelers stayed only as long as was necessary. Water was a premium and meals and lodging were unheard of.

Boyd's Station was also known as Halfway Station. Boyd's Station was built of mortared stone and had rifle portholes for defense against Indians. Boyd's Station gets its name from Bud Boyd, a station keeper who lived there. Living conditions were extremely crude. The partially dug out, rock-walled living quarters contained bunks which were built into the walls. Furniture consisted of boxes and benches. Life at the isolated station was lonely. Activities of the station keeper, spare rider and blacksmith were centered on caring for the horses. Only two riders arrived and departed each day. Only a portion of the rock was that once provided protection now remains.

Burgin was a town in the Tintic Mining District.

Callao/Willow Springs was a small settlement that began mainly because of the Pony Express. It died out when the Pony Express was discontinued. In 1892 a gold boom at Gold Hill and other places in the area began. Callao became the center point for much activity again and acquired a post office in 1895. Callao was isolated and its tiny post office probably handled more business, due to its central location, per capita than any post office in Utah. There was a small store next to the post office.

When Gold Hill became the metropolis of the West Desert, Callao fell from importance again. When auto travel became popular, the Lincoln Highway was developed from coast to coast and went through Callao and again the town blossomed. There were two service stations, a post office, store and hotel, plus the one-room schoolhouse which held twenty or more students. Population peaked at 100 people around 1936. The old Willow Springs Pony

Express station is one of the best preserved in the state, although largely unrecognized as such. It was purchased in 1885 by Charles Bagley and has been in continuous use for over 120 years. The station is a frame structure, while almost all of the other western stations were stone. A log building was erected on one side and a summer porch on the other. As of 2014 there were 27 residents mostly in outlying ranches, the store was gone, a couple of gasoline pumps stood off the road and the adobe hotel had become a residence. Many old abandoned houses line Main Street. The old log post office was still sitting by the side of the road at the Six-mile ranch. There were several log buildings on the ranch built from timbers of the old Express station corrals. The one-room school house, probably the last left in Utah, was still used for the six students in the area. There were many very old log buildings lining the streets.

Callao 2013 Photos by Penny

Camp Crossman was established in 1858 as a temporary Federal Post located six miles west of Nephi. The post was used to observe Ute movements and protect government herds.

Camp Eastman was a Federal Post located in Levan on Chicken Creek 14 miles south of Nephi. Established in 1859, the post was used to observe Ute movements and protect government herds.

Canyon Station Post was established in 1864 as a fortified Pony Express station northeast of Goshute, 12 miles from Deep Creek Station.

Cherry Creek was a small hamlet which flourished for a few years after 1883. In 1883, work on a pipeline began from a dam on Cherry Creek across the desert floor to Eureka. It supplied drinking water for the town 20 miles to the east. After the dam and pipeline were completed, the tent town of Cherry creek soon disappeared.

Diamond was a mining town about six miles south of Eureka. Diamond was first settled in 1870 when a Jewish lapidary discovered crystals in the area that he cut and sold as valuable gems. Other prospectors were finding brilliant crystals and claiming diamond mines. An adjoining canyon was named Crystal Canyon. Within a year Diamond had four stores, three hotels, five saloons, a post office, a boot maker's shop and a newspaper. A huge miller mill was built in 1873. Diamond City was one of the smaller camps in the Tintic Mining District. Ore from the mines was so rich that it was shipped to Wales for smelting. In the 1870s Diamond was visited by Capt. John Codman, a noted world traveler and author who wrote, "Diamond is the chief camp of the Tintic District and is one of the quietest mining camps in Utah. It has been several days now since a murder has been committed!" The last house in Diamond was moved in 1923, and the only thing remaining is a small cemetery hidden in the cedar trees.

Dugway Station/Express Station was a station that offered the most primitive accommodations for travelers. One visitor described it as a dugout in the ground, roofed with cedar logs and operated by two half-drunk boys. The station had no table or chairs and greasy stew was eaten while standing. There was no feed for livestock or water for passengers.

Dutchtown was a town in the Tintic mining district where a school was started in 1881.

Eureka/Ruby Hollow, Eureka became the financial center for the Tintic Mining District, a wealthy gold and silver mining area in Utah and Juab counties. The district was organized in 1869 and by 1899 became one of the top mineral producing areas in Utah. Eureka housed the "Big Four" mines—Bullion Beck and Champion, Centennial Eureka, Eureka Hill, and Gemini, and later the Chief Consolidated Mining Company. The Chief was developed by the Walter Fitch family, who not only had their own mine in Eureka, but also the company headquarters, family residences, and family cemetery, a most unique feature in any western mining town. As with other mining towns, Eureka developed from a camp to a settlement before becoming a town. Fire destroyed most of the business district in July 1893, and recovery was very slow. It benefited from competing transportation services of the Union Pacific (1889) and the Denver and Rio Grande Western (1891) railroads. Census statistics indicate the following population figures through 1930, when the impact of the Depression changed its fortunes: 1880 - 122;

1890 - 1,733; 1900 - 3,325; 1910 - 3,829; 1920 - 3,908; 1930 - 3,216. Eureka's population was typical of a mining town. By the 1980s the population fell below 700, and the population in 2010 was 669.

Fish Springs was one of the state's least known mining camps. It should not be confused with Fish Springs Station which is 15 miles east on the opposite side of the range. In 1899 silver lead ore was discovered at what would become the Galena Mine and within only a year both it and the nearby Utah Mine were paying their stockholders regular dividends. There were no mills or smelters at Fish Springs since there was no water to operate them. Ore was hauled by a 16-horse team to smelters at Wyno. With its mines booming, the new camp grew rapidly, claiming 150miners, camp followers, several stores and a saloon. By 1904 Fish Springs was a wild place, with no laws except miners' law. By 1910 the miners were gone and the tough little town on the rocky slopes of the Fish Springs Range was abandoned.

Fish Springs Station started as a Pony Express and Overland Stage station, which got its name from the fish that populated the springs. This was a popular stopping point for travelers because some springs were hot for washing up and some were cold and great for drinking.

Fort Nephi was located in Nephi, and was a fortified Mormon town, established in 1851. The walls were 12 feet high and surrounded by a moat. Many of the original buildings remain in the town.

Goshute was a small Indian community on the Goshute Indian Reservation. The Goshute people are of Shoshoni extraction and their name means "dust" or "desert" people in the Ute language.

Ironton was first established in 1871 near the present junction of US 6-50 and U-36 or the Tintic Junction two miles southwest of Eureka. Ironton was an ore shipping and supply town for local mines. The town included a row of stores, shops and saloons. As railroad construction crews moved on, Ironton became a ghost town.

Jericho was an early sheep shearing corral, midway between Eureka and Lynndyl, on the Los Angeles and Salt Lake Railroad line. Later, it became a U.S. Civilian Conservation Corps camp. The name came from the sandy, isolated, and desolate surroundings.

Joy/Detroit/Drum was a mining town with a smelter. It was located about 30 miles northeast of Delta, Utah, on the Juab-Millard county line. Harry Joy was a mining engineer from Detroit, Michigan. In 1872 he and his partner, Charles Howard, organized the Detroit Mining District with the new town of Joy as its center. Joy became the supply center for miners and ranchers in the area. Dwellings were erected as well as a hotel, café and store. Isolation and the cost of transporting ores and supplies forced the mine to shut down. The town subsequently died out. In the late 1990s many remains of the town and mine could be seen.

Juab/Widbecks Station was established in 1860 and received the name Chicken Creek from the creek the settlers built on. Shortly afterward, the town was abandoned, then resettled as John C. Widbecks Overland Stage Station. When the Utah Southern Railroad came through in 1876, Widbecks Station became an important railroad stop and John C. renamed it Juab. The railroad built a first class depot, a large warehouse and shops where many men were employed. There were two large hotels, a co-op, a Mormon ward, school house, post office, dance hall and several saloons. In 1879, when the railroad extended its line to Milford, Juab gradually declined in importance and population. As of 2014 only farmland remained.

Knightsville was located in the East Tintic Mountains on the northern slope of Godiva Mountain, approximately two miles east of Eureka. Jesse Knight came to the Tintic Mining District in 1896, with little money and no previous mining knowledge or experience. Against the advice of experienced geologists, he sank a mine shaft that quickly reached a rich body of ore. In response to those who had doubted, he named it the Humbug Mine. Opening about six mines in the east Tintic area, he became one of the region's richest mine owners.

His membership in the LDS church was conspicuous in an industry dominated by non-Mormons, and his successes brought him the nickname "the Mormon Mining Wizard." Knight disapproved of the drunkenness and other vices of the typical mining camp lifestyle. He decided to build his own model town to house the miners near the Humbug Mine. He started Knightsville by having 20 houses built on Godiva Mountain. He soon expanded to 65 homes and two boarding houses. There were stores, churches, hotels, and a post office. But Knightsville became known as "the only mining camp in the United States without a saloon or red light district; as the landowner Knight would not permit a saloon to operate in town. Jesse Knight took on a father figure attitude toward his workers and tenants. He was the first area mine owner to close his mines on Sundays, increasing daily wages to compensate for the lost day of work. He encouraged the miners, most of them Mormons, to attend church on their day off. The operation became known as the "Sunday School mines." By 1907 the population of Knightsville grew to 1000.

In 1915 the valuable ores in Knight's mines began to run out. Some of the mines were gradually closed. Houses were moved out of Knightsville, many of them to Eureka. By 1924 only two mines were still running, and by 1940 the entire operation was closed down. The site of Knightsville was emptied. As of 2014 nothing remained but some assorted debris and the schoolhouse foundation, which is listed on the National Register of Historic Places.

Knightsville

Little Salt Creek was a small polygamous settlement began in about 1870 at the mouth of Little Salt Creek, six miles south of Levan. It consisted of the families of Martin, Norman and Crispin Taylor. A one-room schoolhouse was built which also served as a church. In about 1881 the Taylor family sold the ranch and moved away.

Mammoth was located in the Tintic Mining District. Mammoth was located three miles south of Eureka in the Tintic Valley. The settlement received its name in 1870 following the discovery of rich ore in the nearby Mammoth mine. Miners rushed in and began a boomtown. The area was remote and the environment harsh; no water was to be found nearby. The mines piped in water for industrial use, but residents had to buy drinking water for ten cents

a gallon. Activity in Mammoth peaked around 1900–1910, with a population of 2500–3000. The town had a school, four large hotels, a dozen saloons and other businesses typical of a town its size. Mammoth was officially incorporated in 1910, but began to decline soon after. By 1930 the population was down to 750, and the town was dis-incorporated in 1929.

Tintic Hospital at Mammoth

Mills was a crossing named for Henry Mills, who was the superintendent of construction for the crossing. In the spring of 1880 he supervised the Union Pacific railroad crossing the Sevier River on a grade. The settlement had earlier names of Suckertown and Wellington. The

railroad also named the surrounding valley after Mills. An alternate claim is that the settlement was named for some nearby mills. It was located 24 miles southwest of Nephi. A few miles behind the giant plant is Mills. Some structures remain in 2013.

Mills 2013 taken by Penny

Nortonville was a small ranching community about four miles north of Nephi. Nortonville was first settled by three men from Arizona, who didn't stay long. The land was later homesteaded by the Norton brothers, hence the name. The land was sold again and in

1888 a one-room school house was built. A larger school was constructed later. By 1911 the population had declined.

Partoun was founded in 1949 by the religious group called the Aaronic Order, and named after a town in Scotland. About 35 settlers built homes, drilled wells, cleared land and built a church that was also used as the school. Citizens agreed to erect a school building if the Tintic School District would supply the equipment and hire a teacher. Before the negotiations were completed the entire community got together and within five days they constructed one of the finest school buildings on the western desert. On Sept. 9, 1949 every man, woman and child in the community reported for work and in record-breaking time constructed a building that would be the pride and joy of any community. About 15 students began the 1949 school year and before it ended there were 29 students. There were only nine families living in Partoun in 1998.

Robinson was a mining town near Mammoth, which was booming, but not everyone was happy. A mining engineer named G.H. Robinson moved down canyon and started his own town, naming it after himself. Soon Robinson was thriving, with businesses that equaled Mammoth's, as well as being the terminus for the newly completed Utah Western Railroad. Mammoth and Robinson expanded until they grew together, and to make things more confusing each had its own post office. Mail authorities finally ended the confusion by discontinuing both offices and establishing a new one where the two towns met.

Roseville was a small settlement where a large mill was built to process Diamond's ore. There was a dependable water supply. A small town grew up here because of the mill and the water. Directions: Roseville can be reached by traveling two miles along the road to Paul Bunyan's Woodpile, on a dirt road that turns to the east. It was located 13 miles south of Eureka.

Salt Creek was a small settlement near Fish Springs in west Juab. A school began there in 1914.

Silver City was located southwest of Mammoth, in the east Tintic Mountains, northeast

Juab County. It was a silver mining town in the Tintic Mining District and also produced bismuth, copper, gold, and lead. The settlement began in 1869 when silver was found. Lacking the placer deposits of many Utah mines, extracting Silver City's riches required labor intensive hard rock mining. Jesse Knight decided to build a smelter in Silver City because it had the flattest ground in all of the Tintic Mining District. By 1890 there were several mines but they developed slowly. Gradually the town grew from a mere tent city with a saloon and a blacksmith shop, to include a claims recorder and assay office, a telegraph branch, stagecoach line, post office, and eventually numerous stores, hotels, and restaurants. There were even two railroad depots, as both the Salt Lake & Western Railroad and the Tintic Range Railroad ran lines into town. Economic conditions improved, and by 1899 Silver City's population reached 800. Silver City began to dwindle, and miners left in even greater numbers after a 1902 fire devastated the town. In 1904 Silver City had a total of 18 businesses. In 1907 Jesse Knight, already a successful mine owner in the Tintic area, revitalized Silver City by establishing the Utah Ore Sampling Company and the Tintic Smelter. He nearly transformed Silver City into a company town, but for the fact that he didn't own the land. Knight built a power plant, some 100 new homes, and yet another railroad, called the Eureka Hill Railroad. By 1908 Silver City's population surged to its peak of 1500, most of them Knight's employees. That year the town held a special celebration called "Smelter Day" in conjunction with Utah's annual Pioneer Day holiday. Silver City's resurgence was short-lived. Due to dropping freight rates, Knight's smelter proved unable to compete with those in the Salt Lake Valley. Records show that by 1912 the population was already down to 300, and only eight businesses remained. In 1915 the smelter was shut down. Silver City was inhabited until 1930. Some foundations remained in the early 2000s.

Starr was a small, scattered agricultural settlement three miles north of Mona. In 1858 the soldiers of Johnston's army established a ranch for holding government livestock. When it became available to the public in 1880, Albert W. Starr and his son William A. Starr purchased the property. In 1880 settlers constructed a school, which was also used for church and social gatherings. By 1900 about a dozen families were living in the settlement. Starr's name was used for the settlement that has been absorbed into nearby Mona.

Tintic was a small community in the Tintic Mining District settled in 1903. It was the main supply town for the mines at Mammoth. Businesses at Tintic included Jennings General Store, Freckleton's store, the Cameron Mining Engineers Building and Mary Madison's

Dress Shop. Tintic (Tintick) was a renegade Indian chief of a small local band of Goshute Indians.

Tintic Mills was an early mining town. The Shoebridge Mine was located in 1870 high in the canyon east of Diamond. By the next year a mill was built, 25 miner's shacks were built on the mountain side, and a general store and saloon were in business. As the camp grew into a town, miners living there decided to name it Tintic Mills, but was often called Shoebridge for the mine. The mines produced so much so fast that the Shoebridge mill couldn't keep up, and Crimson Mill was built in 1877. The town continued to grow with more businesses and well-built homes. Samuel McIntosh built an extravagant mansion, which was equal to any in Salt Lake City. By 1890 the Shoebridge mine began to fail and so did the town. A long dirt road runs between Dividend and Silver City and Tintic Mills is in between the two.

Trout Creek was located in the west central part of Juab County. It was settled by ranchers to graze their sheep during the winter months. There was also some mining in the vicinity. At one time the population was listed at 50 and the town supported a store, schoolhouse, and a post office. Most of the original buildings were destroyed by fire. It has one of the most remote Mormon chapels in Utah, with a short section of paved road, being the only paved road for over 50 miles. The church still stood and some residents were still living in the town in 2011.

West Tintic was a farm settlement located at the south end of the West Tintic Mountains near the edge of the white sand dunes. The town site was established in 1920 as a "cooperative farm settlement" or Polygamist settlement which sprang up throughout Utah's west desert country every few years. Ten families moved to West Tintic the first year and their industry was soon responsible for a small village of log cabins, frame houses, barns and corrals and a cooperative store. A large barracks building purchased at Fort Douglas was moved to the new town and used as a storehouse. A garage, blacksmith shop and power plant soon followed.

<u>York</u> was a prominent terminal and railroad center on the old Utah Southern Railroad approximately 15 miles north of Nephi. York quickly became a prosperous little town. For two years it was the closest railroad station to the rich Tintic mines and shipped thousands of tons of ore to the smelters in the Salt Lake. Hundreds of carloads of produce were also shipped out by the farmers, while building material and hardware was brought in. The town consisted of railroad buildings, a depot, water tower, coal station and warehouses, plus several homes for railroad employees. Several farmers also built their homes in town, a busy hotel, store and restaurants were erected. York lasted for several years until the next terminal was established to the south of Juab. York was then promptly abandoned.

CHAPTER 13
Kane County

Adairville was located 45 miles east of Kanab on US-89 then north from the road one-half mile near the Paria River. Adairville was one of the most isolated settlements in southern Utah. Thomas Adair and a group of farmers founded the settlement in 1872. After severe flooding in 1883 and 1884 most of the residents moved upstream, and it was completely abandoned by the 1920s.

Butlerville was a short-lived settlement located south of Henrieville. The predominant settlers were Butlers.

Clif/Clifton was a settlement on Yellow Creek was called Clif, but as more people moved in the name was changed to Clifton. Ebenezer Bryce lived in Clifton (the man that Bryce Canyon is named after.) Bryce said of the area, "sure it's pretty, but it's a hell of place to lose a cow!"

Fort Berryville was located in Glendale from 1864 to 1870. It was a Mormon settlers' log fort. The town was originally known as Berryville until renamed in 1871.

Fort Kanab was located in Kanab. It was a Mormon settlers' fort from 1865 to1870 and was partially destroyed in an accidental explosion.

Fort Meek was named for a Mormon bishop who was traveling with Jacob Hamblin. A Mormon settler's home was once at Fort Meek, located about 40 miles northeast of Kanab. The Mormon Militia built a fort next to it to protect the area from Ute Indians.

Fort Wah Weep was built in 1869 to guard the Paria Crossing of the Colorado, a place favored by Navajos to ambush travelers. It is located north of Lees Ferry, Arizona.

Johnson was a settlement east of Kanab. Johnson was a movie set that was home to Gun Smoke and over 1950s movies. It is privately owned and is sometimes open to the public for tours. The movie set isn't the town, and all that is left of the town is the graveyard containing 20-25 headstones. It is fenced off and is located on an LDS church farm. Johnson was a town commissioned by the LDS church and founded by Joel Hills Johnson who is buried in the cemetery. In 1871 it was known as Spring Canyon Ranch. It had a brick school, a post office, blacksmith shop and two stores. Directions: Johnson Canyon/Skutumpah Road can be reached from Glendale by heading east on Glendale Bench Road, or from Kanab via US-89. The church farm is located just off the road, and the family/care takers are very nice and might grant access. The television series of Gunsmoke ran from 1955 to 1975 and is said to be one of the longest running prime-time shows on television. There were 635 episodes and many of the outdoor scenes for this show were shot in Johnson Canyon near Kanab, Utah. The setting of Gunsmoke is Dodge City, Kansas during the 1870s. A replica of the Hollywood set was created just three miles outside of Kanab. This Johnson Canyon movie set is perhaps the largest movie set constructed in the Kanab area. It can still be viewed from the road but is not accessible due to its state of general disrepair. As of 2012, many dilapidated structures could be seen.

Gun Smoke movie Set

Gun Smoke movie set 2012 photo taken by Penny

Paria/Pahreah was a settlement 42 miles northeast of Kanab at the Junction of Cottonwood Creek and the Paria River from which it receives its name. In 1865, Peter Shirts (Shurtz) became the first white man to settle there. About 47 families built sturdy sandstone houses but many of these were washed away during frequent floods. In 1870, William Meeks and a party of Mormon Missionaries arrived to educate the Indians. Before long before log cabins and buildings of adobe and stone were being built. During the polygamy trials of the 1880s Pahreah was a favorite hiding place for polygamists because of its isolation. A post office operated from 1892 to 1914. The settlers were tired of fighting floods and drought

and moved to other areas. When everything looked the worst, gold was discovered. Miners moved in and built cabins. But the mining boom was short-lived because the flour gold couldn't be recovered economically. By the 1890s only eight families still remained. Four families remained by 1910 and soon there was only one old bachelor miner who stayed until 1929. Pahreah was a popular stopping place for river travelers such as explorer John Wesley Powell. In about 1963 there was another brief burst of activity in the area when a movie set was built about a mile from the old town for the filming of a western movie. Pariah is the movie set and about two miles farther along the road is Pahreah, the original Mormon town. Paria was destroyed by a fire set by arsonists in late 2006. As of 2012, nothing remained of the town, although the drive there is beautiful.

Pipe Springs Fort was a fort laid out by the LDS church in 1870 for the settlers of Pipe Springs. The fort was 152 feet long and 66 feet wide. The fort was dubbed Winsor Castle because of its unique two-story construction.

Ranch was a settlement north of Glendale. There was a population of 54 in 1895 and a post office was established in Ranch.

Rockhouse was a small settlement on the Pahreah River, established by Peter Shirts in 1865. It was located in a wide spot in a canyon near a large sandstone ridge. Shirts built a sturdy sandstone house, which was the first in the village and the town became known as Rockhouse. In 1870 the people moved away.

Shirts Fort was four miles south of Paria on the Paria (Pahreah) River. Peter Shirts and others built this small stone fort in 1865. For safety reasons, the settlement moved up-stream to the site of Paria.

Skutumpah/Clarkdale was an early pioneer settlement of ranches that the Clark and Lee families established at the head of Skutumpah Canyon in 1870. Never more than about ten families lived here. Dellenbaugh of the Powell surveys camped at the settlement one night in 1871 and called it Clarkdale because three of the few families there were Clarks. The town was also called Skutumpah for the creek. A sawmill in the hills supplied the necessary lumber. Dairy products and farm products were traded, but it was decided that the town was just too isolated. In about 1879 the townspeople moved to Arizona. As of 2018 Clarkdale was private ranch property. Skutumpah is 14 miles southeast of Upper Kanab, 16 miles up Johnson canyon.

Upper Kanab was a small ranching village was established in 1882. Homesteaders came in the 1880s, built homes and developed farms in the drainage of the creek. They raised wheat, hay and potatoes. A sawmill was built up in the hills to provide lumber and shingles for the town. Many farmers had milk cows and a creamery was erected, butter and cheese sufficed for money. A boarding house and post office made up the rest of the business district. A small rough, frame schoolhouse was built in 1885. Winter was rough in the high mountain valley. Students had to ski or snowshoe to school. In the first part of the twentieth century, streams began to dry up, farms went sour and people moved out. Directions: The town site is about two miles east of Alton on a dirt road.

White House was located three miles downstream from Adairville. White House survived the floods of the 1880s, but the settlement ended in 1890 from drought.

CHAPTER 14
Millard County

Abraham is about nine miles northwest of Delta. Abraham was settled in 1890 and named after Abraham H. Cannon, a Mormon elder who settled the area.

Adelaide Park is located six miles up Corn Creek southeast of Kanosh. James Mills Paxton and his wife lived there and homesteaded, under the Squatters Rights Act. In 1935 the spot was dedicated as a park.

Antelope Springs was a virtually unknown resort built during the 1860s. Located about seven miles southeast of Black Rock, it is on the old Devil's Gate & Meadow Valley Stage Road between Black Rock and Cove Fort. Long ago, it featured a hotel, saloon, livery stable and barn where settlers and outlaws came from miles around to dance and party.

Black Rock was an area where Father Escalante's group reputedly spent several days around the nearby springs. Many stockmen used the spring to keep milk cold. In 1893 a store was built there to supply area farms and people traveling through the area. The store became the local first aid station for everything from rope burns to minor fractures. A post office and the railroad were built to load livestock from the area ranches. A school operated for 40 years, closing in 1941, and the railroad moved to bigger towns, causing the town to die. When the railroad was hauling silver ore from the mines of the Star District, Black Rock was an important place, with many fine homes and well-constructed buildings. As of 2018, only a few shacks and the old depot remain. The depot had a red tiled roof and yellow adobe walls. It may be torn down so the Union Pacific can avoid paying taxes on it. The depot is located off highway 257, 24 miles north of Milford.

Bob Stinson's was a cave house in Marjum Canyon. This canyon was the way west until they rerouted U.S. Highway 6-50. People relied on Bob to keep the road free of rocks that frequently rolled from the mountainside. For several years, Bob was the resident "rockkeeper" in the pass. Bob made his home in a cave that he enclosed, a few hundred yards up a canyon in the House Range. It was called Hermit's Cave House. He earned money trapping bobcats and coyotes, and mixed poisons for the government to kill grasshoppers. He occupied the dwelling from the mid-1920s until about 1946 before finally moving to Delta where he passed away in 1961. Bob reportedly grew a vegetable garden, had water from a nearby spring, and brewed his own moonshine. Friends from Delta looked in on him regularly. The cave is located 45 miles from Delta. Directions: From Delta, travel west on highway 6-50 for 33 miles and turn right at the "U-Dig Fossil" sign. Travel north on the gravel road for about ten miles to a four-way intersection. At this intersection turn left to the Marjum Pass; drive west for about 13 miles. The rock house is located in a narrow canyon, which is the last small side canyon on the north side of the Marjum Pass Road.

<u>Burbank</u> was a Mormon farming community that dates back to the 1870s, located 11 miles from the Nevada border. There was a post office and a store started at the Dearden's Ranch, near present day Baker. Farmers at Burbank and Garrison sold their produce and livestock for gold, often Mormon gold coins. There were no banks in Snake Valley, or even a business with a safe, so post hole banks and backyard caches hid many farmers life savings. Burbank was right on the "Horse Thief Trail," often used by rustlers to move livestock stolen from Mormon farmers to the mining camps of Nevada. After chasing horse thieves and fighting summer droughts and winter blizzards, Burbank's settlers began to move, leaving a forgotten Mormon settlement in the Snake River Valley south of Prues Lake. Just west of U-21 in Millard County, a ranch house and some weathered log cabins could be seen in 2018.

Historic Dearden's Ranch near Garrison Utah

<u>Camp at Fillmore</u> was a camp located in Fillmore in 1858. It was established as a temporary Federal Post to protect the then Territorial capital.

<u>Champlin</u> was a railroad siding located eight miles northeast of Lynndayl on a dogleg in the highway.

<u>Clear Lake</u> was a siding developed by C.S. Aldrich, a representative of a New York firm in 1897. Clear Lake became a shipping point and an agricultural and stock-grazing center.

Aldrich used the nearby lake for naming the operation. The area had natural wild hay and winter grazing, and several families eventually settled in the area. Water fluctuations, increasing soil alkalinity, and other problems prevented further development and the project slowly deteriorated. As of 2018 the area has been converted to the Clear Lake Water fowl Management area, which is owned and operated by the Utah Division of Wildlife, located 19 miles south of Delta.

Cline was a railroad town located four miles southwest of Lynndyl.

Corn Creek was settled by Peter Robinson around the 1850s. The settlement was in the southeastern part of Millard County, located on a small stream by the same name.

Cove Fort was a military fort made of volcanic rock and limestone in 1867. It was a way station for settlers and travelers in the 1800s. The early settlers were afraid that local native tribes might attack travelers. There were never any conflicts in this area, and the fort was closed down after 1900. The walls of the fort form a square which is 100 feet on each side. The walls are comprised mainly of black volcanic rock and dark limestone laid up in lime mortar, and are 18 feet high. There were four guest rooms with different levels of accommodations. A private room cost more money. Cheaper rooms were available for men traveling alone. The fort was self-sufficient, and also served as a Pony Express pickup and delivery station. Cove Fort is located immediately northeast of the junction of I-15 and I-70, in the southeast corner of Millard County, 24 miles north of Beaver. In 2014 it was still an active tourist stop where the LDS Church operated tours.

Crafton/**Laketown** was a small pioneer village hidden away in the salt marshes of the Sevier River about 19 miles west of Delta. In 1874, farming ventures were attempted along the river. Several families, including the David Craft family, settled together and called their location Crafton or Laketown, as the Crafts had built a reservoir. A small post office supplied the nine or ten families in the hamlet. Crafton was abandoned in 1906-08 due to drought and continued crop failure. The location of Crafton is 12 miles west of Fort Deseret.

Eskdale was a small agricultural community in the Snake Valley west of the Conger Range. It was founded as a religious community, The Order of Aaron, by the spiritual head, Dr. M. L. Glendenning who was of royal background and very fond of his history. The family was from Scotland. The community was located south of Gandy.

Flowell was located five miles west of Fillmore. Many flowing wells can be found in the region. Flowell was known in earlier days as Crystal.

Fort Buttermilk was a Mormon settlers' fort built in 1851, located near Holden. The fort stretched 150 feet long north and south by 75 feet wide. Facing each other and standing 30 feet apart were two rows of adobe houses. The fort's gateways were in the north and south walls. The location of the fort is 100 E. 100 N. in Holden Utah.

Fort Deseret was located ten miles southwest of Delta and must hold the record as the fastest built fort in the west. Made of adobe mud mixed with straw, it was erected in 18 days by 93 men divided into two competing teams. It was 550 feet square with walls ten feet high that tapered from a thickness of four feet at their black lava rock base to one and a half feet at the top. The Fort was actively used during the Blackhawk War of 1868-69. Once, a party of 45 men traveling south from Tooele raced Chief Blackhawk and a band of howling Indians from Pack's Bottom to the fort. Once safe inside, the battle became a standoff.

GUN PORT IN THE FORT WALL

Fort Deseret photo taken by Penny Fort Deseret Gun Port

Fort Scipio was located about two miles south of Scipio, built in 1857. Originally it was called Round Valley and later Graball. At the beginning of the Blackhawk War in 1866 a fort with adobe mud walls was built around the settlement. A log schoolhouse and a general store were built there. There was no drinking water at the fort except the open irrigation ditches. The fort was later moved to Scipio along with the cabins, and the only thing that remained was the adobe wall.

Gandy was a small ranching community in the Snake Valley three miles from the Nevada border, 35 miles southwest of Fish Springs. The Pony Express and Overland Stage traveled just north of Gandy. One of the original homesteaders was Almond Rhoades. Rhoades planted an orchard and brought the first threshing machine into the valley. He also planted the poplars imported from Italy which make up the beautiful lane leading to the current Bates' home. Water from the area comes out of nearby Gandy Mountain from a spring-fed cavern. Gandy was originally known as Smithville. However, to avoid confusion with other Smithvilles it was changed to Gandy, named after the oldest resident, Isaac Gandy, 1835-1904. As of 2015, seven families remained in the area, supporting a small ranching community. Mail delivery is twice per week. A delightful attraction in Gandy is the Crystal Ball Cave. George Sims discovered the cave, in 1956. It is located about 30 miles north of Highway 6-50 on the Utah/Nevada state line.

Garrison was originally founded as a cattle-rustling and outlaw community in the 1850s. The town of Garrison later became the center of mining interests. The name comes from the Garrison family who farmed in the area. After mining interests subsided, the Garrisons ran a livestock and hay ranch. Mrs. Garrison was a schoolteacher who also handled the mail, and the town's name honors her. Garrison is located in Snake Valley east of the Nevada State line, and some of the town's farms and structures are legally in Nevada. It was a small ranching community in 2015.

Gilmore/Salisbury was a stage stop, which included a small store, a dining room and sleeping facilities for travelers. Nearby was a barn where the mail was dropped off and the horses were changed.

Graball was a settlement in Round Valley. Several families moved there from Holden in 1861. The settlers built dugouts and log cabins in the south end of the valley on the west side of the stream.

Greenwood was a town site ten miles northwest of Fillmore on the road to Delta. The town boomed early and died quickly. It was named for Frank Greenwood, an early settler.

Hatton/Petersburg was a small agricultural community three miles northwest of Kanosh. It was settled around the 1850s where the old immigrant trail to California crossed the creek. There was quite a bit of activity, as travelers came through bound for the west coast. The name was changed to Hatton when the post office was taken over by Richard Hatton. It was a main stop on the Overland Stage route to Pioche, Nevada.

Ibex was an old trading center for stockmen and miners. It contained dwellings, corrals, a post office, boarding house and several windmill water pumps. It faded away when the mining subsided and sheep men left. The windmills and houses burned down many years ago. The village site is hidden up in a tiny canyon around the southern tip of the Barn Hills in one of the most remote spots in Millard County. Directions: Take the second dirt road west of Sevier Lake, about 54 miles west of Delta, off U.S. Highway 6-50. Travel southward for eight miles to Ibex Well. A few hundred yards past the well a rough truck road swings westward around the hills seven more desolate miles to the location. Not much remains of the settlement.

Ingersoll was a colony of homes and a post office established by a group of Quakers. They settled in 1893, building the Swan Lake Reservoir and farming 10,000 acres of alfalfa. The town was abandoned when the dam gave way, around 1909. The colony was located about 11 miles along a dirt road that leads westward from State Highway 257, a half-mile past old Fort Deseret, and eight miles southwest of Delta.

Lucerne/Alfalfa was near Sugarville, with the northern most community of the Carey Lands settled in 1909, one year before the general land boom. In 1925 the Union Pacific Railroad built a spur from Delta through Sutherland, Woodrow, Sugarville, and Lucerne. Many people settled, land sold well, and the sugar beet future looked good. Mines in the Detroit District were sending ore and bullion and Lucerne became a profitable shipping point. There were several large warehouses and loading docks. By 1931 the mines were at a low and sugar beet development took a downturn. The sugar factory was moved to Delta, the tracks taken up and buildings taken down or moved and people left. There is nothing remaining except portions of the railroad grade and the wye for turning locomotives around, crumbled foundations and mounds of debris.

Lynndyl got its name from a telegraph operators' shoe. The operator was testing the equipment, and the recipient asked the name of the town and she gave the brand name from her shoe. It was a railroad community with a stop in town. Later on, the train had to be flagged down to catch a ride. The town originally had two hotels, a bar and many other businesses. Living in the town today are farmers, workers for a power plant, and retired people. There were over 4000 residents during the early 1920s. Lynndyl is located on Highway 6, just south of Eureka, Utah.

McCornick was a settlement and a siding on the Union Pacific Railroad located 11 miles northwest of Holden. In 1918 the settlement was established through a high-pressure advertising and selling scheme. A number of families and bachelors arrived and began farming in early 1919. During that year the canal broke, flooding the farms of about 15 families who had made their homes near the mouth of Whiskey Creek. Despite the damage, the plentiful water produced excellent harvests for most of the farmers that year, enabling them to build 40 good permanent homes. The next year the canal broke a second time, and some families moved away. Reports of the settlement's success continued to bring new settlers. In 1920 it began to take shape as a real town. People of the LDS faith built a chapel and organized a ward with 83 families. A small post office was established and a schoolhouse and general store were built. McCornick's population reached its peak of about 500 in 1921, but died by 1930 because of alternating floods and drought.

Mcintyre was a railroad siding north of Jericho.

Neels was an end-of-the-line Rail Road Camp. It was located about five miles north of Borden.

Oasis was a small farming town between Delta and Deseret. Oasis was an outgrowth of Deseret, and was established in 1891. Unfortunately the agricultural opportunities in the area were limited due to water issues, and the little town faded. Today around 100 folks hunker down in this moldering old town along the railroad. There are some large agricultural-related buildings along the tracks.

Shem was a mine smelter camp in 1902. At Shem ore was smelted into bullion. The Blocks (Bullion) were hauled to Modena and shipped away for further refinement. The Apex Mine was about ten miles from the smelter. Shem hummed with activity for about ten years. The old mine is still the scene of limited and sporadic operations.

South Tract was located southeast of Delta, beginning in about 1911. By 1913 there were several homes, and a one-room school house was built for the 33 school children.

Sugarville was a small community northwest of Delta. The early settlers named it Omaha for Omaha, Nebraska. The name later became Alfalfa because the grazing plant grew so well in the region. As the sugar industry developed and the sugar beet crop became successful, the name was changed to Sugarville. There were several stores, a lumberyard, a school and several different church groups. As of 2014, a small farming and ranching community remains.

Sunflower was located about four miles west of Sugarville. The community was settled in 1912 and named for the most common plant in the region. There were several homes close together which formed the town, with other farms nearby. A one-room schoolhouse was struck by lightning and burned down. They tried growing sugar beet but the soil was too poor even with irrigation, and by the late 1920s the town had died. As of 2014, there was no trace remaining of the town except the foundation of the school. Several farms remain in the area but many are abandoned.

Sutherland was located four miles northwest of Delta. This faded agricultural community is one of the oldest settlements in this area, dating to the 1890s. It currently has about 120 people and has a large Mormon church and a cluster of homes, but no commercial buildings. During the early 1900s, the Union Pacific Railroad undertook a campaign to draw farmers to the isolated area, and those farms would ship goods and require goods and services in return. Most of the land in the area was available for settlement under the Carey Land Act, and a land boom quickly developed. Unfortunately, water was not easy to obtain and most of the farms died out. Acreage was consolidated and most of the new, farming boomtowns quickly faded. Some survived, at least in name. Nothing of historical interest remained as of 2014.

Topaz was one of ten internment camps built in 1942. Thousands of Japanese were held there during WWII when all people of Japanese ancestry (most of whom were American-born citizens) were taken from their homes on the West Coast. Of the 110,000 sent to the camps, Topaz housed about 9,000 making it the eighth largest city in Utah.

The Camp closed on Halloween in 1945. As early as January 1942, secret meetings took place between Delta residents and government officials. By June, work had begun at the site for the 17,000-acre Central Utah Relocation Center, later re-named Topaz Relocation Center after a nearby mountain. Located 15 miles west of Delta, the residential area of one square mile was located at the far western boundary of the camp. The camp opened in 1942 although many barracks as well as the schools were not yet completed. Japanese-Americans from the San Francisco area were transported to Delta, Utah, by train. The population of the camp soon reached about 8,000. Once located, some internees finished building their own barracks and other structures at the site. Two elementary schools, a junior/senior high school, and a hospital constituted the major structures of the camp. Administration buildings, warehouses, and government workers' housing were located in the first few blocks of the 42-block camp. The remaining blocks were for internee housing. Each block had twelve apartment buildings, a recreation room, and latrines for men and for women, and a mess hall. The apartment buildings were sectioned into six apartments of different sizes to accommodate families of two, four, or more people. Larger families were sometimes given two apartments. Apartments were heated by coal stoves, but cooking in the residential area was discouraged. Furniture for the apartments included only army cots, mattresses, and blankets. Some residents constructed rough tables and shelves out of scrap lumber left lying around the camp. The barracks, crudely constructed of pine planks covered with tarpaper as the only insulation, and sheetrock on the inside, provided little protection against the extreme weather of the semi-arid climate.

The first killing frost was recorded the end of September 1942, and the first snowfall was on October 13. Some of the apartments still had no windows installed at that time. The winter temperatures in the area typically hover near or below zero, and in the summer soar to the nineties.

Internees were employed at different jobs around the camp and were paid wages ranging from $16.00 up to $19.00 a month for doctors and other skilled workers. Residents could obtain passes to shop in nearby Delta, and some found employment in that community.

In 1943 James Wakasa, age 63, was shot by a guard when he was standing near the southwest section of the fence. After an outcry from the camp population, guarding procedures changed. In January of 1943, President Franklin D. Roosevelt announced that volunteers would be accepted in a Japanese-American combat unit. At about the same time, residents seventeen years of age and older in all the camps were given a questionnaire. Two questions became sore points for more than just the first-generation Japanese, who were not permitted citizenship in the United States. Question 27 asked, "Are you willing to serve in the armed forces of the United States on combat duty wherever ordered?" Question 28 followed: "Will you swear unqualified allegiance to the United States of America and faithfully defend the United States from any or all attack by foreign or domestic forces, and forswear any form of allegiance or obedience to the Japanese emperor, to any other foreign government, power or organization?" Since the Issei, or first-generation Japanese, were denied citizenship in the U.S., answering "yes" to question 28 would leave them without a country. After a protest by many residents, the question was altered; but damage had been done. Some became "No-No boys" by answering "No" to both questions. Dissidents from all ten relocation camps were sent to Tule Lake, California. Of those qualifying for military service, 105 volunteers soon left Topaz for active duty. Camp life at Topaz settled down and residents continued the routine of cultivating gardens, attending classes at schools or the recreation halls, and working. In 1943 residents with sponsors were encouraged to leave the camps and move farther inland. But the camp didn't close until 1945. The buildings were then dismantled; some were moved to other locations, leaving cindered roads, foundations for latrines and mess halls, and an episode that sullied the history of American democracy and it's Constitution. In 1976 the Japanese-American Citizen League erected a monument near the site of the camp. In 1988 President Ronald Reagan signed a redress bill into law, issuing an apology to those interned and calling on Congress to budget compensation for the survivors. As of the 2000s there were foundations and a plaque remaining at the site.

White Mountain Station was about 11 miles south west of Fillmore and was a stop of the Devil's Gate and Meadow Valley route during the 1860s.

Willden Fort was a wooden palisade fort constructed near present day Cove Creek in 1860 by Charles William Willden and his son Elliott. They first constructed an adobe house then enclosed it with 150 foot-square cedar post stockade. The posts were about nine feet high, placed close together to form a solid wall. The fort was occupied from 1860 to 1865, abandoned, and then occupied briefly in 1867 during the construction of Cove Fort. Willden Fort also briefly housed the telegraph office during the construction of Cove Fort, making it the site of the first telegraph in Millard County, Utah.

Woodard was settled around 1910 and was a farming community. There was a post office, school and store along with many farm houses. By 1950 the store was closed and the post office shut down. The school was moved to another town. The old town site today is all farm lands.

Woodrow was located seven miles northwest of Delta, on road Ut-16. By 1910 there were many settlers, and by 1917 there was a small store, post office, school and social hall. Homestead life was hard, even when there were many other families nearby to help. Many religions were represented, and they all got along with each other, with Mormons being the majority. By 1950 the schoolhouse had been moved to Sutherland and the store and post office were gone. By the 1970s, the town faded, and only scattered houses and an abandoned hall remained.

Wyno was a strange town, one that moved around a lot. During the 1870s a smelter was needed to make bullion from the silver and gold ore being mined at Joy and Ibex, but there wasn't enough water at either camp to take a bath, let alone run a smelter. About 14 miles west of present-day Hinckley, several springs promised an adequate supply of water, so a smelter was built in 1881. Shortly a store, a saloon and a row of cabins turned into a small town which, for an unknown reason was named Wyno. The springs that looked so promising in April dried up when summer's heat scorched the Sevier Desert. When the springs failed, Wyno's citizens founded Smelter Knolls, 11 miles to the northwest, where there seemed to be plenty of water to operate their smelter. Wyno was rebuilt at the new location. Soon ore shipments began arriving from Joy and Ibex, but then more troubles developed. The water was heavily laden with salt and other minerals which impaired the process. The entire plant was sold to the Tintic Mine and moved to Eureka. Wyno moved again in 1888 when a blast furnace was built at Hot Springs, 11 miles north of present day Abraham. The new plant proved to be a success. Cabins and shacks that could be moved were dragged form the old camp and others were built. A regular little town grew up by 1890. Then disaster struck; the fine new smelter caught fire and burned to the ground.

CHAPTER 15
Morgan County

Carbonit Hill. The mine at Carbonit Hill had a two-story bunk house and a blacksmith shop located at the mine site. A tram was installed to transport ore from Carbonit Hill down the slope to the bins. Ore from the other mines was hauled by team and wagon. The road from the mine was so steep, drivers had to "rough lock" the back wheels to make the descent safely. The Pembroke Mine consisted of three mines with patented claims designating them as the Argenta Mining District. Morgan Chief Mine was operated from 1900 to 1905. Arbuckle mine operated until 1947. Located in Cottonwood Canyon on the north slope of Durst Mountain were the Carbonit Hill Mine, Carbonit Gem Mine, Pembroke Mine and Morgan Chief Mine. The mines were located in Mills Gulch and Arbuckle Hollow.

Devil's Slide began in 1907 by the Union Portland Cement Company. The Weber River runs between the town site and the mountain. Devil's Slide was the only planned community in Morgan County. The town had a two-story hotel (boarding house) with 20 bedrooms upstairs and a huge dining room where 40 people could be seated. There was a reading room, two VIP bedrooms, and living quarters for the operators downstairs. There was a building about a half-block from the hotel that was the general store, drug store, and post office. A butcher shop and ice house operated until 1923. The butcher shop was torn down and a tennis court put in. In about 1918 the company built a beautiful club house. There was a two-room school house which was also used as the LDS meeting house. There was a Union Pacific Railroad depot called the Croydon Depot a mile north of the village across from the rock formation known as the Devils Slide. There were four-room houses without bathrooms built, with water and sewer added in 1921. There were five-room homes with bathrooms built, along with larger homes that were constructed for the superintendent, the company physician, and an emergency hospital. Jap Camp was a little village built by the first Japanese employees of the Union Portland. There, homes were constructed from surplus grain doors salvaged from railroad cars, used sheets of corrugated tin, poles, old boards, logs or even sheets of heavy cardboard. Some of the shacks had dirt roofs, others were tin. In about 1918 the Union Portland built three new apartment buildings for the Japanese employees and their families with each building providing a special room for Japanese ceremonial bathing customs. Greek Town and Italian Town were nearby but Jap Camp, Greek Town and Italian Town were all considered part of Devil's Slide. In the 1960s a super highway was added and many of the employees bought and built permanent homes in surrounding areas. As homes emptied the company tore them down. In 1987, the last resident moved and the house was demolished. Cement roads, sidewalks and a few garages were all that remained in the early 2000s.

Dixie Station was also known as Carson House, just over the tip of Hogback Summit, a half-mile inside Morgan County. The site can be found just west of the Mormon Pioneer Trail in a grove of cottonwood trees. The station was vulnerable to attacks, but the Indians didn't disturb them. Overnight lodging was available but the station was crude and the food was bad.

Fort Thurston was located near Milton.

Littleton was nearly three miles west of Morgan, near the mouth of Deep Creek. This small agricultural community was named in 1856 to honor Jesse C. Little, its founder. Flooding forced the settlers to relocate to Morgan.

Monday Town Hollow was located between the base of the hills and East Canyon Creek from 1865 to 1866. Early settlers on the South Morgan side of East Canyon Creek were flooded in 1862. Pioneers dismantled their cabins, took them across the creek, and reassembled then in Monday Town Hollow. Named after the day of the week the settlers moved, the area was small with little room for expansion. After several years they moved their homes back to South Morgan, on higher ground away from the creek side. Some moved to Littleton.

Mountain Green Post was located in Mountain Green in about 1825. It was a short-lived Hudson's Bay Company trading post built by Peter Ogden.

Porterville was four miles southwest of Morgan at the junction of Hardscrabble and East Canyons. It was named for Sanford and Warriner Porter, the first settlers who came over the mountain from Centerville. The Porters also built the first sawmill there. The Mormon Flat Breastworks (fortification structures listed on the National Register of Historic Places) are located in Porterville. They consist of horizontal rock breastworks built by Mormons in 1857 to defend against "Johnston's Army" in the Utah War. The walls were originally built about four feet high, with trenches dug for riflemen. A dam was also built on the nearby creek to force enemy soldiers to travel underneath them. These fortifications were not used in battle, and their exact location is restricted. A church was still standing in the early 2000s.

Richville was a settlement located between Young Street on the north and Porterville on the south. The town was named for John and Thomas Rich who settled in 1859. About six homes were built in 1861. Richville had the first gristmill in Morgan County, which began in 1863 and ended in 1866, located at approximately 1425 S. Morgan Valley Drive. The school house was built in 1862 and also served as the LDS church, located at about 1480 South Morgan Valley Dr.

Como Springs was a settlement named after springs of volcanic origin that has been in existence for ages. During the early settlement of Morgan in the 1860s, the river would overflow and wash into the springs. This formed a gutter which retained the water, forming a pool or a lake, which was the beginning of Como Lake. The warm water lake provided a great fishing hole in the early days. In about 1887 a doctor analyzed the water and found that it held wonderful properties for curing skin disease. The ground was cleared to build a small pavilion, dressing rooms, store rooms and a building for plunge baths. A partition was

built to separate the plunge-bath from the lake. Later a huge pavilion was built to provide a skating rink and dance hall. Revenue that came in was poured back into the building of the resort, including an icehouse for storing refreshments. The economic downfall of 1893 to 1896 caused the doors to close, and vandals destroyed the property. In a few years' time, the buildings were torn down and the pavilion burned. In 1920 Como Springs was purchased by the Heiner family. In 1921 the grounds were cleared and a beautiful dance hall was built, boasting two fireplaces and decorated with fine oil paintings. Dances were held twice a week and the community once again thrived with entertainment. Through the years, the improvements got better and better, and as luxuries such as indoor plumbing became a must, an indoor pool was added. Three concrete pools were added, a diving pool, a kiddie pool and a slide pool. Other developments included a hamburger stand, a bar, cabins, a café, motels, and a merry-go-round, a small roller coaster that went out around the lake, a rocket ride, and boat rides through the lake. The resort stayed open for years, with generation after generation continuing to enjoy the fun in the sun. However, much to the dismay of the community, Como Springs had to close its doors for good around 1986, due to rising insurance costs being more than what they brought in during the summer. The café remained opened on the premise, but everything else was gone. It was later sold to a bottling company, and then as a tropical fish farm.

CHAPTER 16
Piute County

Alunite was the site of an Alunite mine/mill, which was the nation's first commercially available potash ore, discovered in about 1910. It was the only American source of potash during the war years. A small company town built up around the plant with a company store, boarding house, churches, school, post office and several small dwellings. The population of the small town exceeded 100. In about 1914 a reduction plant was built in the mouth of the canyon, to extract the pure potash from the ore. An aerial tramway was constructed from the mine up in the narrow reaches of the canyon, down to additional levels and broader areas. From there the ore was hauled by wagons to the plant. For many years, especially during WWII, there was local hope of reviving the town, but potash and aluminum (another product of Alunite) were cheaper to produce elsewhere. In 1928 to 1930, as potash extraction became too expensive, the mines closed and the mill was torn down. Directions: Located about five miles south of Marysvale on U.S. Highway 89, a good dirt road runs west into the foothills about a mile to the town site. There were active mining and no trespassing signs in 2013.

Angle/Spring Creek/Lower Grass Valley/North Fork/Wilmont was located 15 miles north of Antimony. There was a one-room log school situated on "Clover Flat", one mile southeast of present Otter Creek Reservoir and just north of what came to be the Garfield-Piute County line. There was no business district in the settlement. A post office was established, but ended in 1915.

Angle 11-2013 photo by Penny

Box Creek was named for Tom Box and was located about five miles south of Koosharem. About a dozen families farmed or ranched here. At first, the school was held in various homes. Then the Presbyterian Church built a two-room building that served as both church and school. The church had an organ and several children learned how to play. The

Presbyterians faded away and the building was used only as a school house. Greenwich post office was moved to Box Creek. The people of Greenwich and Box Creek built two small reservoirs, but they were not able to support many cultivated acres.

Bullion City was located a little over five miles west of Marysvale. Established in 1872, it was the first county seat. The town contained 200 residents, a stamp mill, gambling hall, 50 homes and boarding houses and a school that operated on a regular basis until the early 1920s, then intermittently for several years until it closed completely. Although numerous mines were opened, the ore did not come up to expectations; the mill and town shut down in 1882 after producing $500,000 in gold and silver. During its boom in the 1870s, some 2,000 people, virtually all miners, lived there, extracting and milling gold and silver. Directions: From Bullion Canyon, just below where the Canyon of Gold Tour begins, turn right and continue about two miles to town. The exhibits of mining equipment and descriptions of remaining buildings marked along the unpaved road up to Bullion City are exceptionally informative and entertaining. Visit the interpretive mining exhibits on the way up, using the printed guide available from the roadside marker. Much remained to be seen in 2015.

Photo taken 2015 by Penny

Copper Belt Mining Camp had an assay office, a commissary, a boarding house, and a number of small houses. At the Copper Belt mine there was a ten-stamp mill, high grade gold, silver and copper which could net over $400 a ton.

Coyote was a small town Isaac Riddle created, near the mouth of Black Canyon at the north end of Johns Valley. Not long after Riddle's arrival in Piute County, he built a gristmill near the two forks of the Sevier River. There were no stores in Coyote.

Deer Trail was a mining town with company housing for the miners and several ranches. There was a one-room school that taught eight grades until 1923. The Deer Trail Mine produced gold, silver and lead.

Florence Mining and Milling Camp were about a mile from the Deer Trail Mine. Construction of the mill began in about 1916 and houses appeared almost overnight. The camp had no business district or churches because it was near Marysvale, but it did have a school provided by the company.

Greenwich was located in the north end of Grass Valley, five miles south of Koosharem. A small two-room Presbyterian school there taught students until 1928. The school was still standing in 2013.

Photo taken by penny

Hoovers was on the east side of U.S. highway 89, five miles north of Marysvale. Kenneth Hoover brought his 18-year-old bride, Ada Steele to the canyon in 1936. They built what Ada called a "honkytonk". They then built Hoover Complex with a café, gas station, and motel.

Kimberly/Snyder City. Peter Kimberly bought the property high in the North Tushar Mountains in Mill Canyon. In the 1890s several gold strikes led to the upper and lower Kimberly settlements being developed, where gold, silver, lead, and copper were mined. Due to the terrain of the canyon the town was built in two sections. Lower Kimberly was horseshoe shaped around the head of the canyon and contained businesses and the mill.

Gold Mountain Mining District was organized in 1897 where the miners lived in tents. Soon there were cabins and a cluster of other buildings; an assay office, a mine office, boarding house, bunkhouse, and blacksmith shop. Two or three general stores, some specialty shops, three livery stables, three saloons, two hotels, two barber shops, two boarding houses, a schoolhouse, post office, doctor's offices, and dance hall were carved into the hillside with the mill on the far end of the road. From the end of the horseshoe a road climbed southeasterly past an enormous lodge building, to the residential section of Upper Kimberly farther up the tight canyon. There were also several homes and shacks on the hillside east of the stores. Some 500 people lived in town during the boom period from 1901 to 1908. A daily stage arrived from Richfield and ore and bullion wagons crawled up and down the mountain road to and from the railroad at Sevier. Summertime was especially busy; besides the regular residents and employees, two large sawmills were at work turning out thousands of mine supports and lumber for buildings. The brothels were well-known places; the town had several murders and the usual array of drunken brawls and other crimes for which the participants filled what was reputed to be the strongest jail in the state. (This jail is now located in Pioneer Village at Lagoon.) Around the town, Butch Cassidy was seen quite often in his years with the Wild Bunch. Mining resources were being depleted by 1908 and by 1938 the town had died. Families lived there, but the town was a wild, hard-drinking and hard-brawling place.

Webster was a small town built up around the Daniel Webster gold mine about two miles west of Bullion City. A cyanide mill was built in 1914 but the gold ores in the district contained so much Sulphur that the cyanide process was unworkable and the plant was rendered worthless. Webster had stores, saloons, a blacksmith shop and other businesses.

Winkleman was a mining town that grew up in Marysvale Canyon, just south of the Sevier County line where Deer Creek empties into the Sevier River, making a wide spot in the canyon. The mine that supported the town was operated until after WWI. A school operated in the early 1920s. When the mine closed, the only establishment that survived was a place called Winklemen's Resort, with an open-air dance hall, bar, and cabins. It operated for a few years until the paving of U.S. Highway 89. A highway rest area now occupies the former town site.

CHAPTER 17
Rich County

Argyle/Kennedyville was located three miles southeast of Randolph on Big Creek. John Kennedy led a party of Mormon farmers to the area in 1874. A church and schoolhouse were built in 1906. In 1910 the population had increased above 125, so a second room was added to the schoolhouse, but the town grew slowly, because it was too cold for farming. The school house was also a local gathering place for social events. The town was renamed Argyle in 1895 because many of the towns' people were from a town in Scotland with that name. When autos came into general use, many people moved to Randolph and commuted to their farms. In 1915 the schoolhouse was closed.

Chimney Town/Meadowville was a small community by Round Valley, seven miles southwest of Pickleville. It was settled in 1869, but the people later moved to Mud Town because of trouble with the Indians.

Mud Town was located between Big Spring & Meadowville. Settled in 1865, there were a dozen cabins in Mud Town. By 1866 the people fled the town because of trouble with the Indians.

Pottawattamie was a small community in Round Valley. The people moved to Mud Town because of trouble with the Indians.

Round Valley was settled in 1863 as a farming community. The settlers built log and sod cabins. A sawmill was constructed in 1864. A post office was built around 1902, and a school-church house was added around 1906, along with several fine houses. By 1930 most people had moved away. The Town was absorbed into Laketown.

Photo by Penny

<u>Round Valley Post</u> was located in Round Valley in 1857 and was established as an Army post.

<u>Sage Creek</u> began in 1870. It was only eight miles north of Randolph but may as well have been 80 miles, for the country was rough and the wagon roads seemed even rougher. There was a church and schoolhouse located in the town. Lessons were taught in private homes until a log schoolhouse was built on a ranch. School in those days was restricted to a few weeks or about three months during the dead of winter. In 1909 a substantial brick school building was erected and classes began to run for six months. The student attendance fluctuated from just a few to as many as 40. In 1926 the school closed and the students were transported to Randolph. Dances were held in the schoolhouse, and when the small children got sleepy, beds were made under the benches along the wall. There were no goods or services available in Sage Creek.

<u>Sly Go</u> was a small cluster of homes located at the south end of Round Valley. The people moved to Mud Town due to trouble with the Indians.

CHAPTER 18
Salt Lake County

Alta was named because of its altitude. Silver ore was first discovered there in 1864. By 1873 there were 26 saloons in town. The population was upward of 5000 people at times. When the mine was depleted by 1895, Alta became a ghost town. A few of the mines were re-opened again in 1904 and worked until 1936.

At one time Alta was considered 'the bloodiest town this side of Kansas because it suffered more than 500 murders in one year. One of its mines nearly caused a war between the United States and Great Britain. An Englishman purchased one of the mines, and 3 days later the Wasatch Fault slipped the mine has never been found. One of the investors was an English Lord, but the U.S. stepped in and averted a disaster.

By 1872, the town's population had boomed to 3,000 and there were 180 buildings. Alta's first settlers neglected to obtain claims for the land upon which they built their businesses and homes. The Walker Brothers and Company applied for and received claims for the Alta town site; the company offered the land to the settlers at $50 to $250 a lot. Most of the "squatters" eventually settled accounts although some simply moved. By 1873, the decline in silver value caused Alta's population to decline. By 1880, the population of the town had fallen to only 300, and production fell from a peak of $13.5 million in the 1870s to $1.3 million.

Alta experienced a boom in 1904 with new discoveries being made by the Jacobsen Brothers in the Columbus Mine. While the old town site was never reoccupied, the miners were housed in bunkhouses built and maintained by each separate mining company at the center of their operations. The production of silver ore peaked in 1917 and declined steadily thereafter. By 1930 Alta was virtually a ghost town with only six registered voters.

In the late 1930s Alta began its second life. The old town site of Alta is now a ski resort. Boiler Basin got its name because of a boiler that was left there after a train crash. Most people think that the train crash was the end of the train service but that is not true. A car was converted to run the cog railway line to transport people to Alta after the train crash. On November 13, 1938 Alta's first ski lift was officially dedicated; but the lift did not become operational until January 15, 1939. The resort's second season saw the purchase of 86,000 ski lift rides; and its first international downhill and slalom competition was held in March 1940. During World War II Alta became involved in the war effort when paratroopers from the 10th Mountain Regiment trained on its ski slopes.

Argenta was located about seven miles from the mouth of Big Cottonwood Canyon or about a mile below Silver Fork. Argenta began in about 1870 as a silver mining camp, with numerous dwellings, a post office, and a store. It burned down after only ten years and was not rebuilt. Argenta was named after the Latin word for silver, Argentum.

Arthur was a small town established in 1910, when the Utah Copper Company and Boston Consolidated Milling Company merged. A few houses were erected on the north side of the highway, among the mill buildings. The last house was moved in 1958.

Bacchus was a small community located on U-111, on the eastern slopes of the Oquirrh Mountains. Bacchus was the former site of the small pioneer village called Coonville settled in 1853. The name was changed to Bacchus in 1915, after vice president of the Hercules Powder Company, an explosives manufacturing plant. It was a typical company town with a grocery and general store, barber shop, school, library, post office, a small train depot and 42 company houses. Buildings were arranged in a triangle built around a town park and tennis courts. The residents operated a cooperative farm on the edge of town and also kept individual gardens. Between 1930 and 1960 the town deteriorated when improved transportation caused people to move to more favorable locations. The houses were sold for $200 to $300 and moved to Granger or Magna.

Bacchus 1916

Baker was an iron ore mine with a smelter located at the bottom of the mountain. They used a cable system to haul out ore. Directions: There is no road so the only way in is by foot. The area is surrounded by cliffs, making the hike difficult in steep and rugged country. As of 2015 there were no remaining residents. The hotel had been blown down, but the cold room was still visible in the rock under a pine, and the mine entrance was still standing.

Bingham was first discovered around 1848. By 1873 two million dollars' worth of gold was dug out. By 1900 gold and silver mining was put on the back burners and copper became king. The Kennecott Copper Corporation soon took over. There were many brick and solid frame buildings, several hotels, churches, banks, a newspaper, every kind of store typical of a good-sized city, dance halls, theaters, society halls, and by 1900 there were 30 saloons. In 1880 and 1895 fires swept through the canyon destroying business and homes, then again in 1932 a fire took out a large portion of the city. Floods and snow slides destroyed buildings and killed people, but they shoveled out and rebuilt. By 1920, 15,000 people lived in Bingham, but by 1972 the town had died because of the ever-expanding mining operations which are still in full swing. A cemetery remains at the site. At its peak, Bingham was seven miles long but less than a city block wide. A sawmill built at the mouth of the canyon supplied much of the timber used to build the Mormon Tabernacle in Salt Lake City. Early names for Bingham were Bingham's Herd House, Bingham's Gulch and later, Jinx Town.

Camp Bingham Creek was located in Bingham Canyon in 1864. It was an Army post for California volunteers and previously a logging camp of Mormon Pioneers.

Camp Murray was located in Murray, established as an army recruitment camp in 1885.

Caribou City was a mining camp that was located in one of the canyons east of Salt Lake City.

Central City consisted of a saw mill along with several small boarding houses and businesses. The town soon boasted a population of 216; located 850 yards east of Alta. Starting with the Alta Hotel, Central City merchants began relocating their log buildings. The borders of the two communities soon merged, and the name was dropped with its residents absorbed into Alta.

Cheatum was a short-lived mining settlement, established in the late 1800s. The settlement had a boardinghouse, saloons, and ten frame shacks, located in Little Cottonwood Canyon.

Copperfield was in the south fork of Bingham Canyon, southwest of SLC. The alpine mining town was established in 1929 and named for the rich copper ore mined in Bingham Canyon. Copperfield was completely evacuated by the 1950-55 period. Then the ever-expanding Utah Copper divided Bingham. For a while the area was simply called "Upper Bingham". Soon a large thriving community developed as hundreds of families as well as hundreds of single males made their homes there. Many boarding houses, hotels, saloons, stores, restaurants, four churches, a theater and a brothel sprung up. Apartments were abundant and Copperfield Grade School was built in 1919. At first the only way to get to Copperfield was up through the copper pit, but in 1939 a new access was built; a one-mile tunnel with a one-way road and sidewalk. The road was operated by automatic electric red/green lights that didn't work properly, and it was a dirty dark tunnel. The houses were primitive with no running water, sitting on a mine dump that was so poisonous that not even weeds would grow. The house insulation was filled with the same toxic dirt. Outhouses were common and never painted. Later the companies built newer, brick homes and apartments. There were about 20 nationalities of people living in Copperfield. The Jap camp and Greek camp were located high on the right side of the road while Terrace Heights and Dinkyville were high on the left side. There were trains in front and in back of the houses, along with ore-mining equipment on the roads. The unsafe town had trestles and bridges to fall off of and mineshafts to fall into. In the spring there were floods and the residents would pan for gold. By 1958 Kennecott claimed the homes and business.

Dalton was a settlement that grew up around a gold mining claim that was discovered in 1863. It later merged into Lark.

Emmaville was located about a mile north of the mouth of Little Cottonwood Canyon. The settlers were predominantly miners, rock quarry freighters, and various day laborers. It is believed to have been named after the Emma Mine up Little Cottonwood Canyon. The town was first settled in 1868-69 but began to decline in 1871 with improved railroad facilities in the canyon, an epidemic, and a disastrous fire, which changed the course of history. It was an informal stopping point for wagons hauling ore from the mines of Little Cottonwood, teams transporting granite blocks from the Mormon Temple quarry at Granite, stage-lines, travelers, and early sight-seers. Stores, hotels, boarding houses, a blacksmith, livery, and three saloons put Emmaville on the map. Dozens of families, miners, quarrymen, teamsters and more called it home, on a strictly temporary basis. At its height, some 500 people resided there. The decline of the town came when the railroad went through Granite instead of Emmaville. In 2016 there were modern homes where the town once was and a granite rock marker that can be found on the east side of Wasatch Blvd.

Fort Bingham was a small stockade built in 1864, ten miles east of Tooele.

Fort Douglas was built by volunteers and named Camp Douglas until 1876. The U.S. Military Reservation is located in Salt Lake City (1862-Present.) It protected trails from Indian raiders and allowed the Army to keep an eye on the Mormons. In 1910 the post was designated a permanent reservation, used as a training camp during the world wars, and was also used to house German POW's. The Military Museum is in the Quartermaster Victoria Infantry Barracks (1875), and is operated by the U.S. Army Center of Military History. Many of the original buildings remain. Much of the land has been donated to the University of Utah.

Fort Herriman was a Mormon settlers' fort built in 1855 as protection against the Indians. The fort was abandoned in 1858, under instructions of Brigham Young, upon the approach of Johnston's Army. Some of the settlers returned a few years later and established the town of Herriman. The fort was named for Henry Herriman, located at 12685 S. 6000 W. Herriman, Utah.

Fort Salt Lake City was located in Salt Lake City, built in 1847. Mormon settlers built this fort which is actually a combination of two forts, "North Fort" and "South Fort".

Fort Union was located in Union as a Mormon settlers' town fort, used from 1853 to the 1870s. The adobe walls were 12 feet high and six feet thick at the base, with numerous gun portholes. It provided protection for 23 families within the compound. Remains still existed until the 1990s when the site was bulldozed for development. The site is located near 7200 South Street and 1300 East Street.

Galena City was a 1880s mining settlement up Little Cottonwood Canyon above Alta. The town was abandoned when the ore in the mine was depleted and is now located in the middle of a recreational area. Nothing of the old town remains.

Garden City was located in Big Cottonwood Canyon, a small settlement near Brighton in the 1890s.

Garfield was a small mining town located a few miles west of Magna, on the old 21st South road which is now Interstate 201. Interstate 80 runs through the north end of the town. Garfield was founded around 1906 and in 1950 it had a population of over 2,000. In Garfield's early history Indians used to pass by the area. Some of them would stay in a cave at the southwest end of the tailings pond they called Dead Man's Cave, named because a man committed suicide in the cave around 1913. Skeletons found in the cave show that the Indians lived here somewhere between 3,000 and 7,000 B.C. Garfield was one of the unique towns that Utah Copper built. The town housed workers and their families that worked at the smelter, refinery, Arthur, and Magna Mills. A club house was built which later became a school house. There were six hotels on Main Street, a trading store, drug store, Carl's Tavern, a bank, post office, barber shop, library, sweet shop, and a show house; it had everything a small town could want. By 1914 a new school was built. There were many benefits for the workers such as a theater, baseball park, swimming pool and library. For a small fee people could enjoy the Copper Club that was built at the Arthur Mill. It had a dance hall, bowling alleys, pool tables, and may other things for people to enjoy. The wages were small but company had many benefits. Houses rented for $18 a month. Each year the company would paint and fix up things at the houses. There was an LDS and an Episcopalian church. In 1955 Kennecott decided to expand so they let the people buy their houses and move the wood frame ones. The end of Garfield came in 1956-1957.

Gold City was located in Little Cottonwood Canyon. It began in the late 1800s as a small mining camp.

Hangtown was located just below Priesthood Camp where placer diggings had been found. A line of tents and dugouts became known as Hangtown.

Hanks Station/Big Canyon Creek Station was known as Hanks Station for its operator. Hank was one of the 'Avenging Angels' like Porter Rockwell. So very few ever spent the night. Hanks station was located on Mountain Dell creek in Salt Lake County.

Highland Boy was a town established in 1873. Many Yugoslavians, Basques, Italians, English & other ethnic groups lived in the town. There was also a Japanese Camp and Greek Camp. There were many stores, saloons, boarding houses and a school. The area was well-known for great fires and snow slides. Located up from Bingham Canyon in Carr Fork, it can be seen from Sun Shine Peak, accessed through Middle Canyon near Tooele. There was an aerial tramway used for hauling ore over the mountain to the smelter in Tooele. The town was unincorporated in 1971 and demolished to make way for further mining development, and most everything is gone.

Highland Boy Mine

Highland Boy Church Highland Boy Community House

Lark was located three miles south of Copperton and about three miles west northwest of Herriman on the eastern slopes of the Oquirrh Mountains. It was settled in January 1866 as a small mining community. The town had enough Latter-day Saint residents by 1918 to be made a ward, but by 1923 the ward was reduced to a branch. In 1930 there were 234 members. In about 1971 the mines closed and people started moving away. In 1977 Kennecott who had built the town began dumping tailings there. The town once had a population of over 800.

Little Dell was a Pony Express Stage Station.

Modoc was one of the central camps in the City Creek mining area about seven miles north of Salt Lake City, near the Empire Sawmill. A town site was laid out in 1873, although it was mainly a residential place having no business establishments.

Mountain Dell was located in Parley's Canyon where Mountain Dell Reservoir is presently located. The road through the canyon was built by Parley P. Pratt and was opened for traffic on July 4, 1850, under the name of the Golden Pass. In 1860 Leonard G. Hardy opened a rest stop known as Hardy's Place. The name was then changed to Mountain Dell in 1869. A log church house was built in 1868. In time, Mountain Dell became a small farming settlement, a Pony Express stop, and stage station. By 1910, the community of approximately 100 people began to die out because of improvements in transportation. In 1916 Salt Lake City bought the land for a reservoir and recreation site. The town now lies beneath the water of Mountain Dell Reservoir.

Priesthood Camp was located nine miles up City Creek Canyon northeast of the State Capitol building. It was located near the mouth of Cottonwood Gulch. Cabins built by the miners sprang up.

Rockwell's Station was first known as Utah Brewery because of a brewery built near the point of the mountain which separates Great Salt Lake and Utah Valley. The brewery was built at a cost of $17,000. The area was plentiful with grains and wild hops, but the business failed. The property was taken over by Orin Porter Rockwell, and became a station for the Overland Stage. Rockwell's Station was looked forward to by travelers because Rockwell was a fine host, jovial and good-natured, whose tales of early Mormon adventures kept his listeners spellbound for hours. Perhaps the fact that he operated and sold "Valley Tan" Whisky had some bearing in its popularity. Rockwell Station is located at the Point of the Mountain in Bluffdale. Nothing remains of the settlement but a marker made out of the Saloon wall. The marker can be seen against the prison fence on the left side.

Salt Lake City Post was located in Salt Lake City from 1865-1866. This Army garrison specifically guarded the territorial capital.

San Domingo City was located seven miles up City Creek Canyon. It was one of the central camps in the City Creek mining area.

Silver Fork was a small community of log buildings that grew up around two sawmills and a shingle mill. Logging began in 1847, and later the mill moved and the town was abandoned. Then in 1870 the camp became a mining camp with activity at Alta spilling over the ridge. A smelter was constructed; a hotel and commercial buildings followed, and miners took over the cabins. The mining boom only lasted about ten years and the town was abandoned again. The area is now filled with summer homes and cabins. It was located up Big Cottonwood Canyon on a road before reaching Brighton, now all is private property including the cemetery. A monument just south across a bridge on Honey Comb Road can be seen on the site of one of the saw mills.

Tannersville was located seven miles up Little Cottonwood Canyon and is now a picnic ground called Tanner's flat. In the 1850s a small lumber and logging town stood on the flat. A man named Tanner ran one of several boarding houses in town. Other log and frame buildings included dwellings, saloons and livery stables. In the early 1870s it also became a smelting and ore-shipping center. The little town was destroyed by fire in 1872 and never rebuilt.

Telegraph was started as a company town by the Telegraph Mine and later was a company town for the employees of the US Mine. Mining began in 1873 on what is called the Giant Chief Fissure in Bear Gulch. It was located one-half mile above Copperfield.

Traveler's Rest was a small Overland stage station where passengers could rest a few minutes while the horses were watered. It was located in Midvale.

Union City was a small mining community in the late 1800s. It was located up Little Cottonwood Canyon between Galena City and Alta. It became a ghost town when the mines were shut down.

<u>**Us**</u> was the site of the "Big Grove" a group of giant trees (now extinct) that were logged in 1850s by Mormons to build Salt Lake. In 1863 an apostate Mormon, 24 other Mormons and General Connor conspired to develop a mine against the wishes of Brigham Young. His disfavor caused the mining to cease. The Old Jordan Mine was later developed, owned by the US railroad. Miners first lived in tents and dugouts and later the company built the town called Us. The area is best viewed from the top of Middle Canyon at Sun Shine Peak on a road from Tooele.

<u>**Willow Fort**</u> was a Mormon settlers' fort developed in the 1850s at South Willow, located in Draper. The site is now a town park with a monument.

Resorts

<u>**Black Rock Resort**</u> was opened in 1876 and was the site of the first recorded 4th of July celebration. Heber C. Kimball built a ranch house here and then later turned it into a Hotel, and the resort had swings and a merry-go-round pulled by a horse. Black rock once hosted a major sports event of the summer, the marathon swim to Antelope Island. Black Rock went out of business by the mid-1890's.In 1851 people were invited and 150 vehicles and 70 horsemen arrived from Salt Lake City. A huge home-made flag was unfurled. A rock home was erected in about 1860 where the guests were entertained. In 1880, 100 bath houses, a bowery, board walk and other equipment were erected. Steamboats sailing the lake were an attraction.

lack Rock Resort and Heber C. Kimball Residence

<u>**Saltair**</u> opened Memorial Day of 1893 at a cost of $350,000. It was built over the lake itself on 2,500 ten-inch wooden pilings. There were originally 1,000 bathhouses, and the June 8, 1893 dedication brought 10,000 people. The main hall was similar in size and shape to the Mormon Tabernacle. A 50-cent fare was payment for travel to and from Salt Lake, as well as the admission to Saltair. With the ambition to be the "Coney Island of the west," Saltair became a world class resort. By 1919 annual attendance was 450,000, but the resort seemed

a magnet for natural disasters. Two windstorms in 1910 destroyed 200 bathhouses and other structures. A large fire in 1925 caused $500.000 damage, with insurance only covering $100,000 of the repairs. A few months after the fire, Saltair reopened. Another fire struck in 1931, damaging the coaster and amusement rides. By then, there was a tunnel of love, six bowling alleys, a Ferris wheel, fish pond, fun house, pool halls, penny arcade, photo train ride gallery, shooting gallery, indoor swimming pool, bicycle race track and roller skating rink. The resort was described as the "biggest amusement value in the world" during the 1930s. Saltair also had the world's largest dance floor, where 5,000 people could fox-trot at once in the open-air hall. Saltair continued to be plagued by disasters. A 1932 windstorm killed two construction workers, and then a 1939 fire destroyed the pier. The resort closed from 1944 to 1945, during WWII. Another fire in 1955 destroyed many bathhouses, and a freak wind gust destroyed the roller coaster in 1957. By 1959 the state of Utah had taken possession of the crumbling resort and closed it. The abandoned resort burned to the ground in November 1970. In 1983, Wally Wright spent $3 million to build a new Saltair resort about a mile west of the original resort.

Bicycle race track 1908 Bath houses 1907

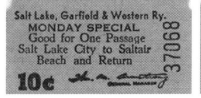

CHAPTER 19
San Juan County

<u>Bluff Fort</u> was located in Bluff beginning in 1880. The site was a Mormon settlers' fort, comprised of about 50 small one-room log cabins erected in a square formation for defense. The original settlement lasted for a few decades before it was replaced by more permanent structures. Dedicated as a historic site by The Hole in the Rock Foundation, the Barton Cabin was restored in October 2008. As of 2018, some of the fort had been recreated and original buildings preserved.

Trading post at Bluff Fort, this Building was still standing and used as a museum in 2018.

Bluff Fort 2018 photo taken by penny

<u>Boulder</u> was located 12 Miles southeast of Monticello. It was a small, short-lived homestead settlement established in 1910.

California Bar was a small mining camp northeast of Halls Crossing. The miners built rock cabins. Mining began in the 1890s and lasted until the 1940s. The camp is now under Lake Powell reservoir.

Camp Jackson was a rough mining camp at the south end of the Abajo Mountains, lasting from the 1880s to 1903. Two brothers found a rich ledge of ore at the top of a steep gulch and started the Gold Queen Mine. Not long after, the Dream Mine opened across the ridge near the head of Johnson Creek. Before the year ended 300 claims had been staked. A 10-stamp mill and other equipment were installed. A second stamp mill was installed in 1901 and a newly-built tramway carried the ore to the mill from the mine. The camp was full of rough miners, there were no fine stores or fancy saloons, but they had plenty of supplies and whiskey. The camp closed in 1903 and was located 11 miles east of Monticello. A campground is located about four miles below the Gold Queen Mine.

Carlisle/Indian Creek was located five miles north of present-day Monticello. During the early 1880s George Washington Johnson built a cabin and started a trap-line. In 1885 a wagon train of immigrants camped near Johnson's old cabin, and decided to settle there. They erected a number of log cabins and corrals, fenced their fields and started an irrigation system. The town was named after a local rancher whose place was reputed to be a hideout for outlaws and rustlers. It was a good place for riders of the Owlhoot trail to hole up, for it was so difficult to get to. The wagons had to be taken apart and lowered down vertical cliffs by ropes before being reassembled to complete their trip to the tough town. Shootouts and killings were common at Carlisle. Farmers discovered that frosts killed their crops nearly every month of the year, while the ranchers stole them blind, and the Indians were bothersome until after the turn of the century. By 1900 most of Carlisle's citizens moved to Monticello and Blanding. Today, most of the area is a large ranch with some cabins that can be seen next to modern ranch houses.

Cedar Point was a small homestead community settled in 1916, located near Monticello.

Crescent City was a mining settlement located near Hite which is now beneath Lake Powell reservoir.

Eastland was a small ranching and farming community that began in the 1920s. The community was located 11 miles east of Monticello and four miles south of US-491 on County Road 312 near the head of Horsehead Canyon and three miles south of US-666.

Fort Montezuma was located at Montezuma Creek, established in 1897. It was originally a small settlement called Montezuma Creek after the creek it was built on. The settlement was often attacked by Indians so a stone fort was built. Later, 200 Mormons settled at the site, building a school house, store and post office. A trading post was built later. Living conditions were very harsh and there was very little farmable ground, causing most of the families to move. In August 1884, two young men were ambushed by Indians on a rocky ledge in view of the fort. The Indians only wounded them but let a pack of wild dogs tear them apart as the families could only watch. This was the final straw and the rest of the families moved to Bluff, 19 miles south. The fort is gone but a trading post with the same name is located by the side of Montezuma Wash on the San Juan River.

Fry Canyon was a uranium boomtown during the 1950s. The tiny hamlet is now a ghost town, located eight miles west-northwest of Natural Bridges National Monument.

Ginger Hill was a small homestead community settled in 1917, located about 14 miles southeast of Monticello.

Gretchen Bar/Schock Bar was gold mining camp that began in 1886 and lasted until the 1940s. A cement rock cabin was built on the riverbank near a spring. Water from the spring was piped to the cabin and was used to irrigate figs, apricots, pomegranates, and grapes planted in the front yard. Gretchen Bar is now under Lake Powell reservoir.

Halls Crossing was a small settlement established at Halls Crossing from 1881 to 1883, but it quickly faded into oblivion. Hall settled at the mouth of Halls Creek and ran a ferry crossing the Colorado River.

Hite was an early Colorado River outpost anciently used by the Indians as a Colorado River crossing. In the early 1870s, Cass Hite arrived in the area. He was a prospector, a former member of Quantrill's Civil War guerrillas, and was considered an outlaw. He settled at the site and became friendly with the Indians. In the early 1880s a small settlement was established, around the ferry. It was located 52 miles southeast of Hanksville, Utah, and now lies beneath Lake Powell reservoir.

Cabin at Hite, Utah Dug out at Hite, Utah

Holyoak was a small settlement established in the 1880s after the Hole-in-the Rock expedition arrived in the area. It was located on the San Juan River above Bluff.

Home of Truth was a short lived religious settlement that was started by Marie Ogden. With a population of 22 in 1933, the settlement grew to about 100. The residents gave up all their possessions for food, clothing and shelter and were not allowed to use tobacco, alcohol or eat meat. During its brief history the town was isolated from the surrounding community socially as well as physically, the residents kept to them. Ogden took over the local newspaper and used it to introduce outsiders to her beliefs. The crisis that led to the downfall of the Home of Truth resulted from Ogden's writings about efforts to raise a woman from the dead. The investigations by local authorities and the intense media attention that followed drove most of the members to abandon the group by the end of 1937. A handful of residents continued to occupy Home of Truth until 1977. The colony consisted of three parts. The first, known as the Outer Portal, was located a half-mile down a dusty road west of U-160. It consisted of a group of well-kept buildings, including a communal house and a dormitory, which had no electric lights or running water. The Middle Portal was about two miles farther along the road and contained more plain but solid buildings and a chapel built of cobblestones. At the end of the road was The Inner Portal, made up of several barracks and six well-built homes, all high on a windswept ridge overlooking the desert below. Today the empty buildings at Home of Truth, are located on fenced private land. The settlement was located along Utah State Route 211, 14 miles north of Monticello and three miles west of U-160.

Home of Truth

Horsehead was a small homestead community settled in 1916. It was located southwest of Lockerby, near Monticello.

LaVaga was a small town located on Spring Creek several miles northwest of Monticello.

Lockerby was settled in 1912, located two miles west of the Colorado border and two miles south of US-666, renamed US-491.

Old Fort Bottom was located on the Colorado River near the extreme northwest tip of San Juan County. The earliest trappers used it, but it was old even then, probably built by Spanish explorers or miners.

Old La Sal was located about 11 miles east of present day La Sal on Highway 46. Settled in 1877, it was named Deer Creek, with about 20 families settled in 1897. The town was at an elevation of 7,500 feet. A post office was established in 1878, and the town's houses were built close together for defense purposes. Because of the cold climate and Indian troubles, settlers moved to New La Sal in about 1930. About five miles farther east is a uranium mining camp.

Peak City was established by John Holyoak in 1882. The settlement was located 25 miles from Bluff, with a few homes and a store that doubled as a post office. Nothing remained of the town in 2014.

Plainsfield/Bueno/Poverty Flat was one of Utah's first uranium mining camps located southwest of Moab, near Cane Springs Park. Several uranium mines were located at Plainfield and along Mill Creek. Plainfield was first settled in the 1870s as a farm and ranching community. There was a post office in the town from 1879 to 1880. By 1886 a church and school were built. The town died when uranium was found in Africa where it was cheaper to mine. Plainsfield was last known as Spanish Valley.

Rincon was a small mining settlement about eight miles above the Escalante River. First they mined for gold, then oil and uranium. The settlement is now under water at Lake Powell reservoir.

Spencer's Camp/Camp Ibex was a short-lived placer gold mining camp on the San Juan River about four miles downstream from Zahn's Camp. During the 1890s when Zahn's Camp was failing, new strikes were made at Spencer's Camp. A trail was built to it and ladders were used to scale the steep cliffs. Two rock wall tent houses were erected, there were no stores. A poor dirt road from Oljito, where an Indian trading post lies south of the San Juan, leads northwest to Copper Creek. The road follows the river, passing high above the site of Zahn's Camp before it ends at an abandoned mine.

<u>Stone Camp</u> was located near Halls Crossing. In 1899 a massive gold dredge was erected at the camp. Before the dredge began operating early in 1901, machinery, equipment, and supplies were hauled in from Green River, Utah by wagon over a hundred miles away, then floated down the river to the camp. Tent houses were set up and a mess hall, ice plant, and blacksmith shop were built. The venture was a financial failure, because the gold was so fine. The cost for extraction was about $100.000 with only about $66.00 in gold taken out. The dredge was abandoned and is now under Lake Powell.

<u>Summit Point</u> was located approximately 30 miles northeast of Monticello. It was named Summit Point because it divides the streams that drain into the San Juan River on the south and the Colorado River on the northwest. Some of the early settlers filed claims in the early teens. By the late 1920s there was a rather large population in the area, with a school house, post office and general store. The first school house was built in about 1922. The second school house was built in 1931. The teacher worked for one-half pay of his wages and donated the rest of his work. It was a one room school house, with all eight grades and one teacher. In 1958 the county couldn't get qualified teachers and the school was closed. It was sold for $500.00 and moved to Dove Creek, Colorado, where it was converted into a home which is still occupied today.

<u>Torb</u> was a small homestead community settled in 1919 located near Monticello.

Ucolo was a small ranching community west of the Colorado border and north of US-666 (renamed US-491.) The community enclosed Piute Springs country and was headquarters for the Carlisle Cattle Company in the 1880s. Ucolo is an anagram for Utah-Colorado.

Urado was a small homestead community settled in 1918 located near Monticello.

Verdure was settled by 15 families that were sent by the LDS leaders to colonize the area, first named South Montezuma. The men that were not needed in the village rode six miles north to the present site of Monticello, and half the population of South Montezuma eventually moved to Monticello to be closer to their land. The remaining families built somewhat more substantial homes, one of which was partitioned off for a store, church and school rooms. One of the first items brought in by the colonists was a cheese vat and press which helped to keep the economy of the village going. By 1893 a post office was established in a family's home and the name was changed to Verdure. The post office lasted 10-15 years. Today Verdure is private ranch property.

Verdure Utah 2016 photo by Penny

Verdure Utah 2016 photo by Penny

White Canyon was located about three miles east of Hite with a store, post office and a few residents. The settlers grew figs and pomegranates. It is now lies beneath Lake Powell reservoir.

White Rock Curve Village was a Navajo Indian community nine miles south of the San Juan River, on the northern slopes of White Mesa.

Williamsburg was a mining camp started by the Williams Mining District in 1892. It was located on the San Juan River. There were rock houses built in the camp, which now lie beneath Lake Powell reservoir.

Zahn's Camp began as a gold camp in 1892; it was one of Utah's most isolated camps. The camp was located in the twisted depths of the San Juan River, about 50 miles west of Mexican Hat. In 1892 the five Zahn brothers discovered fine grain gold in a sand bar five miles below the mouth of Copper Creek. The thousand-foot rock walls that tower above the river widen out at in that area to form a small basin only two miles square. When miners heard of the gold strike at Zahn's Camp, almost overnight 1200 miners moved to the camp. The first arrivals had to risk the extreme rapids of the San Juan and many rafts piled high with supplies were lost to the river. Several prospectors drown when their frail rafts overturned in the boiling rapids. Because of its location, Zahn's Camp was a crude place, with only tents, dugouts and slab-rock cabins, and the camp only lasted a few years.

Stone wall and boiler at Zahn's Camp

CHAPTER 20
Sanpete County

Buckenburg has disappeared completely and is only known to the old-timers.

Camp Clarke was a temporary Federal post in 1859 located in the San Pete Valley.

Camp Fountain Green was a temporary militia camp during the Ute Blackhawk War in 1866, located in Fountain Green.

Camp George was a Nevada volunteer post located in Ephraim in 1866.

Camp Pace was located in Gunnison in 1867 and was a Mormon Militia post.

Camp Paige was a temporary Federal post in the San Pete Valley in 1859, located near Moroni south of Camp Clarke, about 22 miles north of Manti.

Cedar Cliffs was settled in the late 1880s by James Livingston, a polygamist from Salt Lake City, located about three miles south of Fountain Green. The federal prosecution of polygamist men was very active at that time and it is likely that Livingston settled in the small, remote place to provide protection for his families. The place grew large enough to build a school house and an LDS Sunday School. There was nothing remaining in 2013.

Chester/Canal Creek/Chesterfield is located four miles west of Spring City. The town was settled by David Candland in the mid-1800s. In the beginning the town was named Canal Creek after the waterway from which the community received its water. Candland then changed the name to Chesterfield after his hometown in England; it was later shortened to Chester. The town was the only one located in the Sanpitch River bottomlands. Sunday school was conducted under an open-air bowery, until an LDS ward was founded in Chester in 1878. School was initially held in a log cabin until 1893 when a rock school house was erected. A brick school house was built in 1904, which was used as a multi-purpose building. The town was considered the closest to the geographic center of Utah. Some rundown buildings remained in 2013.

Christiansburg was located three miles east of Gunnison near US-89, along the San Pitch River. The town was originally settled in 1873 and named for the Christiansen brothers: Julius,

Theodore, and Titus, who were the first to settle the area with their families to raise fruit. The site proved too cold for reliable fruit production. For a time, there was a chalk mine and a roller miller that produced fine flour from 1885 into the 1920s. Very little remains in 2013.

Clarion was located four miles west of Centerfield on the west side of the Sevier River. In 1911 the Jewish Agricultural and Colonial Association of Philadelphia purchased 6000 acres of land from the Utah State Land Board. The Jewish association dispatched an engineer and an advance party of 12 men (some with families) to survey the area and prepare the ground for homes and crops. Homes, a church, and a school were built, followed by a canal, then a post office in 1915. After six years of crop failures, the colony was declared bankrupt in 1917. The soil was alkaline and inappropriate for intensive cultivation, so the settlers gradually moved. Some of the homes were moved to other towns, but many of the homes remained in place and were used by the new owners, whom were mostly Mormon farmers. In 1919, the population was 140. The schoolhouse was being used as a church on Sundays. By 1925, enough people lived in Clarion that an LDS ward was established, which lasted until 1934. The town was absolutely deserted by 1934 due to a prolonged drought that began in 1933. Japanese families then moved into the area, but WWII disrupted their settlement and the land reverted to the local citizens. Most of the foreign residents of Clarion were gone by 1934. There are a few residents who farm in the area, but the old town with most of the structures is not inhabited. Directions: Most of the homes and foundations are about four miles west of US Highway 89, along a gravel road leading westward from the highway, two blocks south of the old sugar plant at the outskirts of Centerfield. In 2013 two headstones with Hebraic inscriptions remained on a desolate hillside, one for a man who was killed while hauling lumber in 1913, and a baby who died in 1914.

Crowleyville was located between Axtell and Centerfield on US-89. The small settlement was founded around 1890.

Dewey's Camp was a militia encampment founded in 1866 near Fairview.

Dover was a town settled in about 1877 by William Robinson and 45 other families who established homesteads in the area. The town was named after Dover, England, the hometown of several of the settlers. A small one-room adobe school/church/social house was built, and a post office operated from 1879 to 1895. At its peak there were 50 homes, a general store and town hall. During the 1930s a drought struck, then later the river flooded the area, and many residents died of malaria. The following winter was harsh and many died of starvation due to a shortage of crops. The remaining residents fled the area the next spring, forcing the abandonment of Dover. A cemetery with a plaque about the town remains, where many young children and entire families are buried. Directions: The town is located a half-mile south of Fayette on U.S. Highway 89. A dirt road leads off to the west across the Sevier River, and then climbs up to the graveyard approximately two miles from the Highway. .

Fairview Fort was a Mormon settlers' rock-walled town fort, settled in 1866 in Fairview.

Fort Ephraim was constructed in 1854 in Ephraim. A larger fort was built completely enclosing the original fort in 1855. The inner fort was called "Little Fort" and the outer one "Large Fort."

Fort Gunnison was a Mormon settlers' adobe fort in Gunnison from the 1850s to1860s. A stone bastion was built in 1867, but the new stone walls were never completed.

Fort Manti was a Mormon settlers' 50-acre stone and adobe fort that absorbed and replaced the Little Stone Fort that was originally built in 1852. It was located in Palisade State Park.

Hardscrabble was a settlement that has completely disappeared and is only known to the older locals.

Jerusalem was a small agricultural settlement between Freedom and Fountain Green. It was established in 1871 by Lourtz Christensen and Simon Simonson. There was nothing remaining in 2013.

Johnstown was a small settlement a half-mile west of Pigeon Hollow Junction on US-89. There was nothing remaining in 2013.

Little Stone Fort was a fort in Manti used from 1852 to 1854. It was replaced by Fort Manti.

Manasseh was located on the east side of Ephraim. Manasseh at one time consisted of 21 families. The town did not prosper like its sister city Ephraim across the river; the area is now agricultural. Manasseh was home to about a dozen families in 1880. A school was built and the settlers hoped to prosper agriculturally. Today some scattered homesteads with houses, outbuildings, and hay derricks can still be found.

Moroni Fort was built with a stone observation tower in 1865 in Moroni.

Morrison was a coal mining camp about three miles east of present day Sterling in Six-Mile Canyon. A branch of the Rio Grande Railroad was extended to it in 1894. During the 20 years of coal mining activity, several substantial homes and other buildings were constructed to serve the mines and miners.

Mount Pleasant Fort was a Mormon settlers' five-acre adobe fort built in 1859 in Mount Pleasant. The fort encompasses today's Tithing Yard, with a bastion or watchtower in one corner. A second fort directly north was added in 1865 to help protect the livestock.

Mountainville was situated on a small rise between Fairview and Mount Pleasant. It was settled by Mormon Battalion veteran in the mid-1880s. After obtaining land through the Homestead Act, several families drew water from Birch and North Creeks and began irrigating and building a scattered agricultural community. The first log meeting house was erected in 1886, followed by a larger one in 1890. A larger more modern multi-purpose structure was built of brick in about 1917. Mountainville was built up along both sides of the long road going south from Fairview. Several interesting houses and large barns dot the landscape. A dairy was still operating in the area in the late 1980s.

Oak Creek was a small settlement along the road between Fairview and Milburn. It was settled sometime between 1894 and 1912. By 1916 the town was large enough to form an LDS ward. Members met in a building erected as a schoolhouse. Many of the homes and outbuildings remain and the area is still farmed.

Pettyville was also known as Brucetown and Leesbury. In 1873 a group of 15 families from Manti relocated to a site about six miles southwest of Manti and about a mile west of Sterling. Settlers occupied the place as squatters and church meetings were held in homes. A store and amusement hall was built early on, but the settlement was short-lived. The houses and other buildings were either moved or dismantled for salvage.

Pigeon Hollow was located on an unpaved road halfway between Spring City and Ephraim.

Shumway Springs was located three miles southwest of Ephraim.

Spearmint was a settlement where a sugar beet factory was located, operated by William Wrigley Jr., the gum manufacturer. He made many improvements and officially named the railroad spur Spearmint.

Spring City/Allred Settlement/Little Denmark was Sanpete's second oldest settlement. It was settled in 1853 as Allred's Settlement. The village of 15 families built a small fort around the spring which was used by Indians and early scouts. In January 1854 the fort and dwellings were burned by the Indians. The fort was not substantial enough during the Walker War so people moved. Five years later the area was settled again, by Danish emigrants, and new homes were built. The name was changed to Spring City, but it was also known as Little Denmark. Several sawmills were built in town and in the mouth of the canyon in 1860. In 1866 the town was deserted again because of the Blackhawk War. It was resettled again in 1867 and a school and church were built. The early buildings were of log or sod, and more substantial homes were built later. By 1883-84, LDS and Protestant churches were established and Methodists had a parochial school. Many buildings were made from the Eolithic limestone found in the area. Spring City grew gradually but steadily, reaching a population of 850 in 1880 and a peak size of about 1,230. The residents consisted of sheep men, farmers, and cattlemen. About 1300 people lived in the settlement in 1895. (The town is considered a ghost town but has become populated again and the entire town is listed on the Historical Register.)

Spring City Fort was a Mormon settlers' fort built in 1893 in Spring City.

West Point was home to about a dozen families. It was established in 1885 near Manasseh.

CHAPTER 21
Sevier County

Belnap was located in Marysvale Canyon north of Marysvale. In 1894 the railroad reached this point and was discontinued in 1971. This was the end of the railroad town of Belnap.

Brigham River was settled in 1863 by Mormon pioneers from Richfield, who were in search of a suitable livestock grazing area and fertile ground. There was no post office in Brigham River, so the five families that lived there received mail in Richfield. In 1918 the telephone came to Brigham River, and the name was then changed to Brodie Ridge. In 1921 a drought hit the area, causing the residents to move to the Sevier Valley. In 1881 a stage line was put through Brigham River, triggering the beginning of saloons, bawdy houses, and gambling dens. The town was located 28 miles northwest of Richfield in the Sanpete Range. The residents of Brigham River claimed that Butch Cassidy and his gang of robbers blew up the vault in the Miners Delight Saloon on First West. The saloon district of Brodie Ridge still stands, including the bawdy house.

Camp Sevier was a temporary federal post located in Sevier in 1859.

Cove was a small community in a semi-protected area on US-89 about two miles southwest of Joseph.

Gooseberry was located up Gooseberry Creek, 17 miles southeast of Salina. Today there is a U.S. Forest Service ranger station at the site. In 1865 the area was settled by a few ranch families. The name was suggested because the area has numerous wild gooseberry bushes.

Gravelbed was a small town near Sigurd and Richfield.

Lime Kilns were structures built in 1903 by J.H. Kyhl and Jens L. Jenson. The kiln represents a remaining structure important in the development of communities in the Sevier Valley. "Limeburner Jensen" used the kilns to cure lime by heating lime rock. The lime was used to make mortar for rock and brick building, and as a whitewash. Jenson became blind in 1905 due to the intense heat of the kiln. The seven kilns were located near the mountains two miles north of Richfield.

Pittsburg was located at the base of Big Rock Candy Mountain.

Prattville was located four miles east of Richfield. On June 21, 1873 a group of Mormon pioneers arrived and established their community, which was named Prattville after Helaman Pratt. Prattville had a one-room log school house. The settlers soon moved to other locations because the soil was too alkaline and waterlogged.

Prattville 2015 photo by penny

Venice was a small farming village settled by Francis Wall in 1875. Wall thought the area must have rich soil, as the brush and weeds grew so high. He built a cabin on the east side of the Sevier River and sent for his family. In a short time, there were eleven families living at Venice, and a school was built. The village was named Wallsville early on, and when the post office was established around 1894 the name was changed to honor Venice, Italy.

Vermillion was settled ten miles northeast of Richfield. In 1874, white settlers established this small agricultural community on the west bank of the Sevier River. The community had an earlier name of Neversweat because of the midsummer humidity and heat. It was renamed Vermillion because the settlement was adjacent to Vermillion Mountain. The brilliant red coloring of the mountain inspired Brigham Young to name it on Oct. 8, 1876.

CHAPTER 22
Summit County

Altus was located at Parleys Summit, the highest point along the highway between Salt Lake City and Park City. Altus was settled in 1900 as a temporary way station, stage stop and round house, but was soon abandoned. It completely disappeared after the I-80 freeway was built.

Atkinson was near Silver Creek Junction, a company town that suddenly appeared and just as suddenly vanished. The town was the creation of a group of eastern investors, who arrived in Summit County in 1908 with the idea of recovering the valuable minerals washing down Silver Creek from Park City mines. The owners built a mill and flimsy housing for workers and their families. About 150 families, carried by their enthusiasm, moved from surrounding communities to the new town of Atkinson and willingly lived three or four families to a house. It seemed that instant prosperity would come to everybody. The company owners became town heroes. A

one-room schoolhouse was built in 1910, and students traded their old-fashion slates for real paper and pencils. In 1910 the Union Pacific built a depot and also three large bunkhouses to house hundreds of railway workers. Life was rosy until 1918, then suddenly, the principal owners took their families and all the cash, stock, and checks they could find and fled town. Creditors arrived and disassembled the mill. Mill workers left town and the Union Pacific relocated the workers. A few farming families remained, but now all that remains is the old schoolhouse.

Blacks Fork was located about two miles south of Wyoming border near Meeks Cabin Reservoir on U-150. Its history is uncertain; some sources call it an army commissary, saying that it supplied food, wagon repair facilities, pack animals, and equipment for soldiers patrolling the area. Some called it a way station and others call it a timber-company tow. Whatever its beginnings, the town developed into a timber town. Loggers and teamsters hauling wood lived there, and the population was 50 to 100. Blacks Fork lasted from 1870 to 1930. The town's physical layout was built in a semicircle surrounding a large barn. The center of town life was the large company building, which contained company offices, stores, eating facilities and storage rooms. Other log buildings were duplexes, boarding houses and large dormitories. In 2002 there was still a lot to see.

Photo taken by Penny

Camp in Echo Canyon was located near Echo, established in 1859 as a temporary Federal encampment. The exact location is undetermined.

Castle Rock was a settlement started in 1860 around the Castle Rock Pony Express Station. Several families moved close to the express station. By 1867 the express station was closed and the buildings were sold to a French trapper. He moved the buildings a mile above the original site. The trapper raised cattle and sheep for a time and then disappeared. The railroad built down Echo Canyon in 1867-1869 and passed right by the station. The first agent at the location claimed to have bought out the Frenchman and sold the stock to the station foreman. A year later a body believed to be the Frenchman was found in a wash. The original dwellings, church building, and blacksmith shop were built of logs. Homes were built in 1872 and a school was added and continued until 1937. In the early days, some of the boys in town would go down to the Chinese opium dens and climb on the roofs of the low-built shanties, stuff the chimneys with old rags then run off and watch the men come running out with their eyes watering. In the early 1930s there were homes, farms, a gas station, store, windmill, school house, a small depot and a section house. Castle Rock is located 21 miles west of Evanston, Wyoming on private property.

Echo Stage Station was a resting place for thousands of travelers. Echo originated as a stopover along the Mormon trail. Later the town served as a junction between the First Transcontinental Railroad and a spur line to serve silver mines near Park City. The town served as a coaling and watering station for trains entering Echo Canyon. From Echo, helper locomotives were added, to push trains up the steep grade to Wahsatch. There were many railroad buildings located here. By the 1880s over a hundred men and their families lived here. A brick schoolhouse was built in the 1880s and served until 1913. The LDS Church bought the old school and used it as a chapel for another 50 years. Within a month of Echo's birth it had a business district of more than 50 false front business buildings. But behind those wooden false fronts customers found huge white tents. Echo City was a tough place, hold-ups and killings happened every day. Believing the railroad would only be temporary, many saloon owners just dug a pit under their buildings to dump each night's garbage. Many years later digging the site for a new building, a contractor dug into one of these holes and discovered seven human skeletons. He discontinued the saloon and turned the remainder into a first class store, restaurant and dance hall. Echo became the hub of Summit County; the railroad warehouses were full of groceries and hardware. A flour mill operated in the area for 93 years.

Echo Church still standing 2018 Photo by Penny

Echo Canyon Breastworks was located near Echo from 1857 to 1858. Stone breastworks were built by Mormon pioneers along the narrow Echo Canyon Gorge to thwart a potential Federal invasion to suppress a rumored Mormon rebellion. The stonework still remains.

Grass Creek was located about nine miles northeast of Coalville. After coal was discovered along the Weber River and the town of Coalville founded in 1859, Brigham Young sent more searchers in 1860 to explore further. They discovered other coal beds just north over the hill, in Grass Valley Canyon. The LDS Church soon opened a coal mine in the canyon. A few miners' families settled around the mine, calling their settlement Grass Creek.

The silver mining boom in the Park City area in the 1870s created a sudden demand for coal. Non-Mormon investors quickly moved in to develop the canyon's mines. The Grass Creek Fuel Company established its own company town at Grass Creek. The company built homes on the north side of the canyon, with the business district on the south. As the population grew, Grass Creek added numerous buildings, from miners' shacks to fine stone homes for mine owners. There was even a Chinatown.

Until 1873 the coal was hauled by ox teams through Parley's Canyon into Salt Lake City. In 1873 a narrow gauge railway called the Summit County Railroad was built from the Union Pacific Railroad line at Echo through Coalville to Grass Creek.

Grass Creek continued to grow through the end of the 19th century. The canyon's activity peaked about 1881–1910. By 1904 there was a school and post office in town, and in 1907 Ogden millionaire David Eccles bought up more of the Grass Creek Coal Company's coal fields and established the Union Fuel Company. The population of Grass Creek was recorded as 190 in 1910.

Grass Creek's coal was found in soft clay, and the mines began to fill with water, causing dangerous cave-ins. The cost and risk of mining coal made it hard to compete with safer mines that yielded better quality coal. By 1931 the only remaining buyer of Grass Creek coal was the cement plant at Croydon. That year the cement plant shut down, and in 1932 the Union Pacific asked permission to abandon the Grass Creek spur line. All of Grass Valley Canyon is now privately owned and closed to the public.

Hoyt's Fort/Fort Union was built during the Blackhawk War in 1866-1868. During the worst of the Indian problems, 25 families lived in the area. Cabins were built both inside and outside of the fort walls. Hoyt's Fort also served as a stage station, located in Hoytsville. Samuel Hoyt became wealthy and built a stone house and lavishly decorated it with imported marble statues and other costly furnishings. The home is a designated state historical site.

Hoyt Peak was supposedly an old Spanish mine from about 1796. A mine shaft, various remains of cabins and foundations can be found on the way up to Hoyt's Peak. A dirt road is only open to vehicles June 15th to Sept 15th, with snowmobile access in winter. Hoyt's Peak is at an elevation of 10,198 ft. Access can be found from Marion, Utah, where a dirt road heads toward the mountains on the north side of 2972 N. 900 E.

Kamas Fort was a Mormon settlers' fort established in 1868 – 1870 in Kamas.

Kimballs was an Overland Stage/Pony Express Station and hotel built of square cut limestone in the 1860s, located about two miles along Interstate 80 east of the Park City Exit. Passengers traveling east or west found themselves bedding in one of the 11 rooms that were considered some of the finest along the Overland Route. While at the hotel, they ate fresh trout caught by torch light out of Kimball's Creek, wild sage grouse, wild duck and fresh beef. Built in 1862 by William H. Kimball, the son of Heber C. Kimball who was a counselor to Brigham Young, the family owned and operated the hotel until the turn of the century. The Kimball Hotel maintained several successful businesses. When the railroad and automobiles arrived in Summit County, the Kimballs adapted to the changing technology and ways of life. The Kimball family offered a light express stagecoach between Salt Lake City and Park City as well as U.S. mail service. The hotel staff hauled freight and ore from the mines and rented saddle horses, buckboards, sleds and cutters from the Dexter Livery, located at the bottom of Main Street. When the Lincoln Highway Association built the first transcontinental highway in 1913, its route ran right in front of the old sandstone building. But in 1960, when the plans for I-80 were being drawn, engineers were persuaded to veer around the back of the building in order to preserve one of the oldest remaining structures along the Overland Stage and perhaps in all of Summit County.

Lake Flat was built on the shores of a small mountain lake two miles southeast of present-day Park city in 1869. Most of the settlers were Scots. It was also called the Robin's Nest of the Wasatch. There were log cabins and clapboard rooming houses, as well as a store and saloon. Lake Flat residents visited each other by poling across the little lake in the center of town.

Mill City was located high on Gold Mountain, at the headwaters of the Bear River, 11 miles North of Hayden Peak & Mirror Lake. In 1880s logging camp housed 500 gamblers, roughnecks, labors and their families who were employed in supplying timber products to the nearby transcontinental railroad. A store was operated by the logging company. Directions: A short dirt road turns to the west about 11 miles south of the Wyoming border, on State Road 150. A four-mile hike leads to a row of old log cabins. Several bunkhouses and some homes remained.

Needle Rock Station was located near the Utah-Wyoming border. It was named for the Needle Rocks, a prominent landmark used as a guide by all early pioneers. The station was a regular stop where teams were changed and meals and lodging could be found.

North Oakley was an outpost for Anti-Mormons and was destroyed by Mormons. About 300 people resided in the town during its peak population. Directions: Turn north from SR 32, drive one mile north and turn down a dirt road. The town's remains are on private property. A cemetery, some evidence of a fort, and a dam to the north could still be seen, in 2014.

Park City/Mineral City was a mining camp established in 1869 when the Young American lode became the first recorded claim. It was the discovery of the rich Ontario mine that initiated the rapid growth and reputation as a great silver mining camp. In 1872 shortly after the discovery, the mine was sold for $27,000 to George Hearst of San Francisco. It produced some $50,000,000 of ore. By 1879 the Ontario mine was flourishing, with houses springing up near the mine and lower down the canyon. As a camp began to form, primarily wooden structures, a fire destroyed several of the principal buildings in 1882. In 1884 Park City incorporated as a city. Another fire destroyed a building in 1885. On June 19, 1898 fire raged through the Park City commercial district. The blaze was the greatest in Utah history. Main Street lay in ruins, with only a few gaunt walls remaining. Losses were estimated at over $1,000,000, and some 200 business, houses and dwellings were destroyed. With community support the town rebuilt. Commercial activity flourished. Utah business directories reveal that in 1892-93, 112 businesses (not including mining companies) were listed. By 1918-19 the number had declined to 87; and in 1920-21 only 75. The great depression of the 1930s halted development. By the 1950s Park City was almost dead. In the 1960s Park City had a rebirth, when it became a ski resort. In 1978 the Park City Main Street was listed in the National Register of Historic Places.

Rhoads Fort was built in Rhoads Valley (now Kamas). The fort was 30 rods square with 16-foot high walls with gates at the east and west ends. The fort's interior was ringed with cabins where about 50 families lived. The fort was abandoned in 1870.

Rockport /Crandall/Enoch City began in 1860. The town was one-street wide and spread for three miles along the highway on the west side of the valley. In 1866 Indian trouble caused the people to build a stone fort. The town was renamed Rockport because of the rock fort they built around the entire settlement for defense. The wall was two feet thick and eight feet high. In 1872 a concrete building was erected for the general store and the town's first post office. The population was around 200 people. They built a gristmill in 1863, and also had a saw mill. In 1950 the government bought all the land and built Rockport Reservoir where the town once stood. It was located two miles South of Wanship and is now under the water of Rockport Lake.

Sage Bottom Fort was a Mormon settlers' fort settled in 1867 in Peoa.

Stillwater Camp was a timber camp located on the Stillwater fork of the Bear River. A six-mile long feeder flume for logs snaked its way up Stillwater Fork to the timber camp. Bunk houses and bachelor cabins hidden in the dense pine forest now mark its site. Life wasn't easy at Stillwater Camp's 10,000-foot elevation. Lumberjacks must have consumed a lot of whiskey to keep warm during the winter, judging from the hundreds of old bottles that litter the site.

Upton was a small settlement in Chalk Creek, above Coalville, established in 1861. An early name was Huffville for the Joseph Huff family who originally settled on the creek. First a sawmill town, it later had a store and school house. As more people moved in, Huffville became Up Town, and then changed to Upton, as it was "up the creek" from Coalville.

Wahsatch/Wasatch was located eleven miles west of Evanston Wyoming, as a principal camp on the Union Pacific transcontinental railroad that was under construction at the time. It was inhabited from 1868 until the 1930s. From 1868–1869 hundreds dug the 772-foot Echo tunnel through the Wasatch Mountains west of town. Wahsatch soon became a major supply station and railhead, with its own roundhouse, workshops, boarding houses, and warehouses. When the railroad was finished in May 1869, a meal station for waiting passengers was constructed. Wahsatch was known as a wild and lawless place. Laborers spent their wages immediately in tent saloons. Shootings were common, and there is even record of a lynching. Lacking a formal cemetery, the town buried its dead in makeshift hillside graves. This violent period was short-lived. In the early 1870s, the railroad moved most operations to Evanston. The population sharply dropped, and most of the buildings were demolished. Toward the end of the 19th century Wahsatch enjoyed a minor rebirth, as a location central to the area's growing sheep ranches. A number of new dwellings were built as ranchers and laborers began to gather here annually for sheep shearing season. The town grew enough to justify the building of a new school in 1910. In 1916 Wahsatch became the headquarters for the construction of a second railroad tunnel, bringing another temporary surge in population. The railroad built a new depot and section houses in the 1930s, but Wahsatch soon declined, along with the sheep industry. The town was abandoned in the 1930s. The entire town site is on railroad property. Most visitors see little more than an old wooden sign reading Wahsatch alongside the tracks, but there are some remnants of railroad buildings and equipment. The site is located at the Echo Canyon summit between the Weber and Bear rivers drainage system. The camp was named for chief Wahsatch, the local Shoshone Indian chief. Most of his clan converted to the Mormon faith as they sought to learn farming and agriculture in the Mormon manner.

Wanship Station was built in 1861 as a stage coach station to change horses and as an overnight stop for the overland coach. In 1870 it became the Moorehouse family home and in 1877 the Peterson family made it into a rooming and boarding house. The station later served as a granary and was demolished in 1912.

Weber Stage Station was built at the mouth of Echo Canyon in 1854. The settlement was also known as Bromley's, Pulpit Rock, & Hanging Rock. By 1859 there were two groceries, a blacksmith shop, and a mill station. At the time of the Pony Express in 1860, a small village existed here. During it's almost 80 years of service, the solid stone walls of the Weber Stage Station also served as a jail, a fort, and a relay point for the Pony Express. It was demolished in 1931 to build Echo Reservoir. A workman found an 1847 five-dollar gold piece hidden in a crack in the wall, a few pieces of small change, and an old letter from a son and daughter to their parents dated 1873, a pair of glasses, a gun case, and a love letter written on parchment from an Eastern girl to her sweetheart, who was a pony express rider.

Westfork/Timber Town was a settlement located six miles south of the Wyoming boarder. Directions: From SR 150, turn onto a dirt road leading eastward and follow it about 15 miles to Lyman Lake. A rough road turns to the right and follows the West Fork of Blacks Fork upstream. After traveling exactly 5.5 miles, stop and hike into the timber on the road side of the river. In a half-mile some remains of the old log cabins along Main Street can be seen in 2008.

CHAPTER 23
Tooele County

Aragonite was established in the early 1900s as a mining site for the mineral aragonite, used as a decorative stone in building. The site was abandoned after a few years. The mines were reopened later in the century, but there has not been any activity for years. A couple of old buildings and mine shafts remain. Directions: Take I-80 exit 56 to Aragonite. Proceed south on the paved road for about three miles. Just before the Safety-Kleen facility, follow a dirt road to see some remains. The dirt road also follows "Hastings Cut-off," the path followed by the Donner party when crossing Utah. Historical markers can be found on the roadside. In 2013 a few remains were found heading east into the mountains about 3.6 miles.

Arinosa was located 19 miles east of Wendover in the heart of the Salt Flats. Today it is a seldom-used siding with no permanent residents on the Western Pacific Railroad near I-80. In the 1880s Arinosa was a railroad camp, but it was abandoned in 1955 due to a lack of culinary water and because of improved transportation.

Barro was a railroad town west of Knolls.

Bauer/Terminal/Buhl was a mining town located five miles southwest of Tooele before coming to Stockton. It was first settled in 1855 and died out in the 1930s. As of 2013 there was just a big gravel pit. The area has been closed for redevelopment.

Beckwith Camp was a small army camp located on the road beyond Aragonite that climbs up a rocky canyon. In 1853 Lt. E.G. Beckwith led a survey party and established a camp at the site for five years while searching for a route for the railroad.

Benmore was a group of homesteaders under two main families, Bennion and Skidmore, who settled this small village four to six miles south of Vernon. In 2013 nothing but a sign remained.

Blair Spur was a railroad town.

Bullionville was a small mining camp with a store, saloon and a butcher shop that appeared after the first discovery of silver in Dugway in 1870. Bullionville's leading mines were the Silver King, Black Maria and the Queen of Sheba while smaller properties included the Yellow Jacket, Harrison, Cannon and Buckhorn. Distances in the desert country were too great to make hauling ore to the railroad profitable, so a smelter was erected in Smelter Canyon. Mine owners built it at great expense, but after it was completed they learned that smelters require a great deal of water to operate, and water is one thing the Dugway Range had little of. When the smelter proved to be useless, mines closed, and by the late 1880s the town was deserted, with piles of high grade ore stacked up waiting for the day when the proposed railroad would arrive, but it never did. Few know of the old camp in Smelter Canyon, because the north end of the range is off-limits. A sign warns it is part of Dugway Proving Ground, a test area for explosives and poisonous gas. Directions: The town can be reached by following the old Pony Express trail west from Faust and over Lookout Pass to the foot of the desolate Dugway Range. A poor dirt road turns north from the Pony Express Trail and follows the eastern edge of the range almost to its north end, where an almost invisible trail turns up a rocky canyon to Bullionville. It is best to use trail bikes or four-wheel drive vehicles. Be sure to stop and look around at the silver ore that is still waiting, located just west of the Dugway geode beds.

Burmester was a station on the Western Pacific Railroad at the south shore of the Great Salt Lake. It was first known as Grants Station, but in 1906 the name was changed to Burmester after Frank T. Burmester, a landowner. He later sold his land to the Morton Salt Company.

Burnt Station was established in 1859 in Deep Creek Canyon, where the canyon walls were wide enough for a station house and livestock corrals to be built. The station was burned twice by Indian raid in 1861 and 1864. The station sat in a deep twisted Canyon and was a favorite for Indian attacks and a least two soldiers and five station agents and travelers were killed. The stage driver never knew if he would be greeted by a relief driver or Indians. Rough lodging and plain meals were available at the station.

Camp Conness was a camp located in Rush Valley from 1855 to 1869. It was also called Camp Rush Valley and Government Reservation in Rush Valley. This was a grazing area for horses from Fort Douglas and Camp Floyd.

Camp Shunk was established in 1858 as a temporary Federal Post. It was located near Vernon about 25 miles southwest of Camp Floyd.

Canyon Station was located in Overland Canyon. Built in 1861, it consisted of a log house, a stable, and a dugout where meals were cooked and served. In 1863 Indians killed the overland agent and four soldiers, and then burned the station. The overland station was rebuilt in 1863 at the presently marked site, which was a more defensible location. Stone outlines of the 1863 station are still visible. There are remnants of a round fortification built just behind the station which served as a lookout and place of refuge.

Center/Ajax was a small community midway between Rush Valley and Vernon on US-36, settled in 1863 by Welsh pioneers. The community provided hay, livestock and general supplies for nearby ranchers, miners, and other nearby settlements. It was here that Mr. William Ajax and his wife started what became their famous underground store, restaurant and supply center to serve miners, travelers and area residents. A post office for the area was established for a time at the store. A hotel was built above ground providing lodging and meals. Travelers' animals were also provided for with stables for more than 100 horses, 300 cattle and 6,000 sheep. The hotel was abandoned in 1914. It was more than 80 by 100 feet with a dirt roof shored up by huge timbers and served the area from the early 1870s until its closing in 1913. With only a shovel and a wheelbarrow, entrepreneur businessman William Ajax created a unique two-story underground store in 1870. He developed a complete underground department store, cafe, and hotel. Patrons from nearby farms, ranches and mines found a wide variety of merchandise, food, clothing, housewares, hardware, tools and medicines. Goods were arranged in department store style. It was estimated the value of the merchandise was in excess of $70,000. William Ajax died in 1899, but his store was operated until 1914 when the family of William Ajax liquidated the inventory. The town was located about three miles north of Vernon on state Highway 36, but in 2013 there was just a depression in the ground and a marker.

Clifton was a mining town. Located about four miles south of Gold Hill, the road climbs to Clifton Flat. There were several business and buildings but the town didn't last long. Valuable ore (silver and lead) was discovered there in 1858 and in 1872 a smelter and mill were built. Directions: A large sagebrush flat lies between low mountains. Immediately past the rim of the flat, a poor road leads to the left downhill about three miles to the Clifton ruins. In April of 2014 nothing remained of the town, but there was some active mining.

Clive was a maintenance camp and siding for the Western Pacific Railroad that was abandoned in 1955.

Death Canyon was a town that was located at the extreme southern end of the Simpson Mountains. Directions: Turn to the south at the bottom of Lookout Pass on the Pony Express road, then follow the range around to the southern end. Turn north up the canyon.

Delle was established in 1880 as a maintenance camp and dispatch center for the Western Pacific Railroad. It was originally called Dalles Spring but was shortened to Delle for telegraphic efficiency. Delle was located near I-80.

Dolomite was a railroad town, slightly off I-80 to the east of Dell.

Dunbar was a railroad town.

Dunnstein was a small mining camp located near the south end of Tooele County's Lakeside Range. It started in 1905 when silver & copper were discovered, but nothing remained by 1909. Directions: A dirt road leaves I-80 just west of the Lakeside exit and winds back into the hills to the old Monarch Mine. Just beyond on the mountains' east slope, there is an old Indian burial ground. Most of the area is on the Air Force bombing range and permission to enter should be obtained.

E.T. City was a permanent settlement established in 1849 by a group of Latter-Day Saints. They built a sawmill and called the settlement "E.T. City" after LDS Leader E.T. Benson. The alkaline soil in the area caused the settlement to fail.

East Rush Valley was a pass station built as a dugout along the original Pony Express Trail. A stone monument on the flat marks the location of East Rush Valley, or Pass Station. Located about 12 miles from Fairfield and Camp Floyd, not much is known about the structure which was here or its use. It was not listed as a Pony Express contract station.

Ellerbeck was a railroad town.

Faust/Meadow Creek is at the south end of Rush Valley where the old Pony Express Trail crosses the railroad. Faust was named for H.J. "Doc" Faust who rode the Pony Express out of the station, operated a mail station on a local section of the Overland Trail and later purchased the station and surrounding area for his ranch. The station was a two-story stone structure located some distance from the present marker. Today the site is an unimportant siding on the railroad.

Flux was an end-of-the-line railroad camp.

Free Coinage was a mining camp in Timpie Springs Canyon. During 1896 the Free Coinage Mining Company erected buildings at the Humbug mine. Directions: Take Exit 77 for 19.7 miles.

Gisborn/Gisbourne was located a half-mile south and several hundred feet further downstream from Jacob City. Cabins were built on both sides of a windswept ridge. The area was developed by Matt Gisborn around the Mono mine. It was far enough away from Jacob City that even the short distance uphill was very strenuous. There were many businesses in Gisborn. The Mono mine finally pinched out in 1879 but not until a million dollars had been produced. In 2004 some foundation and piles of wood and some open mines remained.

Gold Hill was located in the southwest corner of the county. The Clifton (Gold Hill) district near the Utah-Nevada line had a total production of around 26,000 ounces of gold between 1892 and 1944. There are numerous mines in the area; the Cane Springs, Alvarado and Gold Hill mines lead in production. In the Deep Creek area there were some small copper-lead-silver mines that had a byproduct of gold. This area has also produced large quantities of bismuth and molybdenum. Legend has it that placer gold was discovered in the area in 1858, but the Indians drove the prospectors away. By 1869 the settlement consisted of dugouts and shacks. In 1892 the town of Gold Hill was established. The year 1917 brought the Deep Creek Railroad into Gold Hill and a smelter was constructed. There was a need for arsenic in the cotton fields of the south during WWII, used to control an infestation of insects. Almost 100,000 tons of arsenic was mined from 1943 to 1945 and boosted the population of Gold Hill to over 3,000. However, cheaper arsenic prices from abroad cooled that endeavor. The sizable town in its hay-day had several stores; mercantile, pharmacy, garage, two lumber yards, elementary school, pool hall, grocery & clothing store, the Home Restaurant and Bakery, and a hotel. Gold Hill also had a dentist and doctor, and even a house of ill repute. A newspaper, The Gold Hill Standard carried local news and advertisement to the community. World War II brought a demand for tungsten, and once again the town began to flourish as it shipped out tons of the metal. The town dwindled for a third time as the need for tungsten diminished at the end of the war. Although mining implements, old ore sites and the occasional cabin in the hills lie dormant now, modern technology has kindled a renewed interest in taking another look at the area. As of 2015 a few residents still resided in the area.

Photo by Penny

Grantsville Fort was located in Grantsville. The early settlers build a fort for protection from the Indians. The walls on the north and west sides were made of hard packed dirt and were five feet wide at the bottom and 12 feet high. The other walls were of rock and adobe, three feet wide and 12 feet high.

Harker Canyon was located in the Sheeprock Mountains about six miles south of Vernon. The entire area is National Forest land so you can explore as much as you like. The town is two miles west of Harker Canyon. Artifacts of a town and abandoned mining operations below a natural spring remain.

Ibapah/Deep Creek was an early Pony Express Station that was originally founded in 1859 by Mormon missionaries, who taught the local Indians modern methods of farming. The settlement was originally known as Deep Creek for the name of the creek where it was located. Ibapah was on the orginal Lincoln Highway on the extreme west side of the county. It was one of three early Pony Express Stations in the area and was the last stop before the route entered Nevada. Along with the Pony Express, the Telegraph and the Overland Stage & Mail were also routed through a main station in Ibapah. Ibapah had three stores and four saloons.

Iosepa was located 20 miles south of the Great Salt Lake in the center of Skull Valley. In 1889, with the encouragement of the Mormon Church, a group of converts from Hawaii attempted to establish a colony at this location. At one time over 225 members lived in the colony. There were well-built stores, homes, a schoolhouse, a church and an underground water system. They planted 300 fruit trees, 300 walnut trees, 100 ornamental trees, along with numerous shrubs and roses. Hansen's disease (leprosy) struck the settlement in 1893. When the church built a temple in Hawaii in 1916, many of the Hawaiians returned to their homeland. By 1917 Iosepa was a ghost town centered around a cemetery. The property was later sold to the Deseret livestock Company. "Iosepa" is Hawaiian for "Joseph". As of 2014 the cemetery was still there.

Indian Springs was a mining town in one of the canyons in the Simpson Mountains.

Jacob City was one of Utah's earliest mining camps, built near the head of Dry Canyon. It was reached by means of a steep, winding road which passed Gisborn. A few claims were being worked in Dry Canyon as early as 1863, and the town site was established soon after that. In 1870 a newspaper reporter described Jacob City as "A string-town along the bottom of a steep and narrow canyon, where houses are built leaning against the mountainside to keep them from falling into the canyon below". The camp could not be reached by wagon and horses are doubtful of their foothold on its streets, the streets were paved with boulders and drained by a creek. The city had two stores, two first-class eating houses, two meat markets and other businesses, but there were more saloons than anything. Most of the buildings were made of logs, but the grand hotel was built of "finished redwood." Col. Patrick Connor built the great Basin Mill at Jacob City. By 1876 almost 300 people lived in the settlement. Jacob City was the largest producer of precious metals in the district for a time. The mine played out and other discoveries in the Oquirrh Mountains lured the miners away and Jacob City became a ghost town. Directions: Turn on Silver Avenue at the south end of Stockton. As of 2004, several barred mines and some ruins could be seen.

Junction was an end-of-the-line railroad camp.

Knolls was primarily a train depot used to facilitate the movement of trains. A large wooden water tank was installed on a hill and track was laid to haul water up to this elevated point. Sometimes the train crew would leave a tank car on the hill with some water in it to provide warm water for a bath. Nell Marie (Palmer) Lamus said she lived at Knolls, Utah and that the children traveled to school in a camp wagon that was pulled out to Knolls. It is now a recreation area.

La Cigale was a mining town settled in the 1890s. It was located north of U-73, a mile south of Mercur Canyon, and one-half mile around the bend north of West Dip. La Cigale is French for "the Cricket." La Cigale's mine was not rich enough to support the town without nearby Mercur, causing its abandonment when Mercur died.

Lake Point was an outgrowth of E.T. City settled in 1854 at the north end of the Oquirrh Mountains. Several businesses at Lake Point included a general merchandise store, a dry goods store, a flour mill and the Utah Wool Company. Mine owners found it was cheaper to ship the ore across the lake to Corinne, where mills and smelters were located. Almost overnight Lake Point became Utah's first seaport. The large, steam-powered ships were called the "City of Corinne" and the "Kate Connor."

Lincoln was settled in 1876 at the mouth of Pine Canyon on the west side of the Oquirrh Mountains. Although the original name was Pine Canyon, the settlers changed it to Lake View because the settlements had such a beautiful view of Great Salt Lake. After a post office was established, it was realized that there were numerous "Lake" names in the territory, so the name was changed to Lincoln, in honor of the President of the U.S.

Lofgreen was settled in 1898 by Herman Lofgreen, along the Union Pacific railroad track going south from Lake Point. In earlier days there was a small schoolhouse in the settlement.

The residents earned their living by breaking wild horses and working as section hands for the railroad. The settlement was abandoned after creosote was discovered, since this greatly reduced the demand for section hands. (Applying creosote to railroad ties keeps them from rotting.) Directions: The settlement was located west up a dirt road about two miles south of Vernon.

Low was a Western Pacific Railroad siding at the northern tip of the Cedar Mountains on the eastern edge of the Great Salt Lake Desert. The settlement was established in the early 1880s as a construction and maintenance camp. Local water was unavailable and the camp was abandoned by 1955. The siding was located on a low pass between two mountain ranges.

Marblehead was a railroad town.

Marshall was a railroad town for the track crew. A tipple enabled the crew to transfer sugar beets to railroad cars for shipment. The town was located east of Grantsville.

Martinsville/Slagtown one of Tooele County's first settlements was located three miles south of Stockton, just west of U-36, near the Steptoe Military Camp historical marker. It was a string town that grew up along the now dried-up Rush Lake. Houses were built against one another for support. By 1870 several large mills and smelters were in operation at Martinsville, reducing the rich silver ore being hauled from Jacob City and Gisborn. Among them were the Chicago and Godbe smelters. Martinsville was a lively place while it lasted, with eight business buildings, six of which were saloons. Directions: Southeast of the marker on U-36 a grove of trees can be seen by the railroad tracks. The foundations of an old mill could be seen in 2014 among the trees.

Mercur/Lewiston was first known as Lewiston. Several rich mining strikes were made in the late 1860s and Lewiston became a major mining camp. Saloons, gambling houses, dance halls, frame buildings, and tent sites sprang up, and hotels flourished. The town grew to about 1500, but by 1880 it became a ghost town. There was a rebirth when a prospector came looking for a deposit of gold. He discovered quicksilver, a vein of cinnabar. He named the ore Mercur, but the gold content was more valuable than the mercury. Efforts to get the gold out of the rock proved to be too expensive, and the town died again. Then a group of men with financial resources, succeeded in finding a way to extract the gold from the rock. The renamed Mercur rose again into a boomtown. During the early part of 1896 a fire nearly destroyed the entire town. The town was rebuilt and was destroyed by fire again in 1902, when there were about 12,000 residents. Whiskey was cheaper than water, which was sold door to door for a dollar a bucket. Sugar cost a dollar a pound and canned goods were $2.50 each. Again it was rebuilt and the boom lasted until 1913. By 1925, Mercur was once again a ghost town. In 1934 a side canyon called Horse Thief Gulch was found to be rich in gold and in two years Mercur had risen again to become the second highest gold-producing town in Utah. The end finally came in 1951. Mercur had a total production of 1,115,000 gold ounces. Mercur was totally destroyed by fire and was Utah's only all-gold mining city and was considered to be one of the world's greatest gold camps, where the cyanide process was first introduced into North America. In 1983 the Getty Oil Company reopened the Mercur area and removed most of the remaining structures. Directions: The ghost town can be reached from Route 36 south of Tooele, A short distance south of route 73 turn east to Ophir. Only the cemetery remains part way up the road on the right-hand side on top of the hill.

Morris was a railroad town.

Nowlenville/Batesville was a small settlement located south & west of the mouth of Ophir Canyon. It was settled in approximately 1852 as a farming community, supplying Ophir and other mining camps with farm and dairy produce. Although small, it had several stores and a Mormon Church, something unusual in Tooele County at that time. In later years it became a ranch and is now included in the area of the Deseret Chemical Depot.

Ophir was established in 1865 after soldiers of the U.S. Army noticed that Indians in the territory were using bullets made from silver. The soldiers soon found the source and named the location St. Louis. When the find became public, the site quickly became a town with no official name. In 1870, it was named Ophir after the rich mines of King Solomon. During its heyday, a number of ornamental homes and buildings were constructed, saloons, gambling and dance halls, red-light houses, hotels, cafes and stores. There were drugstores, general stores, theaters, two schools and a post office built of stone with iron shutters to protect viable shipments. A combination town hall and fire station was built. The population peaked at 6,000 people. By 1918 Ophir still boasted a post office, weekly newspaper, general store, daily stage line, railroad and a population of 560. In 1930 a large flotation mill was built at the mouth of the canyon to reprocess the old tailings. Only the foundations of the mill remain. By 1949 a small general store operated, along with a tiny hotel and a post office. A bar was opened in the old rock post office building, which in the recent past served as a drugstore and pool hall. The Ophir Hill mine continues to produce, and the first fatality in 25 years occurred in late 1971. The town is located south southeast of Stockton, four miles up Ophir Canyon. In 2016 Ophir was still a small active town, and the Ophir City Hall that was built in 1870 was still standing.

Orr's Ranch catered to motorists. In 1913 the Lincoln Highway came into being, the first coast-to-coast "motor road" that linked New York City and San Francisco. Its 3,389 miles of mostly one-lane dirt road passed through 12 states, entering Utah at Evanston, Wyoming and departing at Ibapah near the Nevada state line. The Lincoln Highway ran through the heart of Tooele County, with a major stop at Orr's Ranch in Skull Valley. At Orr's Ranch, motorists could buy gas, food and stay the night before embarking across the Great Salt Lake Desert. The ranch still stands today, with a Lincoln Highway marker on site.

Pehrson was a railroad town located east of Vernon.

Point Lookout Station was located eight miles from Faust. Horace Rockwell, brother of Orrin Porter Rockwell, and his wife Libby lived in a small log house at Lookout. There was a store where travelers could buy supplies and Aunt Libby's home cooked meals. They had no children, and Aunt Libby, as she was called, kept several dogs upon which she doted. A stone enclosure was a short distance to the south of the home. Built to protect the cemetery where her beloved dogs are buried. Three emigrant graves are also said to be found within. The cemetery still remained in 2014.

Photo by Penny 2014

Richville was once the county seat of Tooele and the LDS church had several mills built in town. There was a grist, flour, saw and textile mill. The first county hall was a private home purchased by the county, the basement sufficing for the county jail. In 1860 the county seat was changed to Tooele. Afterwards, Richville became less prestigious and remained a small mill town. The town's name was changed to The Mill, Milltown, and Milton. By 1889 the mills were quiet, the town deserted. The most prominent and picturesque building is located near what is now known as Mills Junction of U.S. Highway 40 to the west and State Highway 36 southward. Benson's Grist Mill stands four-tenths of a mile west of the junction. Nearby are many rock and concrete walls of other mills and buildings. Benson Grist Mill was built in 1854 in Lake Point, which was then known as Twin Springs Creek. A tannery and sawmill were also built nearby. After sitting idle for more than 40 years, restoration of the mill began in 1983 to preserve the mill site for present and future generations. Restoration of the mill, which is widely recognized as one of the more intact pioneer-era industrial buildings in Utah, is an ongoing process. The Benson Grist Mill was hailed as the most significant structural landmark between Salt Lake City and Reno, Nevada when it was placed on the National Register of Historic Sites in 1972. The mill is an interesting place to visit; in 2018 educational tours were available.

Photos take in 2018 by Penny

River Bed Station was located about eight miles west of Simpson Springs, built near the end of the Pony Express era. Directions: The road drops into the old bed of the Sevier River and the site of River Bed Station. Substantial structures were found here to serve the stagecoach line.

Round Station was a circular, rock enclosure built in 1858 as a traveler stop to defend against Indians. There was no agent at Round Station, but a traveler could get fresh spring water. There are some ruins at Round Station and the foundation of the station is visible to the south and east across the parking lot.

Photo by Penny

Rowley was used as a truck stop from about 1965 until the mid to late 1970s. The stop is located right of I-80 on the Iosepa exit headed east. Some foundations remain.

Salduro was once a rather sizeable town of 200 located in the salt beds along the Western Pacific Railroad, about nine miles east of Wendover. A potash plant was the basis for the town's existence in the 1930s and 1940s. Salduro is a Spanish word meaning salt. When the potash plant closed down the town collapsed. The remaining structures were gutted by fire in 1944.

Scranton was located east of Tintic Mountains southeast of Vernon in Barlow Canyon. The town was established in 1908 around a lead and zinc mine. The population of Scranton was around 100, with small cottages, bunk houses and a boarding house, a small general store-post office and an assay office. Several of the men managed to wrangle and break some of the wild horses to work in the mine. Two years later the ore played out and the town was deserted. In the summer of 1971 during a National Guard exercise some sagebrush caught fire and destroyed most of the town. Directions: Coming from the north, follow the railroad bed 6.4 miles south of Toplift, then east past a well and corrals 4.2 miles up into a narrow canyon. The road is passable by auto in good weather, although very rough in spots. Coming from the south, at approximately four miles north of the Tooele-Juab county line, travel along a dirt road 5.4 miles to the Scranton road east past the well.

Shambip/Johnson's Settlement was about three miles southwest of Rush Valley. In 1856 it was known as Johnson's Settlement. By 1856 the town had enough population to build a schoolhouse. A stockade was built to protect against Indians, the stockade was torn down in 1868 and used to build a school house at St. John, now Rush Valley. Sagebrush covers the site and the tiny cemetery at the cedar foothills.

Shields was a small railroad town.

Silsbee was a railroad town.

Simpson Springs was established as a mail station in 1858, later used by the Pony Express from 1860-1861, and Overland Express from 1861 to 1869. There was a small store for travelers to buy supplies, and fresh water for the travelers to take with them. Simpson Springs consisted of a stone fort structure, for defense against Indians and outlaws preying on stagecoaches crossing the desert. A number of structures have been built and destroyed in the area over the years. A restored structure is located on a building site which dates to the 1860s and closely resembles the original store.

Six Mile Springs/Mountain Springs/Lost Springs was the site of a cabin, springs and connecting roads, according to an 1875 survey plat. The cabin was possibly used as a station house for a Pony Express stop. Directions: From Callao, follow a rough, jarring road six miles to Six Mile Springs.

Solar was a railroad town.

Steptoe Military Camp was an overland stage station from 1868 to the early 1870s. In 1854 army troops under the command of Col. E.J. Steptoe established a Camp at the edge of Rush Lake. Consisting of two companies of artillery, quarters for 85 dragoons and 136 teamsters were built, as well as billets for Col. Steptoe and his officers. They erected quarters, stables and corrals, and several large barns and were also built. About three miles from Stockton on the west side of the road a monument and grave of a young child could be seen in 2014.

Sunshine was located one mile up Sunshine Canyon near the south end of the Oquirrh Range. The Sunshine mine was discovered in the early 1890s and began seriously producing in 1893 when mercury-laden gold ore was located. After several promising strikes were made, the Sunshine and Overland mills were erected in 1895 for cyanide processing of the gold ore. The town was small but had mine buildings, dwelling and boarding houses, saloons and gambling dens. The sunshine mine had exposed larger bodies of ore, and several hundred thousand dollars were invested, but in 1896 only $7000 worth of gold was recovered. The mills were remodeled in 1908 but by 1910 the mine was depleted. The canyon has been deserted since 1910; most buildings were either removed or have fallen to the elements. A few old brick building foundations are hidden in the sagebrush. Directions: Five miles south of the Mercur turnoff a dirt road which becomes a thin trail leads up to the site of Sunshine.

Timpie Delle was a railroad town.

Toplift was built in about 1875 around the mining of lime rock. The town had several fine stone buildings and several homes. Along the trackside were the depot and railroad buildings and a water tower. The rail line was operated to haul out the crushed limestone, a train load a day. By 1913 most activity had died, but Topliff continued until 1937. All the homes and rail lines were torn down and hauled to Fairfield. Directions: Take I-73 west from Lehi, turn south at the Tooele county line on the paved railroad route. The site lies about five miles south. Several brick foundations, with brick walls near the water tower and west towards the quarry site can still be seen.

Warner was a railroad town.

West Dip/West Mercur was settled in 1895, a fairly large town of mining buildings, homes, a school and church house. The daisy mill was built in 1898 and produced $75,000 in gold that year. In 1910 electrical machinery was added to the mill which yielded better results, but was destroyed by fire in 1917. Most of the buildings were wood framed and were burned. When Mercur was abandoned so was West Dip. Directions: The town was located a few miles northwest of Mercur. Travel a mile from U-73 towards Mercur, then turn left and travel about a mile. About a mile north of Mercur at the cemetery turn left on a dirt road which will lead to the remains of the mine.

West Wendover was used as a Military Army-Air base from 1931-1964. At its peak about 8,000 airmen worked there. After about 1967 there was little military use, and it was left vacant. The town of Wendover has tried to keep the old base up, but due to financial problems on the Utah side the base has fallen. A hanger, bunker, mines, church, and military housing remain.

Willow Springs (Home Station) was a Pony Express station located at the Bagley Ranch on the western end of Callao. The monument and the buildings, which comprised the home station, are still standing and in good condition. This station is one of the best preserved in the United States, and is the only existing home station maintained on private property. Because of the existing structures, the station is one of the most interesting and frequently visited in Utah.

Resorts

Garfield Resort began in 1881, two miles southwest of Black Rock. It capitalized on service via the Steamboat from Lake Side. The boat was renamed "General Garfield," in honor of James A. Garfield taking a ride on it. The boat was anchored semi-permanently off shore of the resort. In 1887 the resort was purchased by the Utah and Nevada Railroad. Some $100,000 in improvements was added, including 200 bathhouses with showers, a restaurant, race track and bowling alley. It was then called "Utah's Great Sanitarium Resort," and 84,000 people visited that year. Five years later, it was still going strong, and the Union Pacific Railroad purchased it and sent another $150,000 in upgrades. It was the lake's first resort to have an electric generator and lights. A fire destroyed the resort and steamboat in 1904, and it was never rebuilt. The steamboat was built to use as a freighter. It had three decks and was 70 feet long, patterned after the Mississippi stern wheel boat. When the railroad came through in 1869 the boat was put into service to carry passengers and freight to the southeastern shores of the Great Salt Lake. The project was unsuccessful and abandoned. For a short time it was used as an excursion boat. When the resort and beaches became popular the boat shored permanently and a bathing resort was built around it.

CHAPTER 24
Uintah Count

Alhandra was a site where a ferry was used to cross the White River. From White River the stage road climbed through a deep, narrow canyon and wound across desert and mesa country to the Bonanza Mine and Kennedy Station; then on to the ditty across the Green River, at what was known as Alhandra, and on to Vernal.

Avalon was settled in 1905 with the opening of the Uintah Reservation to white settlers, located between Randlett and Ouray.

Bennett/Cuneal was located five miles northeast of Roosevelt. It was one of the many town sites laid out shortly after the Uintah Basin was opened to homesteading in 1905. The site was officially laid out in 1914 but had been settled earlier by John Bennett. Before that, James Jones filed for a town site which he wanted to name Cuneal, he was not successful.

Bitter Creek was established in 1904 when cattleman Frank Brewer and his family settled at Bitter Creek in the Book Cliffs about 80 miles southeast of Vernal. Eventually a one-room school house was constructed. In July of 2014, the road was closed and posted no trespassing.

Bonanza was 40 miles southeast of Jensen on U-45. Byron Colton believed his claim on the Gilsonite vein would develop into a very rich strike. Gilsonite is natural asphalt found only in this area. "Bonanza" is the Spanish word for prosperity, a rich strike, or boom. Bonanza was established in 1888. Several stone buildings were built in the early 1900s; a boarding house was built in 1904 and was used as a depot for the old Uintah Stage line. In July of 2014 houses remained and mining was still going on.

Bullionville/Bullion was located at the head of Big Brush Creek in the eastern Uintah Mountains. In the 1880s, a cowboy/prospector named L.P. Dyer was looking for gold, he found a little but there was a lot of copper. A lot of mines opened up soon afterward and Bullionville sprang up to support the miners. There were numerous log cabins built that had iron stoves and chimneys. The town prospered until the early 1900s when the copper veins were played out. In the 1930s the Civilian Conservation Corps gave the site another breath of life when they established a camp in the town. Directions: Located north of Vernal on US-191, travel about 23 miles to the Red Cloud Loop road turning west. Travel toward East Park, about another mile and a half, to where the road turns west to Kane Hollow. About two miles further there is a small two-track road going up a steep hill between a couple of old cabins. The site can be found one-fourth a mile further.

Camp Fudgy was a mining camp settled in the 1880s in the mountains north of Vernal.

China Wall was a Gilsonite mining camp between Watson and Harrison. The camp was one mile long. There were many fine homes in China Wall. The children went to school in Watson. In 1917 Watson lost its end-of-track status as a railroad town and China Wall soon became deserted. Directions: In July of 2014 the paved highway was gated with "no trespassing" signs. A dirt road turned east about a mile back, but the road was windy and very rough for about 35 miles. The road was to rough we never made it to the town so I don't know if there is anything left.

Chipeta Wells was a way station that had stables, barns and inns for travelers. Water wells were hand-dug and lined with rock. Drinking water was hauled five miles to Kennedy Station. Chipeta Wells was located on the road to Fort Duchesne.

Dragon was a settlement that grew up near Black Dragon Gilsonite Mine, approximately one mile from the Colorado state line. The mine began production in 1888. The town of Dragon didn't flourish until 1904, when the Uintah Railway laid tracks. The town boasted a fine hotel, stores, a school, saloons and well-built homes. A public library was built in 1910 and for anyone along the railroad who borrowed a book; the Uintah Railway delivered and returned it for free. It also had a railroad round house and shops. The town boomed until the mine was depleted in 1920 and the people moved to Watson. The town received its name from the nearby Black Dragon Mine where Gilsonite was originally discovered. The mine was named for the imagined shape of the Gilsonite deposit as it appeared on the surface of the ground. Gilsonite or uintaite was used for phonograph records, stove polish and high-grade lacquer paint. This particular type of asphaltum is not known to exist in any other area in the world. Directions: Located south of Bonanza, continue on the paved road until a dirt road veers to the left. A good landmark to look for is a huge rock that looks like a duck on the left side of the road. The road goes for many miles but there is a mileage sign that says Rainbow, Dragon, and Watson. The first ghost town is marked as Watson. In July of 2014 there were "no trespassing" signs. About a mile back there was a rough, windy dirt road that turned east for about 35 miles. Some foundations remained, along with the cemetery and the mine.

Dyer was a copper mining camp built around the workings of the Dyer Mine operation between 1887 and 1900. The site lies four miles north of Bullionville on the eastern slopes of the Dyer Mountains. At its peak Dyer claimed more than 100 miners and their families, and an additional 30 families living at the camp's smelter site two miles to the northwest. The camp's location is about 26 miles North of Vernal.

Eatonville was a settlement of about 26 families and a few single men. It was established in 1896, with a school in operation until 1912. The site is located at the north end of Vernal.

Fort Duchesne was a U.S. Army Fort that operated from 1886 to 1910, located on the Uintah and Ouray Indian Reservation. The fort later became the Indian Agency for the reservation. The Ute Tribal Museum is located in Fort Duchesne.

Fort Kit Carson was located opposite the mouth of the Duschesne River on the east bank of the Green River, south east of Ouray. Some controversy exists over who built Fort Kit Carson. Journals described spending the winter of 1833 at the fort, but not ownership. The fort was quite elaborate, 78 feet wide and 95 feet long, with castle-like turrets at the northeast and southwest corners. It could have been a Spanish Fort judging from its architecture.

Fort Robidoux/Fort Uinta/ Reed Trading Post was established in 1828, when Kentuckian William Reed teamed up with veteran fur trader Denis Julien to travel north to Taos into the Uinta Basin. The Reed Trading Post, at the confluence of the Whiterocks and Uinta rivers, remained in operation until 1832 when Antoine Robidoux bought the location and business from Reed. The business and permanent residences were the first to exist in the central portion of the intermountain corridor. The fort was about 12 miles northeast of present day Roosevelt. The fort consisted of a small group of log cabins with dirt roofs and floors, surrounded by a log palisade. The enclosed area of the fort was about 60 by 60 feet, with gate openings at both the north and south ends.

Fort Thornburgh was first established in September 1881 by Captain Hamilton S. Hawkins near the present site of Ouray, Utah. In April of 1882 the fort was moved to the mouth of Ashley Creek and continued until its abandonment in 1884.

Fort Uintah was a trading post more commonly called Fort Wintey that operated from about 1834-1844. The fort, located at Whiterocks, was destroyed by Ute Indians in 1844.

Harrison was a small mining camp located nine miles up the canyon from Watson. It was a Gilsonite mining camp. The children attended school in Watson. Directions: In July of 2014 the paved highway was gated with "no trespassing" signs. About a mile back there was a rough, windy dirt road that turned east for about 35 miles.

Hayden was located ten miles north of Roosevelt, a temporary settlement during the Uinta Basin land rush of 1905-06. There were many small Indian dwellings scattered in the area, and John G. Davis one of the first settlers used one for a home and also for a church house. By 1908 about 30 families were settled in the town. A post office and store were in operation, and also a blacksmith shop and hotel in the center of town. The community did not succeed as a settlement but was good cattle land. Most of Hayden's residents moved to nearby Neola.

Hill Creek was settled by cattlemen in 1894 to the south of Ouray.

Ignacio/White River Crossing was a stage crossing and community located about three miles south of Bonanza. A wood bridge originally crossed the White River at Ignacio, which was located approximately one mile above the White River Crossing. Due to floods and ice jams washing away the bridge, the crossing was moved to the White River Crossing (now known as Ignacio) where a steel toll bridge was built. A number of homes and a small store were on the hill, just south of the river. Directions: The site is located at the edge of the high bluff above the south side of the river, down a steep, narrow canyon. In July of 2014 the metal bridge was still standing, with a sign on a tree marked "Ignacio Park OE."

Independence was settled in 1905 during the Uintah land run. Independence was a trading and outfitting village along the old road, about halfway between Myton and Ft. Duchesne. The area's alkaline land grew only salt grass, but was advertised and sold by speculators as prime farmland. A number of homes were built and a trading company store was established by the development company. After monies were collected, the promoters skipped town. In 1912 the site was abandoned.

Kennedy Hole was a way station that consisted of stables, barns and inns for travelers. It was located a few miles south of Bonanza.

Leota Ranch was established in 1904 by R. S. Collett and other settlers, named after a local Indian girl. The first public building was completed in 1912, made of blocks with a dirt roof. It was used for church and school. The first school had fifteen students attending who ranged in grades first through eighth. The building was of rough, hewn logs, with one door, one window, and equipped with old-style benches. In 1915 a new frame schoolhouse was completed and used for all public gatherings until it burned down. A brick structure was then erected by the county for the school, used also for social and church gatherings. By 1947 the old town site was completely deserted.

Ouray was first settled by white men in the early 1830s when Antoine Robidoux established a trading post on the confluence of the Green and Duchesne rivers. A few years later the trading post was moved further north. The area later became known as Fort Kit Carson. A few adobe foundations can still be seen on the south side of the Green River. In 1881, an Indian agency was established there for the Uncompahgre band of the Utes. It was named for the Ute Chief Ouray, who was born in 1820, which means 'arrow' in the Ute tongue. In 1886 Fort Thornburg was established there in response to the Meeker Massacre in Colorado. This fort was moved to present day Vernal less than a year later. The town prospered until about the late 1920s when the population slowly dwindled. Postal service ceased in December of 1964. Ouray is the second oldest settlement in the Uinta Basin. Directions: Travel about 14 miles west of Vernal to the intersection of US-40 and SR-88. The site can be found on the north bank of the Green River after traveling south about 17 miles. The town is on the Uintah and Ouray reservation. It is advisable to contact them about applicable laws before any visit. In 2014 there were still a few families living in the area.

Packer was a small settlement west of Hayden. Some of the people of Hayden started a new settlement because the area at Hayden was so rocky. Only a few homes existed in Packer.

Parson's City was a mining camp settled during the 1880s in the mountains north of Vernal.

Rainbow was a small mining community situated over the Rainbow Mine, established in 1912. Located in southeastern Uintah County, four miles southwest of Watson, about 135 people lived there in 1931. Rainbow consisted of two rows of houses, mostly of log construction. Although the Gilsonite mines in the area were developed by 1905, oil was struck in the area in 1920 and the town boomed. The oil wells in Rainbow are still producing today, although the town itself was abandoned shortly after mining operations were relocated to the town of Bonanza in 1938. Some of the buildings were moved to Bonanza. Directions: As of July, 2014, some foundation and cabin ruins among the cedars could be found. The paved highway was gated with "no trespassing" signs. About a mile back there was a rough, windy dirt road that turned east for about 35 miles.

The Strip was segregated from the Uintah Indian Reservation and opened to mine Gilsonite. A wild, lawless mining town quickly sprang up on the isolated strip. It was a short lived town and was a favorite haunt of Butch Cassidy and the Wild Bunch, mainly because of the lack of organized law. In its heyday there were four saloons and at least that many brothels. There were many deaths by gun fight and a great deal of violence. The Strip is located at the extreme western end of Uintah County, between Fort Duchesne and Gusher. Directions: Travel about a mile west of Gusher on US-40, then south .9 miles.

Watson was an important ore shipping point for Gilsonite from mines at Harrison and China Wall. The town of Watson was established around 1900 and inhabited until around the late 1920s. The people who lived in the town were Gilsonite miners and their families, and at one time the town had around 750 residents. The town died after 1917. Directions: From Bonanza travel southward on the paved road, until a dirt road turns to the left. A good landmark to look for is a huge rock that looks like a duck on the left side of the road. This road goes for many miles, look for a mileage sign that says Rainbow, Dragon, and Watson. The first ghost town is marked as Watson. Old cabins were built into the sides of the hill. There are still some collapsed structures standing. In 2014 the paved highway was gated with "no trespassing" signs. About a mile back there is a rough, windy dirt road that turned east for about 35 miles.

Watson 1998

Webster City was established by the Webster Cattle Company in the late 1800s as a centralized location for their operations. Butch Cassidy worked out of the town. The company built a log cabin ranch town for their cowboys, and a combination commissary and saloon, large enough that dances were held there almost every weekend. They also built a school for employees' children and a large first class boarding house with a dining room, known as the Webster City Hotel. It was a wild town, with fights and even a few shoot-outs. There was no law closer than Vernal, which was a hard two-day ride away. Directions: The Webster Site is on the Uintah & Ouray Indian Reservation, permission should be obtained before visiting. Located south of Ouray towards Hillcreek, travel about five miles past Towave Reservoir. From there, a hike along Hillcreek will lead to the site. The site is now covered by a marsh. It can only be reached from Vernal. Webster City was deep into the Book Cliffs, near the head of Willow Creek on the Hill Creek Indian Reservation.

Willow Creek was started in the late 1800s as a gilsonite mining town. The population was about 700 until the mine was depleted. The residents then moved to Bonanza. Directions: Follow highway 88 past Ouray to a "Willow Creek" sign. The site can be found next to a hillside.

CHAPTER 25
Utah County

Beaver Creek Camp was a Mormon settlers' armed camp for defense against the Ute Indians, established in 1849 in Pleasant Grove.

Camp Ashley was a trading post located in Provo from 1825 to 1828. In 1826 it was armed with one cannon. The trading post was later sold to the Rocky Mountain Fur Company.

Camp Battle Creek was an armed camp established by Mormon settlers in the1850s, located in Pleasant Grove.

Camp Dodge was an Army post of Nevada volunteers from 1865 to 1866, located in Provo.

Camp Floyd was a military camp that operated from 1858 to 1862. The camp had the largest troop concentration in the U.S. at the time. The troops were sent to the camp to suppress a Mormon rebellion that never materialized. Camp Floyd was renamed Fort Crittenden in 1861. The Overland Mail Company bought much of the post in 1862. Replaced by Fort Douglas, the Military Interior transferred the reservation to the department in 1884. The site is now known as Camp Floyd/Stagecoach Inn State Park and Museum to which there is an admission fee. The camp once had 400 buildings, but only the cemetery and commissary remain.

Commanding Gerneral's quarter's photo taken 1859

Commissary photo take around 1930 Commissary in 2015 photo by Penny

Camp Rawlins was a temporary Federal Camp that operated from 1870 to 1871, located in Provo.

Camp Timpanagos was a temporary Federal post established in 1859 on the Timpanagos (Provo) River, about eight miles from Provo.

Canyon Station was a fortified Overland Stage station established in 1864. It was located near Goshute, 12 miles from Deep Creek Station.

Castilla Hot Springs was a resort that was developed in early 1891. It included a three story, sand stone hotel, indoor and outdoor swimming pools, dining and dancing pavilions, and other recreational facilities. At the height of the resort's popularity, special excursion trains brought visitors to the resort from all over Utah county and beyond. Castilla was located eight miles southeast of Spanish Fork in Spanish Fork Canyon, along the north side of Highway 6/89.

Cedar Fort was a Mormon settlers' fort from 1855 to 1858. The abundance of cedar trees suggested the name. On January 5, 1856, by legislative act, the settlements of Cedar Valley were organized into a county with Cedar Fort as the county seat. It was raided by US soldiers from Camp Floyd in revenge of the killing of a sergeant. The fort was located on U-73 west of the north end of Utah Lake about four miles north of Fairfield.

Christmas City was a small settlement that was demolished when the highway was widened.

Colton/Pleasant Valley Junction was settled in 1883. In 1940 the population was 327, but the town died around 1950 when railroad operations ended. Colton was located about six miles south of Soldier Summit. Formerly a busy railroad junction on the Denver and Rio Grande Western Railroad, Colton is a landmark on U.S. Route 6 through Spanish Fork Canyon between the cities of Spanish Fork and Price. The site was first settled under the name of Pleasant Valley Junction, where the Pleasant Valley Railroad connected the mining town of Winter Quarters, 20 miles to the south, to the Rio Grande line. This line was soon abandoned, replaced by a Rio Grande branch along a much easier grade between Pleasant Valley Junction and Scofield. Pleasant Valley Junction quickly grew to include a store, hotel, and five saloons. In addition to the railroad, the mining and milling of ozokerite was important in the local economy. Sometime just before 1898 the town was renamed Colton in honor of railroad official William F. Colton. Two years later in 1900 the Scofield Mine disaster dealt the entire area a serious blow, but Colton survived. It remained a busy railroad town even though the town burned and was rebuilt three times. After the introduction of diesel locomotives, Colton rapidly declined with most of the buildings removed by the 1950s. The Hilltop General Store, built in 1880, was moved to highway UT 6-50 in 1937. The store, closed on Sundays, was still in business in 2014, with photos of the old town. The owner had photos of his grandfather with Butch Cassidy.

Colton, Utah   Colton, Utah 2017 photo by Penny

Deer Creek was a railroad town located seven miles up the canyon on the North Fork. The Aspinwall Steamship Company built a railroad into the canyon to bring the ore down from Forest City. The railroad was completed as far as the Deer Creek in 1872, four miles below the Sultana smelter at Forest City. From there up it was too steep for the train to run so the town of Deer Creek came into existence to service the railroad and lumber jacks in the local area. A train terminus was added, along with buildings, a lime kiln, and a large boarding house. The boarding house featured a large dining area where dances were held. Ten charcoal kilns were built at Deer Creek to make fuel for the train, as no coal was available. There was a small cemetery located here in which accident victims were buried. An office was built by the creek on the side of a hill, but it was washed away during a flash flood. Many important mining records were destroyed which caused a lot of problems over claims. It is unknown what the population of the town was. The ore from the mines at Forest City was brought down to Deer Creek by wagons and on mules, and then loaded onto the train. When the railroad closed down in 1878, the town of Deer Creek began to disappear. Deer Creek was located where Tibble Fork Reservoir is now.

Dividend/Standard was a company town built by the Tintic Standard Mining Company five miles east of Eureka. It was a camp of rough cabins in 1916, but by 1918 it included stores, shops, a pool hall, schoolhouse, amusement hall, barber shop, 75 private homes and even a brass band, but there was no church. Before it was granted a post office it was called Standard, but the postal authorities said there were too many towns with similar names. The town was changed to Dividend because of the profits paid out to stock holders. By 1922 over one million dollars had been paid out in dividends. It reportedly was one of the top five silver-producing mines in the world. In 1949 when the mine closed, it had paid out over 19 million dollars in dividends. The town was one of the first in Utah to have indoor plumbing. Directions: A nice drivable road goes through Dividend. The old water tanks still sit above the mine and look over the town site with the words "TINTIC STANDARD" painted on them. Following the dirt road from Highway 6 south through Dividend, what appears to be an old tipple and a gallows were still standing in 2015, both quite picturesque. Dividend once had a baseball diamond, golf course and tennis courts.

Dividend 2010 photo take by Penny

Dobietown/Frogtown was located just over the creek from Camp Floyd. Dobietown was one of the roughest towns in the state, there was every kind of saloon, bordello and gambling hall known. Murders occurred daily, and by 1862 Dobietown had only 18 families left.

Eva Mine was a mining town east of Santaquin, associated with the Eva and Little Eagle mines. The town was established with enough children to set up a school district; but the ore played out and the town faded before it really got started.

Fairfield was located five miles south of Cedar Fort on U-73 on the west side of Utah Lake. The town was established in 1855 when John Carson, his four brothers, and others settled in the valley. John Carson built the Stagecoach Inn in 1858, which served as a stop and hotel in the Overland Stagecoach route. The Inn countinued to operate until 1947, and was still standing in 2015. In 1858-59 Johnston's Army began to arrive. The army established a nearby camp called Camp Floyd. The quiet Mormon town began to resemble a wild mining town, with 17 saloons and gambling halls, prostitutes and gun slingers with a population of seven thousand soldiers, teamsters, gamblers, and camp followers of various persuasions. Shootings were common. In 1860 Fairfield was the third largest town in Utah. The settlement was soon known as Frogtown. Frogtown became Fairfield in 1861 in honor of Amos Fielding, who participated in establishing the community. As of 2015 about 130 people lived in the town.

Fairfield school 2015

Stagecoach Inn in 1959 before it was remodeled. Stagecoach in 2015 Photo by Penny

Forest City was a typical mining town built at Dutchman Flat. The town began to grow around the smelter with mine and smelter offices, supply warehouse, 15 charcoal kilns, a sawmill, livery stables, several homes, bunk houses, boarding houses, stores, hotels, a school and a saloon. Forest City was inhabited from about 1871 to 1880. One winter there was a diphtheria epidemic, killing a number of people inclucing 11 children, and they were buried in a small cemetery, which became known as Graveyard Flat. Population figures for Forest City are uncertain, ranging as high as 2000 to 3000 at the peak. There were enough children that a school was established. The American Fork Railroad, which was intended to serve Forest City and the smelter, stopped short of its destination due to engineering difficulties. Forest City was abandoned when the smelter, mines and railroad closed down.

Fort Peteetneet was built to house 16 families in 1851. The fort was made of logs from the Peteetneet Creek, which was named after a Ute leader who lived in the area. In 1853 the fort was enlarged to about four city blocks square. As of 2014 a walking tour of the fort and Historic Payson was available.

Fort Rawlins was located about two miles north of Provo City on the north bank of the Provo River. It was established in 1870 with two companies of the 13th Infantry from Fort Douglas. Funds were not appropriated for barracks or other quarters, so the men lived in tents with dirt floors without heating stoves until mid-winter. The soliders were very disorderly and drunkenness and desertion was a problem, one-third of the men were court martialed for being drunk on duty. Captain Osborne was very strict and his punishments were severe. On September 22, 1870 the troops staged a riot and shortly afterwards the Fort was closed and the men were sent to Fort Douglas.

Fort Sodom was located two miles north of Goshen, built in 1857. Its adobe walls enclosed two acres, with rows of cabins built along the inner walls. The fort served as protection for the settlers of Southern Utah County.

Fort St. Luke was located at the mouth of Spanish Fork Canyon. Mormon settlers built a high wall around the new townsite to protect their lives and livestock. Only 16 houses had been built when church authorities decided that a more substantial fort should be built.

Fort Utah was established in 1849, located in Provo. Originally called Fort Provo, it had only one cannon for defense. A second fort, nicknamed Fort Sowiette, was built at the same site in 1853. A replica of the first Mormon settlers' fort is on the original site. Original cabins from the second fort are now at North Park Museum in Pioneer Memorial Park. Tours are given by appointment only.

Fort Wordsworth was a Mormon settlers' fort built in the 1850s, located in Alpine. The fort was later expanded. A historical monument can be found in the town.

Gilluly/Upper Tucker was a railroad siding providing water for the old steam engines.

Harold was established high on a steep hillside above the Warm Spring east of Goshen. Harold grew up around the Tintic Standard reduction mill. It lasted as long as the Mill from 1921 to 1925. Harold was a company town and had a company store, a row of look-alike company houses, a company boardinghouse and a post office. In 2015 the crumbling mill foundation was still standing.

Tintic Standard reduction mill at Harold 2018 Photo take by Penny

Homansville/Lawrence was the site of a mill and smelter built in 1871. A post office was established December 20, 1872 at Lawrence which lasted 19 days when the name was changed to Homansville. The town was developed to produce water for the surrounding mining towns such as Eureka. The population was about 300, with a general store, saloons, a post office and numerous homes. Limestone was also mined/quarried near Homansville and the old railroad bed passed nearby. There were also two charcoal kilns in the town that used the cedar trees on the surrounding hillsides. Located two miles northeast of Eureka, the town was abandoned prior to 1900, because the railroad favored the larger smelter in the area. In 1916 the site was used as a lime quarry by the Chief Consolidated Mines.

Ironton was settled by 120 men, 30 women, and 18 children in the 1850s. It was also known as "Iron Mission." The Deseret Iron Company was founded and iron production was under way. The plant was the second only plant west of the Mississippi where ore was made into pig iron. After only eight years of operation, floods, repairs on the furnace, and problems transporting the iron shut the plant down. As railroad construction crews moved on, Ironton became a ghost town.

Ironton

Joe's Dugout was located approximately eight miles west of the City of Lehi. It was named for the coyote hole dugout Joe lived in. There was no water near the station. Meals and lodging were not available at Joe's dugout, although Rockwell's Valley Tan Whiskey could be purchased for one dollar a bottle.

Lake View was a small settlement that began in 1855. When flood waters from the Provo River and Utah Lake rose the inhabitants moved their homes to higher ground in 1861 and 1862.

Lott Settlement was located near Lehi. The settlement was named after Pamelia Lott, who settled at the site.

Lower Goshen was a Mormon pioneer town, settled in 1860 and abandoned by the end of the decade. The town lay undisturbed for nearly 120 years, located three miles northwest of present-day Goshen.

Manning was a town that grew up around a $25,000 mill that was built in the late 1880s on a large flat up in Manning Canyon for treatment of ores from Mercur. The mill and town were largely appendages of Mercur but were located at this site because of the water supply. The town included frame houses, false front buildings, and saloons. The recovery was not good until the mill was remodeled in 1890 into the first major cyanide plant in the United States. In 1898 the plant was shut down. In the 1930s a new, more modern mill worked the old tailings, then in 1937 the mill was dismantled and moved to Mercur. A standard gauge rail line (the Salt Lake and Mercur Railroad) was built between Manning's Mill and Mercur's Ores, completed in 1895. The rail line between Mercur and Manning was 12 miles long, though the actual distance was only about six miles. The switch-backs were so sharp that the engine was often alongside of the caboose. Directions: Manning was located just east of Camp Floyd where a road leaves U73. As of 2004 the area was closed off.

Mechanicsville was a short-lived settlement across the creek in front of the Fort Sodom. Mechanicsville only lasted a few years because of poor soil in the area.

Mill Fork was a settlement located about 12 miles east of Thistle in Spanish Fork Canyon. Mill Fork was important in the development of the railroad through the canyon. The Utah and Pleasant Valley Railroad built through Spanish Fork Canyon in 1875 to 1879. Sometime during this period the railroad established three sawmills at Mill Fork to process railroad ties. A large water tower and a small reservoir were constructed in 1888, soon joined by a general store and housing for railroad employees. A helper engine was also stationed at Mill Fork. The population grew as high as 250. Another use for the area's abundant timber came with the creation of an extensive charcoal business in the canyon; many Mill Fork residents were employed in cutting the wood or working the kilns. The charcoal business closed down around 1890, followed by the store, and Mill Fork was in a serious decline. Most residents had left by 1900; a few homesteaders lasted until the 1930s. The 1940s saw the change to diesel locomotives, and it was no longer needed as a water stop, and with its helper engine obsolete, the Mill Fork railway station was closed down in 1947. The railroad removed its section house in the late 1950s, leaving little besides the cemetery, located on U.S. Route 6 between Spanish Fork and Price.

Mosida was a heavily promoted planned community in the 1910s, located on the southwestern shore of Utah Lake, 12 miles south of Elberta. Mosida was ultimately a failure. The land was purchased from the Utah State Land Board in 1909. They planned to divide the land and sell it in tracts for peach orchards. Within months they sold out to a group of promoters from Denver, Colorado who incorporated as the Mosida Fruit Lands Company. They improved the property and advertised. A pump house was built, and a large boarding house was constructed to house up to 250 workers. In 1911 they cleared and plowed the land and planted apple and peach seedlings. By 1912, 8,000 acres of land had been plowed, 50,000 fruit trees planted, and 50,000 US bushels of grain was harvested. The company built a 25-room luxury hotel which became the town landmark, used to house tourists and prospective investors. No expense was spared to impress the guests; a fine passenger boat ferried them across the lake to and from Provo. The Mosida Fruit Lands Company soon added more houses, a store, a post office, and even a school. They imported two French cooks to provide their workers the best of meals at the boarding house. The company's salesmanship was effective; by 1913 some 400 people had moved to Mosida and were working the farms and orchards. The new residents quickly found that life in Mosida did not live up to the promotional literature's glowing descriptions. The fruit trees began to die; it transpired that the soil was too salty and mineralized for them. Other crops such as wheat and peanuts did better. Transportation to and from the isolated site was a challenge, and became even harder when the Mosida boat was destroyed by fire on April 17, 1913. The lake level dropped and by 1917 most people had left. By 1920 the population was 67. The last resident left in 1924.

Moyle House and Indian Tower was located at 606 E 770 N in Alpine. The property was listed on the National Register of Historic Places in 1992. The listing included two contributing buildings and one structure on 2.5 acres. A dugout home was expanded in about 1859 into a house. A tower was constructed during 1860 to 1866 as a private fort for defense against Indians of the Black Hawk War of 1865-1868, and is the only such tower known to have been built for protection of a single household in Utah. The stone structures were built by English-born mason and Mormon, John Rowe Moyle. His son Joseph Moyle expanded the house in 1917, adding Bungalow/Craftsman elements. A dugout food cellar also was built during 1868. Several structures remained in 2015. Photos by Penny

Homes at Moyle 2015 Tower at Moyle 2015

Pelican Point was a small mining and fishing community. At one time it had over 3,000 residents. Pelican Point is most noted for the unsolved murders of three boys which took place in 1895 on the west side of Utah Lake approximately six miles from Lehi.

Pittsburg was a mining community that started around the Pittsburg mine. Some sources state there were 40 to 50 men living and working in Pittsburg, other sources cite 400 to 500. Pittsburg was located above Forest City in the 1870s.

Sandtown was established in 1859 one mile southeast of Fort Sodom. Sandtown only lasted a few years because of the poor soil.

Santaquin Fort was constructed in 1856 when Mormon settlers began the second settlement in the area. A rock schoolhouse was built in the fort that served the public for many years, and a church building was constructed in 1896 which is now used as a senior citizen center and veteran's memorial hall. In addition to farming, early industries included sawmills, a flour mill, a molasses mill, and a furniture shop. Several mines were discovered on Santaquin Ridge in 1875.

Summit Creek Fort was settled in 1856, located in Santaquin. A fort was built when Mormon settlers returned after abandoning the original settlement that began in 1853 as a result of the "Walker War." The town was originally known as Summit Creek until sometime after 1866.

Thistle was a farming and ranching community in 1883. By 1890 population was 228. The town included a depot, beanery, water system, post office, schools, several stores, a barber shop, pool hall, and saloon. Thistle was also a locomotive maintenance facility, which included an eight-stall roundhouse, water tanks, a coal triple, and a machine shop. In 1983 a mudslide moved part of the mountain, blocked the river, and made an earth dam. The water backed up, which flooded and covered the land where Thistle was located. Thistle was almost completely destroyed; only a few structures were left partially standing. Federal and state government agencies claimed this was the most costly landslide in United States history at the time. The landslide resulted in the first presidentially declared disaster area in the state of Utah. Some ruins remained in 2014.

Tucker was a railroad town located seven miles below Soldier summit on U.S. Route 6 through Spanish Fork Canyon. Tucker started as a railroad junction, between the main line of the Denver and Rio Grande Western Railroad and the spur of the Utah and Pleasant Valley Railway, which extended to mines at winter Quarters near today's Scofield Reservoir. A station was built at the site to house the helper engines used to push freight trains over Soldier Summit. It quickly grew into a town with a population of 500 to 1000, called Clear Creek. A boarding house, company store, two saloons, two hotels, a roundhouse and dozens of hastily constructed houses filled the small valley. By 1900 the name was changed to Tucker. After the town was abandoned, the state of Utah used the town site as a rest area. In 2009, the site was buried as part of a project to re-align a portion of US-6's western approach to Soldier Summit. To honor the town, the state of Utah built a replacement about two miles downstream from Tucker, called the Tie Fork Rest Area. This rest area, which is designed to mimic an early1900s era train depot and roundhouse, was voted one of the most beautiful buildings in Utah in a contest sponsored by the American Institute of Architects.

CHAPTER 26
Wasatch County

Buysville was a small settlement that began in about 1891 between Daniels and Charleston.

Center Creek was located five miles south southeast of Heber City and two miles north of the mouth of Daniels Canyon. In 1860 the town received its name from the creek on which its community first settled.

Hailstone/Elkhorn was homesteaded in 1864 by William and Ann Hailstone and others. Mining, ranching and lumbering were the reasons people settled here. In 1929 conditions changed when lumbering moved elsewhere. Hailstone was located at the junction of US-40 and US-189, seven miles north of Heber City, and is now beneath Jordanelle Reservoir. The Junction's earliest name was Elkhorn and later changed to Hailstone.

Keetley was a camp on Silver Creek and US-40, three miles east of Park City. The earliest name was Camp Florence. It later became a Pony Express Station and mining and lumbering center. The name was changed to Keetley in honor of John B. (Jack) Keetley, a Pony Express rider and the supervisor of mining construction work in the region. The community was slowly abandoned with diminished mining and lumbering. Keetley is now beneath Jordanelle Reservoir.

Soldier Summit was located at the summit, midway between Thistle and Helper. Several soldiers either became ill and died at the summit or were caught there in a blizzard, and are buried at the summit. The small community of Soldier Summit developed in 1862. The community boasted a classification yard, passenger and freight trains, a round house, locomotive shops and facilities, plus 70 employee homes, a large hotel, swimming pool and YMCA building, totaling over a million dollars. Non-railroad buildings were three stores, two automobile garages, a restaurant, billiard hall, real estate office and a schoolhouse. Three years later activity was so heavy on the railroad that 50 more homes were built. Over 300 people lived in town from 1925-1930. In 1930 the division was moved to Helper.

CHAPTER 27
Washington County

Adventure was located about a mile west of Rockville, on the south side of the Virgin River. Adventure was a small settlement, part of the cotton growing colony, founded in 1860. Adventure was a substantial community, with well-built homes and farm buildings, it did not have a business district. It was destroyed by the great flood of 1862 and settlers moved to what is now Rockville. Nothing remained of the settlement in 2012.

Anderson/McPherson's Flat was located about three miles north of Toquerville and a few miles south of Pintura. Anderson's Ranch (now called Anderson's Junction) was a natural stopping place on the road for weary travelers. Escalante noted camping near there before the pioneers came to the area. Because its location was on the junction between the Toquerville road (which now leads to Zion National Park) and the highway along the Black Ridge to Cedar City, Anderson's Ranch received a steady flow of visitors.

Atkinville was located ten miles south southwest of St. George. At one time there were many brick buildings in the settlement, built by William Atkin and his sons. Atkinville was notable because Wilford Woodruff, President of the Council of the Twelve, spent several years there in exile from the U.S. Marshals. When the marshals were seen coming down the road from Price City, he was hustled into a boat with his bedroll, food, fishing tackle and books, then hidden among the heavy growth of cattails in Atkin's pond and was never captured.

Babylon was a town associated with the Stormont Mill along the Virgin River, 12 miles northeast of St. George. It was established in 1877 by a group of mill workers and their families. The town's name came from the Babylon of Biblical times, and was probably chosen to distinguish themselves from their Mormon neighbors. About twenty families, totaling between forty and fifty people, lived in the town. There were no businesses, so the families traveled to Leeds and Silver Reef for their needs. Directions: From Old Highway 91 just north of Leeds, travel south on the Babylon Road about seven miles to the Virgin River to reach the site.

Bloomington /James Town, was settled in 1861 by William Carpenter and his family on the north east side of the Virgin River. William and his sons each built homes here. They raised cotton, sugar cane, made molasses, and started a broom making business. In 1875 the named was changed to Bloomington. By 1950 no one remained.3

Bonanza City was a mining town that began in 1875 when William Barbee found an outcropping of silver ore at a place where a wagon wheel had broken the edge of a rock. Barbee staked the Tecumseh claim on what he called Bonanza Flats, and made a shipment of $500 worth of ore to a mill in Slat Lake City. He staked out a townsite he named Bonanza City, and in less than a month it became a boom town. As Silver Reef expanded, it eventually swallowed up Bonanza City.

Calls Landing was a planned community on the muddy river for growing cotton.

Camp Lorenzo was also known as Brigham City. The camp was a short-lived cotton mission a mile southeast of Harrisburg.

Conger was a small camp that grew up around the smelter known as Conger. The Black Warrior mines had been operating as early as the 1870s, and the owner erected a smelter on what was called "the old Conger farm."

Crawfordville : William Robinson Crawfor was sent by Brigham Young to settled the area. It was a small collection of farms in Oak Creek Canyon near what is now the museum on the western edge of Zion National Park. It was the home of the Crawford family and others in the late 1800s and early 1900s.

Dalton was established in 1864 by a group of Mormon settlers. Dalton might have become prosperous, but the people were forced to leave during the Black Hawk war. Only a few people returned, by 1870 there were only 30 people. By 1880 Dalton was a ghost town, located 1.5 miles up the Virgin River from Virgin.

Duncan's Retreat was located on the upper Virgin River between Rockville and Virgin City. It was settled in 1861, and in 1863 about 70 people lived here. In 1863 a post office was built. A school and meeting house were added in 1864. In the late 1860s the town was abandoned during the Blackhawk Indian War. After the war the people barely resettled before the Virgin River flooded. Many people moved away but new settlers came. In 1866 floods took a toll on the town and over the next few years high water from the Virgin river destroyed the fields. By 1891 the town was deserted. Directions: Located just off the Highway halfway between Rockville and Virgin City. As of 2013, Nancy Ferguson Ott's gravesite and headstone remained.

Photo taken by Penny

Fort Clara/Fort Santa Clara was a fort constructed in 1854, which was 100 feet square and built of "hammered rock," with walls three feet thick and 12 feet high. The inside was partitioned off into 25 rooms, with rifle portholes in each. The doors all opened to the center and there was only one opening where wagons could enter. Fort Santa Clara was the forerunner of today's city of Santa Clara.

Fort Harmony was founded in 1851 by a band of emigrants led by John D. Lee, located southeast of New Harmony. Brigham Young said it was the best planned fort he had seen and by 1854 it was the strongest fortification in Dixie. The east and west walls had a row of cabins built against their inner sides. There was a school house and a 100 foot-deep well to insure a water supply during siege. The fort was in constant use until 1862 when a 28-day rain fell in January and undermined its walls. Lee was told to abandon the fort but he refused. During the night the wall began to collapse, and at the break of dawn the roof beams fell, landing across the bed of his sleeping children, killing his son and daughter instantly. The fort was not rebuilt, and people moved to New Harmony or Kanarraville, three miles to the northeast. Today the old fort's stone corners and the two stone pillars which stood at each side of its heavy gates remain, and in the center of the fort is a sunken hole that was the well.

Fort Pearce was located 12 miles southeast of St. George. The fort was built in 1866 to 1870 to protect the trail from Dixie to the Arizona settlements. The fort was small, only 30 feet square, but it was sturdily built of stone and had a high tower equipped with portholes for riflemen. Fort Pearce was intended as a way station where travelers could defend themselves from Indians. Workmen hauling timber and stone used in construction of the Mormon Temple at St. George often sought refuge there. A stone corral with walls 5 feet high protected their livestock from raiding Indians.

Goldstrike was a mining camp with an amalgamation stamp mill. Gold was discovered in the area in the late 1800s. Directions: Located a half-mile west of Gunlock road, a narrow dirt track leads north. The stage station was 11 miles to the north. At the bottom of a steep down grade 19 miles from the highway, the East Fork of Beaver Dam Wash comes from a deep dark canyon to the right. A two-mile hike up the canyon reveals an old house and an ancient looking barn. After another mile several large tunnels dug into the solid-rock cliffs can be seen. Several miles farther upstream there is a frame house. The remains of the Hamburg Mine lie in the canyon below. To get to the Hamburg mine five miles northeast of Gunlock, a steep, rocky road turns up Cove Canyon. A BLM sign proclaims it to be the Goldstrike Road, but it offers no distances or clues how to get there. Beyond Maple Ridge, 13 miles from the Gunlock road, a four wheel drive trail turns to the left and drops steeply into the head of East Fork Canyon. It is about five miles to the old frame house in the canyon below the Hamburg Mine. Head-high sagebrush hides the rock ruins of some buildings. It is difficult to get to Goldstrike, as one road is impassable and the other is impossible.

Grafton/Wheeler was first settled in 1859 one mile below its present town sight as part of a southern Utah cotton-growing project ordered by Brigham Young, with each farmer receiving about an acre of land. The community dug irrigation canals and planted orchards, some of which still exist. In January of 1862 the town was completely washed away by a flood. The people rebuilt the town a mile further upstream at its present site. By 1864 about 28 families had settled in the town, constructing many log houses, a post office, church, school and community hall. The town was deserted in 1866 due to Indian attacks, but the people returned in 1868. By 1920 only three families still lived in Grafton. The town ended when the local branch of the Church of Jesus Christ of Latter-day Saints was discontinued in 1921. The last residents left in 1944. Several movies have been filmed in Grafton, one of which was "Butch Cassidy and the Sundance Kid." Directions: Grafton is located right off the highway. The first house, the church and two buildings are viewable by the public. There is a long dirt road that leads to an area where there is another house, but it is blocked by a locked gate and "no trespassing" signs. There was much to see in 2014.

Old barn & corral in Grafton Schoolhouse at Grafton, built in 1886.
Photos taken 2014 by Penny

Hamblin was a small community at the north end of Mountain Meadows, settled by Jacob Hamblin and a small group of Mormons in 1856. There were a few cabins, a school, an LDS church and a fort that was never finished. The fort was not finished by the time of the Blackhawk war, but the town was set up to offer some protection. All of the houses were built along one street, the east end of town was closed off by the church and school house and the Hamblin Co-Op Store at the opposite end, giving the appearance of a fort. The residents made a living selling butter and cheese to the emigrant trains passing through. Overgrazing and floods eventually caused the people to relocate and the site became a ghost town by 1890. Directions: Hamblin is located six miles southeast of Enterprise. Travel three miles northeasterly along a good dirt road, then a poor road leads north uphill to 0.6 miles. An old cemetery remains 0.4 miles to the west. Hamblin can be found between Little Pinto and Highway 18.

Harrisburg/Cottonwood was established in 1862 when a flood destroyed the settlement of Harrisville, forcing the residents to move elsewhere. They named the new settlement Harrisburg after Moses Harris. About 200 residents lived in the town by 1866. Many houses were made of stone, as well as the barn and church. As the men cleared their land for planting they used the loose rocks to separate their lots and fields instead of post and wire. A church was built and there was a school attended by 60 students. Population reached its peak in 1868 at about 200. In 1869 many people started to move away due to grasshopper plagues and flooding. Indian raids also chased many away. By 1895 the last people had moved away and Harrisburg became a ghost town. Directions: Today Interstate 15 runs through the middle of the old town. The town site remains on the east side of I-15, now an RV Camp. There were several old stone houses and walls left standing at the site. A one-lane road that goes under I-15 from the RV Camp leads to the remains of Harrisburg on the west side of I-15.

Harrisville in 1859 Moses Harris and other settled on the Virgin River and named the settlement Harrisville. In 1862 floods drove them further up Quail Creek to the Cottonwood Creek Fork.

Heberville/Price City was located five miles south of St. George on the Virgin River, first settled in 1858 as a cotton mission. Heberville prospered with its farms, producing an abundance of crops. Disastrous floods destroyed a large part of the Heberville. Brigham Young visited in 1870 & directed the settlers to rename the town Price City. The town was rebuilt with homes, business and farms cultivated to grow fruit, 700 trees were planted. Price City might have prospered but the curse of the United Order of Enoch was inflicted upon it. (Under the United Order of Enoch, settlers were required to place all of their worldly goods into a cooperative pool, so everyone could share equally in the fruits of their labors. Unfortunately, some were sharing more than others.) When the United Order failed the saints left Price City.

Hebron/Shoal Creek was first known as Shoal Creek, and in 1868 the name was changed to Hebron. The town Shoal Creek was discovered in 1862 by people driving cattle. Several farms were started and in 1868 the settlers built a fort out of logs with a spring in the middle to protect themselves from the Paiute Indians. The community grew because of mining at nearby Silver Reef and Pioche, Nevada. In 1867 a school house was built, followed by many shops, stores and homes. Hebron was the largest town in the area. The farmers raised crops, milk cows and beef, and sold them to other towns in Utah, as well as supplying many mines in Nevada. In 1900 many people began to move away due to water problems. In 1902 an earthquake destroyed much of the town, and by 1905 the town was deserted. Directions: Hebron was located 5.6 miles west of Enterprise on State Highway 120, where a dirt road turns north about .04 miles through a cattle gate and across Shoal Creek.

Holt was a small farming village about three miles north of Hamblin. It was built along the creek bottom on the Old Spanish trail. Settled in 1874, it grew into a thriving mountain village. Holt died away after being plagued by drought and floods.

Johnson's Mill was a small village that was established for people that worked at the sawmill. Located 1.5 miles upstream from Mountain Dell, the mill furnished lumber to many other towns including Virgin City and Duncan's Retreat.

Marshalltown was established in the early 1900s. A brick factory at Marshalltown provided fired bricks for buildings in southern Utah without having to haul them long distances.

Middleton was a small cotton community that lasted only briefly, located between Morristown and St. George. There was some excitement in Middleton when Ben Polack was warned that horse thieves were going to steal several of his prized mares. Pollack with the Sheriff and two deputies were hiding near the corral when three men approached in the darkness. Sheriff Hardy yelled "throw up your hands." There was gunfire and when it was over, two rustlers were seriously wounded, the third escaped. The men were outlaws who were wanted at Pioche, Nevada. A few days later two men claiming to be lawmen from Pioche arrived at Middletown. The sheriff turned the two injured men over to them and watched them ride out of town. The next day the bodies of the two rustlers were found on the trail still wearing leg-irons and shot through the head. The so-called lawmen were never seen again.

Milltown was a mining town located on the backside of Silver Reef.

Photo by Penny

Morristown was a short-lived cotton mission, located between Camp Lorenzo and St. George.

Mountain City was an agricultural colony a few miles northwest of Hamblin.

Mountain Dell was settled on North Creek in 1861. Even though good farming ground was scarce along the narrow canyon at the bottom of North Creek, settlers started arriving and the town grew. A church was built in 1863. Mountain Dell was abandoned during the Blackhawk War, but the Indians never burned the town so the homes and shops still stood when the people returned. During the 1890s a series of dry years caused many to leave and Mountain Dell was a ghost town by 1900. The settlement was located four miles up North Creek from Virgin on private property.

New Castle was land that was purchased by a developer who plotted out a town. He then built a hotel, trying to entice people to buy a plot of land. He was unable to sell the land, and a few years later the hotel was destroyed by fire.

Northrup was located at the confluence of the north & east forks of the Virgin River, one mile from the Kane County line. The farming community was settled in 1861. By 1867 only 30 acres were under cultivation, growing mainly sorghum cane and corn. A sorghum mill was built in town which handled all the cane for most of the adjacent villages. By 1890 there were only 20 people remaining, and the town was deserted by 1900. The area is now part of Springdale.

Overton was a planned community on the muddy river for growing cotton. Life was very bleak.

Pine Valley is a small isolated community, located in the Pine Valley Mountains north of St. George. It was settled in 1859 near the head of the Santa Clara River. There were as many as seven saw mills and shingle mills built in Pine Valley and the lumber was used in the area mines. During the early years the town became a small but stable community with many luxurious homes, a tannery, cheese factory, flour and grist mill. A barrel factory also produced buckets, churns and tubs for southern Utah. Significant landmarks include Pine Valley Ward Chapel of the LDS Church, designed by shipbuilder Ebenezer Bryce in 1868 using the scheme of an upside-down boat. Pine Valley Chapel is the oldest Mormon chapel in continuous use. As of 2012, the charming town had a few permanent residents.

Pine Valley LDS Chapel 2012 Pine Valley Tithing Office 2012
Photos taken by Penny

Pinto was a small town that began when the Spanish Trail became a main thoroughfare for travelers. One group was the Fancher party, a collection of Missouri and Arkansas rowdies, who had been badmouthing Mormon towns all the way through Utah on their way to California. In Pinto the rowdies tried to buy or trade for food and supplies but were refused, so some of the party stole what they wanted. This added more fuel to the already growing embers which burst into flame, culminating in the Mountain Meadows Massacre a day or two later. A few of the surviving children were taken back to Pinto where they were cared for until soldiers from Camp Floyd came to pick them up. In 1867 the population was about 100. The town included houses, some two-stories, shops and a log church which was later replaced with a rock building that also served as a school house. The historical marker at Pinto is built from the stone of the old church. Pinto can be found 12 miles east southeast of Enterprise.

Pinto taken in 2012 by Penny

Pintura/Ashton/Bellevue was a farming community located on Ash Creek and I-15 between Cedar City and St. George. It was settled in 1858, then abandoned because of a lack of water, then resettled a second time. It was first named Ashton because it was located on Ash Creek. In 1863 it was renamed Bellevue (Bellview) by Jacob Gates and James Sylvester because the landscape resembled the shape of a bell and the view was superb. Population at its peak was 150, but by 1920 only a few families remained. In 1925, at the suggestion of Andy Gregerson, the name was changed to Pintura, a Spanish word meaning "painting," in reference to the nearby brightly colored hills.

Sherm/Jackson was an all Mormon mining camp, which was unusual in view of the church's opposition to mining. Sherm was a small mining town that developed around the Apex Mine. Some old maps show the town as Jackson instead of Sherm. The town died when the Apex mine failed.

Shunesburg/ Shonesburg was a farming community located deep in a dark, narrow canyon. In 1861 Oliver DeMille and several other families purchased land from Chief Shunes of the Paiutes. Shunes wasn't paid much and continued living with the pioneers doing some work and begging the rest of the time. The town was a sister city to Northrop, and by 1868 there were homes, barns, many other buildings and a church/school community center. Most of the farms were destroyed by grasshoppers. By 1880 population was 82 and by the turn of the century only Oliver DeMille and his family live there. In the 1990s the DeMille house still stood. The house was located east of Springdale on a private ranch. No visitors are allowed.

Silver Reef was a mining town that began between 1866 and 1870. In 1875 there were 22 mines in the area. In 1876 Silver Reef became an established town. Main street was over a mile long. Silver Reef had over 2000 people, with homes, hotels, nine stores, six saloons, a bank, several restaurants, a hospital, two dance halls, two newspapers, a China town, Catholic Church, barber shop, boarding house, telegraph office, Masonic & Odd Fellows Hall, and cemeteries. In 1891 the last mine shut down. About 25 million dollars worth of ore had been taken from the mines. In 1901 another $250,000 of ore was taken out of the area. As of 2012, the old Wells Fargo Express office was on the National Historical Register and was a museum. The old bank had been transformed into a gift shop.

Simmonsville was a planned community on the Muddy River for growing cotton, but the area was so bleak that many either refused or upon arrival chose to leave.

St. Joseph was a planned community on the Muddy River for growing cotton, but the area was so bleak that people either refused or upon arrival chose to leave.

St. Thomas was a planned community on the Muddy River for growing cotton, but the area was so bleak that many either refused or upon arrival chose to leave.

Tonaquint/Lower Clara was a farming town that began in 1855 and was named for the Tonaquint band of Indians. The missionaries helped the Indians build dams and irrigate their farms. Jacob Hamblin planted some cotton seed in the fertile river bottoms at the confluence of the Santa Clara and Virgin Rivers. A pioneer woman had brought the cotton seed across the plains in 1847. The harvest of 1855 was carded, spun and woven into cloth which greatly interested the church leaders. Thus the origin of the Cotton Mission. The town had many nicknames, Lower Clara, Lick Skillet, Seldom Stop and Never Sweat. Most of the buildings were small adobe, log and willow cabins. Tonaquint was in the southernmost settlement in Utah Territory, located at the junction of Santa Clara Creek and the Virgin River.

Wheeler was a cotton-growing settlement established in 1859. It was largely destroyed on the night of January 8, 1862 by a weeks-long flood of the Virgin River, part of the Great Flood of 1862. The town was rebuilt about a mile upriver and renamed New Grafton.

Zion was a small settlement inside Zion Canyon. Named by Isaac Behumin, who had, along with many other Mormons, been driven from town to town, state to state, across the plains and now found a haven from their troubles. The first families moved to Zion in 1863 and began farming where Zion Lodge, Grotto Campground and Emerald Pool are located today. Many settlers came until the 1866 Indian scare. Behumin built an irrigation ditch for farming, and other settlers raised cattle, chickens and pigs. By 1874 the settlement was abandoned.

CHAPTER 28
Wayne County

Aldridge was settled in 1882 and by 1890 developed into a small farming community, located at the mouth of Pleasant Creek on U-21. It was 11 miles east of Capitol Reef Park Headquarters, about at the Sleepy Hollow Bend. The settlers produced fruits, alfalfa, melons, and a variety of vegetables. A small schoolhouse was built for the children of the town. It was abandoned by 1900 because of the poor quality of the land. Nothing remained of the settlement in 2013.

Caineville was a settled in 1882 by the Mormon Church's Elijah Cutler Behunin, and during the winter of 1882 several families moved in. Behunin was the first man to take a wagon through Capitol Wash (now known as Capitol Reef Gorge) in the Capitol Reef National Park. The town he established was named to honor John T. Caine, Utah Territory's representative to Congress. A sorghum mill was built in town and employed many of the non-farmers. The townspeople built a community center. Periodic flooding caused the people to abandon their homes in Caineville and much fertile land was lost. Erosion and abandonment eventually reverted this area to open range and ranch land. As of 2013, some of the area was still farmed and the old church was still standing. Caineville was located on the left bank of the Fremont River, 65 miles southeast of Loa.

Caineville Church 12-2013 Photo by Penny

Elephant was settled in 1887 when a wagon train was led to where the high bluffs along the Dirty Devil widen out to form a small valley. There they staked out a town site. They built homes and the next year more settlers came and built more homes. Flood washed out the dam and irrigation ditches and within three years the town was abandoned. Elephant was located between Giles and Caineville. As of 2013, nothing remained but some fence posts.

Fruita was settled in the late 1870s by a few stout LDS pioneers. Initially the name of the town was called Junction, because of its location between the Fremont River and Sulphur Creek. It was changed to Fruita in 1904. Early pioneers raised crops such as alfalfa, various vegetables and sorghum (a tropical cereal grass used for molasses and syrup.) Fruit trees by the thousands, planted below the spectacular cliffs of the Water Pocket Fold by the early settlers, still thrive in the good soil of the bottom land. A thousand years earlier the Fremont Indians, whose petroglyphs are found in the area, relied on the same river for their crops. Prior to 1904, a spectacular cottonwood tree, still alive and doing well, served as the "Post Office", a shady place to congregate and anxiously await the arrival of the mail. A one-room schoolhouse built in 1896 and renovated by the National Park Service in 1966 served the Fruita community for nearly 50 years not only as a school but as a place to hold social events. At times it was also used as a place of worship and town hall. Fruita never had more than 10 families living there at one time. By early 1937 Fruita was absorbed into the newly created Capitol Reef National Monument. In 1971 the National Park Service purchased Fruita and created the Capitol Reef National Park. Today the trees and remnants of Fruita are maintained by the park.

Behunin cabin 12-2013 Elijuah Cutler Behunin built this sandstone cabin in 1890. The cabin has one window, a door and a fireplace. He lived here with his wife and 10 children.

Giles/Blue Valley was farming town located seven miles west of Hanksville. Giles was originally named Blue Valley until 1895. The developing community was named to honor their religious leader and prominent citizen, Mormon Bishop Henry Giles. A sawmill was built in the Henry Mountains to the south. The town also had a blacksmith shop, a school/church building, post office and a store. Alternating water shortages and floods with accumulating salts in the soil ruined the crop land and by 1919 the town was abandoned. Directions: A building can be seen on Highway 89. The town site is a little west of the building, then south on a dirt road for about 2.5 miles. In 2013 there was some farming in the area.

Giles   Giles 12-2013 Photo by penny

Grover was a ranching settlement that began in 1880, located on the north side of Boulder Mountain on U-24. When the town was granted a post office in 1890, it was named for the U.S. President Grover Cleveland. The town was first known as Carcass Creek for the creek located adjacent to the town. The first school classes were held in 1892, and the first school constructed in 1900.

Kitchen Town was a very small settlement located near Giles. During ghost town hunting travels, a woman in Henrieville, Utah spoke about Kitchen Town where her grandfather was born. Some structures remained at the settlement in 2013.

Kitchen Town 12-2013 Photo by Penny

Nielson Grist Mill was built in 1883. It was then destroyed by fire and rebuilt in 1890 by a Danish carpenter, Neils Hansen for a miller, Hans Peter Nielson. The tall sandstone foundation walls allowed for easy access to the machinery beneath for repair and maintenance adjustments. A wooden frame structure rises two and a half stories above the foundation. The structure houses a mill that contains all of the original equipment, everything needed for the workings of a pioneer flour mill. Nielson operated the mill until his death in 1909, the mill continued until its closure in 1935. The mill is located three miles southeast of Bicknell Utah and was placed on the National Register of Historic Places in 1975.

Nelson Grist Mill 2013 Photo by Penny

Notom/Pleasant Creek was settled in 1885 by a wagon train of Mormons led by Jorgen Smith. Smith maintained a regular apothecary at this home for many years, he was also the town blacksmith, Justice of the Peace and the postmaster. First called Pleasant Creek, Notom was expected to be a farm settlement and with great effort crops were grown, but it was at the edge of a drifting sand desert, and the fields were always covered with sand. The town was abandoned before 1900 and the people moved to Aldridge. The settlement was located near Pleasant Creek on the east side of Capitol Reef National Park. In 2013 a historic marker for the town could be seen on the side of the road.

Pleasant Dale/ Floral was a small settlement between Notom and Aldridge. Directions: A dusty road leaves U-24 just east of Capitol Reef and passes by Pleasant Dale. Some farms were still being worked in the area, and the ruins of several rock houses stood stark and bare.

Thurber was a settlement located eight miles southeast of Loa on the southwest slope of Thousand Lake Mountain, south of present-day Bicknell. The first homes were built in Thurber in 1875 and businesses soon followed. In 1881 a 20 foot square log school house with a dirt floor and roof was built. In 1890 a new school was built which was elaborate for a pioneer village. It boasted two cut-glass chandeliers, used when they held dances. In 1909 a stone school house was constructed. Thurber had problems with flooding of farms and sometimes houses were washed away. Also the drinking water came from open ditches that froze in the winter and were filled with sand in the summer. Several cases of Typhoid fever were blamed on the water supply. The settlers soon moved to Bicknell.

CHAPTER 29
Weber County

Bagley was a ralroad siding on the Lucin cut-off, located east of Promontory Point.

Bingham's Fort was located north of Second Street and west of Washington Boulevard on the banks of the Ogden River. It was a Mormon settlers' adobe and rock fort, its walls enclosing 40 acres. About 700 people sought shelter from Indian attacks there in 1853. The fort remained occupied for several years, more than 50 cabins were built along the walls. A historical marker can be found on west Second Street.

Bingham cabin once located at 317 W. 2nd St. Ogden,
Is now in Pioneer Museum, Lagoon, Farmington, UT

Bonneville/Hot Springs was an important loading station for ore being mined in the El Dorado Mining District high on Mount Ben Lomond. At the mines they built long tramways to carry their ore to mills built near the Hot Springs at what later became Bonneville. The little mill town never amounted to much since it was so close to Ogden. Ogden Hot Springs was reached by the Utah and Northern branch of the U.P. railroad and also by motor line every hour from Ogden. Hot Springs became a popular resort around 1875. Its history began with its exploration by John C. Fremont in 1873, but it was not until near the 1880s that Rason H. Slater, a Salt Lake horse doctor staked it out as a homestead. He used the boiling waters for horse medicine and found it worked for people, also. Soon people were coming from all areas to soak in the hot, curative waters and in 1889 Mr. Slater sold the property for $50,000. A full-scale race track operated during the 1890s, and at one time there was a hotel, saloon, restaurant and dance floor.

OGDEN HOT SPRINGS,
REACHED BY U. & N. BRANCH U. P. RY ALSO BY MOTOR LINE EVERY HOUR.

Bridge was a small telegraph station on the north shore of the Great Salt Lake built in 1930. Built up on twenty-ton boulders, Bridge consisted of two railroad tracks, the telegraph station, a box car, and two small shacks. In 1945 as the demand for telegraph operators declined, Bridge was abandoned.

Camp Defiance was constructed in 1832. A Rocky Mountain Fur Co. Trading Post was located at the camp, somewhere on the mythical "waters of the Bonaventura," as mentioned in William Sublette's journals. This was probably the Weber River, somewhere near Ogden.

Farr's Fort was built in 1850 at the mouth of Ogden Canyon, where Lorin Farr had located his grist mill a year earlier. It enclosed only five acres, but provided a place of refuge during Indian scares. A historical marker can be found at 1050 Canyon Road.

Fort Buenaventura/Browns Fort was located in Ogden from 1846 to 1852. Originally it was a stockade, four-cabin trading post called Miles Goodyear's Fort. The Mormons bought the post in 1847 for $1,950. In 1850 a flood wrecked the fort so it was moved southeast on higher ground and renamed Capt. James Brown's Fort. It was the first permanent white settlement in the state. The current structure is a faithful reconstruction on the original site, at 2450 "A" Avenue. Goodyear's original cabin is now on display at the Daughters of the Utah Pioneer Museum on the corner of 2104 Lincoln Ave. in Ogden Utah. The fort was founded in 1846 just east of the Weber River, west of current downtown Ogden, Utah. The fort and the surrounding land was bought by the Mormon settlers in 1847 and renamed Brownsville, then later Ogden. The land on which the actual fort stood is now a Weber County park. The purpose of the fort was to serve as a trading post for trappers and travelers.

Fort Kingston was a Mormon settlement built in 1853. It was located at the mouth of Weber Canyon. It was first known as Kingston, consisting of a church, a school, a bowery and two rows of log cabins. When Indians threatened, a wall was built, and it was then known as Fort Kingston. It was abandoned in 1857. In 1859 the false prophet known as Joseph Morris and his followers resettled it. Joseph Morris claimed he was chosen by God to replace Brigham Young as leader of the Mormon Church. When that failed he started his own church and took 600 fanatic followers. The Mormon Militia attacked the Fort and killed Morris. Interstate 80 passes near the site just west of US-89, where there is a historical marker.

Malan's Basin/Malan's Heights Resort was named after an Ogdenite, Bartholomew "Tim" Malan. In 1892, Malan and his family carved out a path up the mountain side. Malan charged visitors $1 per person to be hauled up to the hotel in a horse-drawn wagon that had a "poke" stick which prevented the wagon from rolling backwards down the hill. They built Malan Heights Hotel a two-story hotel, a sawmill, seven log cabins, a campground and a club house. Passengers were treated to beautiful panoramic views, excellent meals, and lodging at $6 per week (steak included). Unfortunately, the Hotel burned down in 1906 and the only evidence of its existence left is the old cast iron boiler lying in the grass near the stream which leads to Waterfall Canyon. A plaque at the old Hotel location shows Malan Heights Resort from 1893-1913.

Horse Buggy on Malans Basin Boiler

Mound City was an off-shoot of LaPlata just across the border from Cache County.

Mound Fort was constructed in 1853 at the request of Brigham Young. The Mormon settlers' fort was located around a natural clay mound, which was an Indian burial ground, in the vicinity of today's Washington Boulevard and 12th Street. A historical monument is located near an LDS church at the top of the mound.

North Camp was a railroad camp located at the mouth of Weber Canyon.

North Ogden Fort was planned and started in 1853 because of Chief Walker's Indian uprisings. There were only 35 families available to build this massive stone wall. In 1854, 47 families lived in or near the fort. Inside the fort area was a church, school, Relief Society building, tithing office, family homes, a blacksmith shop and the bishop's home. The fort was not completed before the Indian uprising subsided.

Ogden Stockade was a Mormon settlers' adobe fort complex constructed in 1854 in Ogden. It was located between present-day 20th and 28th Streets, and Madison and Wall Avenues. The fort was never completed.

Ogden Station was a Federal post constructed in 1878 in Ogden.

Thompson's Settlement was a settlement that became a main junction for travelers. The Union Pacific went south from Ogden to Jack Thompson's Settlement before turning east toward Weber Canyon. Jack Thompson's Settlement was called Taylor's Mill before the railroad arrived, and after the iron rails were laid it quickly became a booming place. From a sleepy village it blossomed into a town that had no less than eight restaurants, where meals cost $2 each, more than most people there had ever seen before the railroad came. It had the usual saloon but not the usual drinks, for only beer could be served. The settlement has been swallowed up by city Riverdale, which was incorporated in 1946.

Miscellaneous Information

Fan-tan is a gambling game similar to roulette. A square is placed on a table, with the sides marked 1, 2, 3, and 4. A double handful of small objects (button, beans, etc.) are placed in the center and covered with a bowl. Bets are made on the numbers and placed on the side of the square matching the number selected. The dealer removes the bowl and using a stick, scoops out the objects four at a time until the final batch is reached. Depending on how many objects (1-4) are left in the final batch, the winning bet would match the numbers on the square. Bets are paid 3 to 1, less 5%.

Typical Mormon Fort in Utah

Typical Box Car Home

Index

Chapter 1 Pages 1-9
Beaver County

Adamsville
Aragon
Arrowhead
Beaver bottoms
Blueacre
Bradshaw city
Cruz
Elephant City
Florida
Fort Cameron
Fortuna
Frisco
Granpian
Greenville
Harrington
Hay Springs
Hickory or Old Hickory
Indian Creek
Laho
Lincoln
Lower Beaver
Manderfield
Moscow
Mercury Springs
Murdock
Newhouse
North Creek
Opal
Pine Creek
Pine Grove Creek
Shauntie
Shenandoah
Smyths/Read/Reed
South Camp
Star City
Shenandoah
Smyths/Read/Reed
South Camp
Star City
Sulphurdale/Morrissey
Thermo
Troy
Upton
Wah-Wah

Chapter 2 Pages 10-33
Box Elder County

Appledale
Belfour
Beppo
Blue Creek/Deadfall
Boone
Booth Valley
Boston Terrace/
Newfoundland
Bovine
Buel City
Camp Cedar Swamp
Camp Church Buttes
Cedar Creek
Cedar Springs
Camp Church Buttes
Cedar Creek
Cedar Springs
Clear Creek/Nafton
Colin
Connor
Copperfield/Copper Hill
Corinne/Burg on the Bear
Cropley
Dathol
Dove Creek
Elinor
Etna
Evans
Fort Bear River
Fort Calls
Fort Davis
Fort Malad
Golden
Fort Davis
Fort Malad
Golden
Gravel Pit
Groome
Grouse Creek
Grouse Creek Fort
Hampton's Ford
Hardup
Hogup
Iowa String
Jackson
Junction
Kelton/Indian Creek

Knowltonsburg
Kolmar
Kosmo/Cosmo
Lake
Lakeside
Lakeview
LaMay
Lampo
Last Chance
Lamar
Little Valley
Loy
Lucin/Pilot Peak
Lucin Cutoff
Lynn
Matlin
Medec
Metatarsus
Midlake
Monument/Parker's Camp
Muddy
Nella
Nerva
North Promontory
Old Terrace
Olney
Ombey
Painted Post
Park Valley
Pegion
Penrose
Peplin
Promontory/North Pass
Promontory Point
Quarry
Rambo
Red Dome
Romola
Rosebud
Rosette/Victory
Rozel/Camp Victory
Russian Settlement
Victory
Saline
Scandia
Seco
Speery
Standrod/One Mile
Stokes
Strong Knob
Subon

Surban
Teck
Ten-Mile
Terrace
Tresend
Umbria
Unia
United Order
Vipont
Walden
Washakie
Water cress
Woodrow
Wyben
Yost/George Tow/Junction
Zias

Chapter 3 Pages 34-35
Cache County

Buster City
Camp Relief
Fort Logan
Fort Richmond
LaPlata
Mineral Point
Porcupine City
Smithfield Fort
Willow Valley

Chapter 4 pages 36-48
Carbon County

Blackhawk
Castle Gate
Clear Creek
Coal City/Great Western
Consumers/Gibson
Fort Nine Mile
Franham
Hale
Heiner/Panther
Hiawatha
Kiz
Latuda/Liberty
Little Standard
Martin
Mutual
National
New Peerless

Nolen
Peerless
Rains
Royal/Rolapp/Cameron
Scofield
Spring Canyon/Storrs
Standardville
Stewart
Sunnyside
Sweets
Wattis
Winter Quarters

Chapter 5 Pages 49-51
Daggett County

Bridgeport
Brown's Park/Brown's Hole
Fort Davy Crockett
Greendale
Linwood
Sweat Ranch
Sweet Ranch

Chapter 6 Pages 52-53
Davis County

Bountiful Fort
Farmington Stockade
Kaysville Fort
Simkins
Lake Park Resort
Lake Shore Resort
Lake Side Resort
Syracuse Resort

Chapter 7 Pages 54-58
Duchesne County

Altonah
Antelope
Basin
Bluebench
Blumesa
Bridgeland
Cedarview
Cresent
Emigrant Springs
Falls
Harper
Hartford
Hyland
Ioka
McAffee

Meadowdell
Midview
Montwell
Mount Emmons
Palmer
Smith Wells
Starvation
Stockmore
Upper Strawberry/Riverside
Utahn
Woodbire

Chapter 8 Pages 59-65
Emery County

Austinville
Cedar
Cliff
Connellsville
Desert
Desert Lake
Emery/Muddy
Grassy
Lawrence
Mohrland
Moore
Nolan
Quitchupah
Sphinx
Temple Mountain
Victor
Wilsonville
Woodside/Lower Crossing

Chapter 9 Pages 66-70
Garfield County

Asay Town/Aaron
Bromide Basin
Castle
Clifton/Cliff
Eagle City
Georgetown
Greens
Henderson
Hillsdale
Losee/Loseeville
Osiris
Panguitch Fort
Spry
Ticaboo
Warm Creek
Widtsoe/Adairville

Chapter 10 Pages 71-80
Grand County

Agate
Archeron
Castleton
Cisco
Cottonwood
Cresent/Cresent Junction
Crystal Carbon
Dolton Wells Camp
Daly
Danish Flats
Dewey
Dolores Triangle
Elgin
Elk Mountain
Fort Moab
Halfway Stage Station
Harley Dome
Hittle's bottom
Little Grand
Marrs
Mesa
Miners Basin/Basin
Picture Gallery
Pindhook
Pinto
Polar
Richardson
Sagers
Sego/Neslin/Ballard
Solitude
South Mesa
Thompson Springs
Utaline
Valley City
Victor
Webb Hollow
Westwater
Whitehouse
Wilson Mesa

Chapter 11 Pages 81-89
Iron County

Aberdeen
Avon
Beryl
Beryl Junction
Buckhorn Springs
Cedar Fort
Chloride
Desert Springs
Duck Creek Camp

Ford
Fort Louisa
Fort Paragonah
Fort Stanford
Gold Springs
Grimshawville
Hamilton's Fort/Walker Fort
Hamlin Valley
Heist/Escalante
Iron City/Iron Town
Iron Springs
Johnson Fort
Kerr
Latimer
Little Pinto/Page Ranch
Lund
Marchant
Midvalley
Modena
Nada
New Castle
Pikes Diggings
Pleasant Valley
State Line
Stevensville
Sulphur Springs
Summit
Tomas
Uvada
Yale
Zane/Sahara
Zenda

Chapter 12 Pages 90-100
Juab County

Black Rock Station
Boyd's Station
Burgin
Callao/Willow Springs
Camp Crossman
Camp Eastman
Canyon Station Post
Cherry Creek
Diamond
Dugway Station
Dutchtown
Eureka/Ruby Hollow
Fish Springs
Fish Springs Station
Fort Nephi
Goshute
Ironton
Jericho
Joy

Juab
Knightsville
Little Salt Creek
Mammoth
Mills
Nortonville
Partoun
Robinson
Roseville
Salt Creek
Silver City
Starr
Tintic
Tintic Mills
Trout Creek
West Tintic
York

Chapter 13 Pages 101-104
Kane County

Adairville
Butlerville
Clif/Clifton
Fort Berryville
Fort Kanab
Fort Meek
Fort Wah Weep
Johnson
Paria/Pahreah
Pipe Springs Fort
Ranch
Rockhouse
Shirts Fort
Skutumpah
Upper Kanab
White House

Chapter 14 Pages 105-117
Millard County

Abraham
Adelaide Park
Antelope Springs
Black Rock
Bob Stinson's
Burbank
Camp at Fillmore
Champlin
Clear Lake
Cline
Corn Creek
Cove Fort
Crafton
Eskdale
Flowell

Fort Buttermilk
Fort Desert
Fort Scipio
Gandy
Garrison
Gilmore
Graball
Greenwood
Hatton
Ibex
Ingersoll
Lucerne
Lynndyl
McCormick
Mcintyre
Neels
Oasis
Shem
South Tract
Sugarville
Sunflower
Sutherland
Topaz
White Mountain Station
Willden Fort
Woodard
Woodrow
Wyno

Chapter 15 Pages 118-122
Morgan County

Carbonit Hill
Devil's Slide
Dixie Station
Fort Thurston
Littleton
Monday Town Hollow
Mountain Green Post
Porterville
Richville
Como Spring Resort

Chapter 16 Pages 123-126
Piute County

Alunite
Angle/ Spring creek
Box Creek
Bullion City
Copper Belt Mining Camp
Coyote
Deer Trail
Florence Mining and
Milling
Greenwich

Hoovers
Kimberly
Webster
Winkleman

Chapter 17 Pages 127-128
Rich County

Argyle/Kennedyville
Chimney Town/Meadowville
Mud Town
Pottawattamie
Round Valley
Round Valley Post
Sage Creek
Sly Go

Chapter 18 Pages 129-141
Salt Lake County

Alta
Argenta
Arthur
Bacchus
Baker
Bingham
Camp Bingham Creek
Camp Murray
Caribou City
Central City
Cheatum
Copperfield
Dalton
Emmaville
Fort Bingham
Fort Douglas
Fort Herriman
Fort Salt Lake City
Fort Union
Galena
Garden City
Garfield
Gold City
Hangtown
Hanks Station
Highland Boy
Lark
Little Dell
Modoc
Mountain Dell
Priesthood Camp
Rockwell's Station
Salt Lake City Post
San Domingo City
Silver Fork
Tannersville

Telegraph
Traveler's Rest
Union City
Us
Willow Fort
Black Rock Resort
Saltair

Chapter 19 Pages 142-149
San Juan County

Bluff Fort
Boulder
California Bar
Camp Jackson
Carlisle/Indian Creek
Cedar Point
Crescent City
Eastland
Fort Montezuma
Fry Canyon
Ginger Hill
Gretchen Bar/Schock Bar
Halls Crossing
Hite
Holyoak
Home of Truth
Horsehead
LaVaga
Lockerby
Old Fort Bottom
Old LaSal
Peak City
Plainsfield/Poverty Flat
Rincon
Spencer's Camp
Stone Camp
Summit Point
Torb
Ucolo
Urado
Verdure
White Canyon
White Rock Curved Village
Williamsburg
Zahn's Camp

**Chapter 20 Pages
150-154**
San Pete County

Buckenburg
Camp Clark
Camp Fountain Green
Camp George
Camp Pace
Camp Paige

Cedar Cliffs
Chester/Chesterfield
Christianburg
Clarion
Crowleyville
Dewey's Camp
Dover
Fairview Fort
Fort Ephraim
Fort Gunnison
Fort Manti
Hardscrabble
Jerusalem
Johnstown
Little Stone Fort
Manasseh
Moroni Fort
Morrison
Mount Pleasant Fort
Mountain Ville
Oak Creek
Pettyville
Pigeon Hollow
Shumway Springs
Spearmint
Spring City/ Little Denmark
Spring City Fort
West Point

Chapter 21 Page 155-156
Sevier County

Belnap
Brigham River
Camp Sevier
Cove
Gooseberry
Gravelbed
Lime Kilns
Pittsburg
Prattville
Venice
Vermillion

Chapter 22 Pages 157-165
summit County

Altus
Atkinson
Blacks Fork
Camp in Echo Canyon
Castle Rock
Echo Stage Station

Echo Canyon
Echo Breastworks
Grass Creek
Hoyt's Fort/ Fort Union
Hoyt Peak
Kamas Fort
Kimballs
Lake Flat
Mill City
Needle Rock Station
North Oakley
Park City/Mineral City
Rhoads Fort
Rockport/Crandall
Sage Bottom Fort
Stillwater Camp
Upton
Wahsatch/Wasatch
Wanship Station
Weber Stage Station
West Fork/Timber Town

Chapter 23 Pages 166-184
Tooele County

Aragonite
Arinosa
Barro
Bauer/Terminal/Buhl
Beckwith Camp
Benmore
Blair Spur
Bullionville
Burmester
Burnt Station
Camp Conness
Camp Shunk
Canyon Station
Center/Ajax
Clifton
Clive
Death Canyon
Delle
Dolomite
Dunbar
Dunnstein
E.T. City
East Rush Valley
Ellerbeck
Faust/Meadow Creek
Flux
Free Coinage
Gisborn
Gold Hill
Grantsville Fort

Harker Canyon
Ibapah/Deep Creek
Iosepa
Indian Springs
Jacob City
Junction
Knolls
LaCigale
Lake Point
Lincoln
Lofgreen
Low
Marblehead
Marshall
Martinsville/Slag Town
Mercur/Lewiston
Morris
Nowlenville/Batesville
Ophir
Orr's Ranch
Pehrson
Point Lookout station
Richville
River Bed Station
Round Station
Rowley
Salduro
Scranton
Shambip/Johnson
Shields
Silsbee
Simpson Springs
Six Mile Springs
Solar
Steptoe Military Camp
Sunshine
Timpie Dell
Toplift
Warner
West Dip/ West Mercur
West Wendover
Willow Springs
Garfield Resort

Chapter 24 Pages 185-181
Uintah County

Alhandra
Avalon
Bennett/cuneal
Bitter Creek
Bonanza
Bullionville/Bullion
Camp Fudgy
China Wall

Chipeta Wells
Dragon
Dyer
Eatonville
Fort Duchesne
Fort Kit Carson
Fort Robidoux/Fort Uinta
Fort Thornburgh
Fort Uintah
Harrison
Hayden
Hill Creek
Ignacio/White River Crossing
Independence
Kennedy Hole
Leota
Ouray
Packer
Parson's City
Rainbow
The Strip
Watson
Webster City
Willow Creek

Chapter 25 Pages 192-204
Utah County

Beaver Creek Camp
Camp Ashley
Camp Battle Creek
Camp Dodge
Camp Floyd
Camp Rawlins
Camp Timpanagos
Canyon Station
Castilla Hot Springs
Cedar Fort
Christmas City
Colton/Pleasant Valley
Junction
Deer Creek
Dividend/Standard
Dobietown/Frogtown
Eva Mine
Fairfield
Forest City
Fort Peteetneet
Fort Rawlins
Fort Sodom
Fort St. Luke
Fort Utah
Fort Wordsworth
Gilluly/Upper Tucker

Harold
Homansville/Lawrence
Ironton
Joe's Dugout
Lake View
Lott Settlement
Lower Goshen
Manning
Mechanicsville
Mill Fork
Mosida
Moyle House and
Pelican Point
Pittsburg
Sandtown
Santaquin Fort
Summit Creek Fort
Thistle
Tucker

Chapter 26 Page 205-206
Wasatch County

Buysville
Center Creek
Hailstone/Elkhorn
Keetley
Soldier Summit

Chapter 27 Pages 207-217
Washington County

Adventure
Anderson/McPherson's Flat
Atkinville
Babylon
Bloomington
Bonanza City
Calls Landing
Camp Lorenzo
Conger
Crawfordville
Dalton
Duncan's Retreat
Fort Clara/Fort Santa Clara
Fort Harmony
Fort Pearce
Goldstrike
Grafton/Wheeler
Hamblin
Harrisburg/Cotton wood
Harrisville
Heberville/Price City
Hebron/Shoal Creek
Holt
Johnson's Mill
Marshalltown

Middleton
Milltown
Morristown
Mountain City
Mountain Dell
New Castle
Northrup
Overton
Pine Valley
Pinto
Pintura/Ashton
Sherm/Jackson
Shunesburg
Silver Reef
Wheeler
Zion

Chapter 28 Pages 218-221
Wayn County

Aldridge
Caineville
Elephant
Fruita
Giles/Blue Valley
Grover
Kitchen Town
Nielson Grist Mill

Notom/Pleasant Creek
Pleasant Dale/Floral
Thurber

Chapter 29 pages 222-226
Weber County

Bagley
Bingham's Fort
Bonneville/Hot Springs
Bridge
Camp Defiance
Farr's Fort
Fort Buenaventura
Fort Kingston
Malan's Basin/Malan's Heights
Mound City
Mound Fort
North Camp
North Ogden Fort
Ogden Stockade
Ogden Station
Thompson's Settlement

References

A History of Beaver County
A History of Box Elder County
A History of Cache County
A History of Carbon County
A History of Daggett County
A History of Davis County
A History of Duchene County
A History of Emery County
A History of Garfield County
A History of Grand County
A History of Iron County
A History of Juab County
A History of Kane County
A History of Millard County
A History of Morgan County
A History of Piute County
A History of Rich County
A History of Salt Lake County
A History of San Juan County
A History of Sanpete County
A History of Sevier County
A History of Summit County
A History of Tooele County
A History of Uintah County
A History of Utah County
A History of Wasatch County
A History of Washington County
A History of Wayne County
A History of Weber County
Grand Memories
Online Utah .com
National-gold.com
Piute.org/history

Utah Place Names John W. Van Cott
grandcounty.net/abouthtm
North Ogden Historical Museum
Serra Madre West: The History of the
Mines below Willard & Ben Lomond
Peaks by Mike and Steve Holmes.
Utah History Encyclopedia
Utah Home town Locator
Utah Division of State History
GhostTownGallery.com
Utah Rails.net
Tooele County Guide to Historical Attractions
Utah Mining Uintah Basin Teaching American History
Project
Utah History Resource Center
Used by permission, Utah State Historical Society
Legends of America Ghost Towns and Mining Camps
Utah Outdoor activities resource to the Utah Outdoors
Utah Historical Markers on Waymarking.com
History of 2nd street, Ogden Utah
History of Ogden, Utah in Old Post Cards By D. Boyd
Crawford
Images of Railroads Around Helper
LaPosta: A Journal of American Postal History
Ghost Town Seekers
Utah History to go
Ghosttowns.com
Washington County Historical Society
Summitpoint.net
Images of America Coal Camps of Eastern Utah
http://www.legendsofamerica.com/ut-carboncounty3.html
http://wrbaldwin-connect.blogspot.com/
http://www.carbon-utgenweb.com/towns.html

I hope everyone enjoys this book and goes out and explore these place's it is a lot of FUN.

Penny Spackman Clendenin

About the Author

I was born and raised in North Ogden, Utah. I graduated from Weber High School, and I have a Bachelor's degree from Weber State College. I married my husband Rod Clendenin, we were married 1 day short of 37 years went he died, I had 3 children my youngest died in a motorcycle accident in 2019 and 2 months later my husband died of cancer. I have 7 grandchildren and 1 great grandchild.

Rod and I started an auto repair business together, now I run it myself with the help of my wonderful employees. I started going blind with Macular Degeneration, when Rod was very sick with cancer and it progressed very fast. We loved snowmobiling and riding our 4 wheelers exploring ghost towns, not just Utah, but all over Idaho, Montana, & Nevada.

I am a member of the Daughters of the Utah pioneers, and on the board for the North Ogden Historical Museum.

I have always been fascinated by ghost towns and the history and stories they tell. This fascination led me to write the *Shadowy Remains of Utah's Towns*, which is a comprehensive guide to many of the ghost towns in Utah.

Many years of research went into writing *Shadowy Remains of Utah's Towns*, to give you the most accurate information possible. Research included; books, internet, museums, experts, people familiar with the area, and a personal trip to as many locations as possible.

–Penny Spackman Clendenin

Printed in the United States
by Baker & Taylor Publisher Services